Marshall Turenne

Turenne

\RSHAL TURENNE

BY THE AUTHOR OF

"\R KENELM DIGBY," "THE ADVENTURES OF
_____" "THE LIFE OF A PR___" ETC.

W__H AN INTRODUCTION BY

__IER GEN_E__AL FRANCIS LLOYD, C.B., D___

WITH ILLUSTRATIONS,
AND A M__

NGMAN, GREEN, AND CO.
49 PATERNOSTER ROW, LONDON
NEW YORK, BOMBAY, AND CALCUTTA
1907

MARSHAL TURENNE

.

BY THE AUTHOR OF

"A LIFE OF SIR KENELM DIGBY," "THE ADVENTURES OF
JAMES II.," "THE LIFE OF A PRIG," ETC.

WITH AN INTRODUCTION BY

BRIGADIER-GENERAL FRANCIS LLOYD, C.B., D.S.O.

WITH ILLUSTRATIONS

AND A MAP

LONGMANS, GREEN, AND CO.

39 PATERNOSTER ROW, LONDON

NEW YORK, BOMBAY, AND CALCUTTA

1907

PREFACE

To apologise for a book dealing with the campaigns of a celebrated General, but written neither by a soldier, nor by that far higher authority upon such subjects, a civil "military expert," would be useless; for it is inconceivable that such an apology could be accepted. To the obvious retort, "Then why did you write the book?" the Author can only reply by saying, "Why do most of us do many things which we ought not to do?" and by expressing a hope that any ludicrous blunders to be found in the following pages may amuse his military readers as much as it has amused him to make them.

Whatever apologies may be due for the book itself, no apology is required for its Introduction, for which the author cannot sufficiently thank the talented, experienced and distinguished officer who has so kindly and so ably written it. While that officer is absolutely irresponsible for anything in the book except its Introduction, the book is responsible to the officer, not only for its Introduction, but also

for a number of exceedingly useful hints and timely
warnings. The author also wishes to express his
gratitude for some very valuable suggestions, as
well as for much assistance, from that kindest and
most competent of critics, Mr. Walter Herries
Pollock. Of the help always so readily and un-
selfishly placed at his disposal in his own family,
the author will say nothing.

CONTENTS

CONTENTS

CHAPTER VI.

1644.

PAGE

CONTENTS

CHAPTER XI.

1649—1650.

CHAPTER XII.

1651—1652.

CHAPTER XIII.

1652.

CHAPTER XIV.

1652.

CONTENTS

CONTENTS

CHAPTER XXVII.

1675.

LIST OF ILLUSTRATIONS

INTRODUCTION.

"READ and re-read the campaigns of the great captains," said the greatest of all captains, and foremost among those of modern times he placed Turenne. But did he not practically contradict this "Maxim" by gathering in the threads of thought and action of all previous leaders and reweaving them in the loom of his powerful and almost omniscient mind into lessons of warfare for all time? For all time certainly, so far as we can see, as regards the greater lessons of strategy, even allowing for the infinite possibilities of the future. Tactics, however, have altered so much that the Napoleonic battlefields are to us little more instructive than those of the Thirty Years' War and the Fronde, much less so than the battles of Turenne were to Napoleon himself, who practically swept away the old methods. Even strategy may in some degree now be said to be affected. Had Turenne undertaken the passage of the Alps, science would have aided him little more than it did Hannibal. When Napoleon performed that wonderful feat, with the exception of rather better roads than Turenne would have had to deal with, the mechanical means at his disposal were

little greater than those on which the great Cartha-
ginian could count. Were a general, however, to
attempt a like invasion in these days, he would have
all the accessories of iron, steam and electricity to
materially forward his project.

As regards the weapons and equipment of the
Napoleonic wars, armour had practically ceased to be
worn. ' The pike, the harquebuss and the wheel-lock had
given place to the musket and bayonet, pike and wheel-
lock in one. Cavalry had ceased to charge at the trot,
and the firing of "piece and pistol before setting on with
the sword" had yielded to shock tactics proper. In
fact the highly trained infantry of the age of Napoleon
had considerably curtailed the liberties taken by
cavalry in the age of Turenne, and certain modifica-
tions in mounted tactics were the inevitable consequence.
The conqueror of Austerlitz and Jena, the victor on a
hundred fields, remodelled the tactics and altered the
system of war, from that which had prevailed in the
time of his predecessor, to suit the different conditions
under which he led the armies of France into nearly
every country in Europe. But although he might
alter the conditions of attack and defence, although he
no longer laid his armies up in winter quarters, nor sat
down before fortresses when there yet remained an
army in the field to defeat, still with all the momentous changes he made, he could not alter the great
principles of strategy. On the other hand, his cam-

paigns exemplify every principle upon which Turenne acted, and with the wider field in which he exercised his greater ambitions, he not only mirrored to us all that Turenne thought and said and did, but added to them the fire of his own genius for war. But the great principles of strategy as affected by the configuration of frontiers, the necessity for a secure base, the command of the sea, and the strokes of attack and defence, which these demanded, must remain immutable for all time. The great principles of Turenne are the same as those under which Von Moltke and Oyama worked, and although it may be better worth the time and the study of the military student to read and re-read the campaigns of Napoleon and the great masters of the art that have lived since, than to turn to the pages of a biography of Turenne, still there may be much there that even the most advanced of modern soldiers will find of value.

Are we, however, quite certain that the last word has been said on the principles of warfare? Surely no one would dream of asserting that tactics are not changing day by day? Is it not possible that developments since the Russo-Japanese war, even of [the last few months, may entirely revolutionise strategy as well as tactics? Is it not possible that some modern "Trafalgar" or "Battle of the Sea of Japan" may be fought in the air, that the warship may give place to the airship, that a "secure base" may be looked for

among the higher Alps or in the Himalayas, and that
not only our swords but possibly our rifles and our quick-
firing guns may find final resting-places in museums,
beside the armour and equipment of past centuries?

But unlimited as are the possibilities of the future,
we can only deal with things as they are, and that being
so, the student will find much that will interest him in
the campaigns undertaken, and nearly all brought to
a successful issue, by a great general who commanded the armies of France in the middle of the
seventeenth century.

The careful study alone of the strategical marches,
which began in 1647, and formed a new development
in the art of war—new, indeed, so far as the Middle Ages
and modern times are concerned, but in reality only a
reapplication of that art, as understood by the greater
captains, among the ancients—will well repay the reader.

Turenne's march to effect a junction with Wrangel
at Friedburg is one that has rarely, if ever, been surpassed in the annals of war, be it taken either as an
exemplification of endurance on the part of an army,
organisation on the part of a staff, or moral courage
on the part of a leader.   No doubt a severe discipline accounts for the first.   But the second is another
matter.   Even in these days with good roads, with
more than one road to march over, and with a well-
organised and trained staff to direct and work out
details, the movement of an army is not the easy matter

that it may appear on paper. Considering the difference of the conditions in the seventeenth century, the
complete absence of even one good road, and the non-
existence of a staff in the modern sense of the word, I
think there can be little doubt that to the leader himself belongs the chief credit of the organisation that even
in those times was at any rate to some extent an
absolute necessity. Still more than this, what shall
we say of the decision and moral power which enabled
Turenne to make up his mind to enter upon so
hazardous an undertaking? This march, if nothing
else, should place him for all time among the great
captains of the world. Certain it is, that if the modern
soldier learns nothing else from the study of the
campaigns of Turenne, it will be borne in upon him
more than ever that all practices, and all principles,
may pass away from the conduct of war save one—the
moral. Of this Turenne was as great an exponent as
the Corsican himself. It won them both many a
battle, as much later it enabled Lee, aided by his great
lieutenant, to keep at bay for so long the concentrated
might of the Federal cause, and as it will decide many
an action of the future, be it fought with the quick-
firing guns and far-reaching rifles of to-day, or the
boundless possibilities of the future, such as airships
armed with unknown weapons, of which we only see
faint indications in the present.

Again, even if it be acknowledged that the great

Napoleon has caught up all the threads of thought from the captains that went before him, including the subject of this book, whom, as leader, strategist and tactician, he ranked so high, are there no other reasons for studying his career? Can the story of a life such as Turenne's lie unnoticed on the pages of the past? Or is it possible that the memory of an honest, upright man of genius, who played so great a part on the stage of the world, can fade away entirely without having left his mark, not only on the century in which he lived, but on the race to which he belonged? The student of history will find much in his career that affected the politics of his time, while the soldier will read of his campaigns and battles with more than a passing interest; for they are not only examples of the battles and sieges, marches and countermarches of that great century of war, the seventeenth, but also illustrations of the perpetual truth, that the leader who understands how to "set a squadron in the field" and "the division of a battle knows," is more important than many squadrons, that numbers do not make an army, and, above all, that even a trained army is nothing without trained and capable leaders, or without a supreme, trusted and highly experienced commander at its head. This great fact no one knows better than the private soldier, possibly better even than the critic, able though he may be. Did not the "private men" of the Peninsular Army say that they would rather see the "Duke's" great nose on the morning of a battle than hear that an extra division was coming up? And when the love of the soldier is combined with this respect, as it was in so marked a degree in the case of Turenne, success should indeed follow. The great Marshal studied his profession from youth upwards, both theoretically and practically; theoretically, in such books as were then to be obtained, practically, in the best of all schools, successful and unsuccessful war. Early in life he rose to high command, but he never ceased to practise the lesson learned in his youth, "that diligence and activity are the great cause of success in military affairs". Finally, the words of the old soldier to the young grumbler would be an epitaph worthy of Turenne, words that might well be printed at the beginning of every British soldier's "Small Book": "What makes you complain? You do not know our General; when we are in distress, he suffers more than we do. At this moment his thoughts are wholly employed in contriving how to extricate us from this difficulty. He is awake when we are asleep. He is our Father. It is easy to see you are but young."

To all who are interested in the life-long work of a man whose character was written in such glowing words by a subordinate, I commend the fascinating pages that follow.

FRANCIS LLOYD.

ALDERSHOT,
September, 1907.

CHAPTER I.

ENGLISHMEN are pardonably apt to look at everything from an English standpoint, therefore it may be well, before embarking upon a study of certain events abroad, to ascertain where we stand in relation to things in England, at the starting-point of our story. Half a dozen years had passed since the attempt to blow up King and Parliament in a gunpowder explosion, and James I. was now engaged in trying to raise money by instituting a minor hereditary honour, which he entitled a baronetcy and offered at the fixed price of £1,095. If a literary landmark should also be required, we may observe that we start five years before the death of Shakespeare.

Meanwhile in France, with which we shall be much more concerned than with England, a boy only ten years old had been a year on the throne, with the title of Louis XIII. His mother, Marie de' Medici, the first of several women connected with politics whom it will be necessary to notice, was Regent, and she was so badly served by her ministers that some of the greatest Princes of France, including the Prince of Condé and the Dukes of Nevers, Mayenne, Longueville, Vendôme and Bouillon—the father of our hero—with-

drew from the Court and formed a league to protest
against the incompetence, maladministration, and uncon-
stitutional conduct of the Government. Soon afterwards the Ministry was recast, and, five years later,
Richelieu was made Minister of State, with the port-
folios of War and Foreign Affairs. This League of
the Princes, so near the moment of our outset, deserves
special notice, because subsequent Leagues of French
Princes, some of whom bore the same names, led to
many of the complications and wars to be described in
these pages.

Another cause of warfare at that period was religion,
or at any rate what went by that name. Protestantism,
in the usual acceptation of the word, was scarcely a
century old, and it had become, to a large extent, a
political plaything; nor were certain Catholics of high
rank, or high office, above taking a hand in the game
which was provided. During a great part of the second
half of the previous century, civil wars, undertaken in
the name of religion, had been waged in France between
the Catholics and the Huguenots; and the King, who
was assassinated the year before our point of departure,
had fought as a Protestant against the Catholic King,
before he himself became King and Catholic. And
while the Christians, in Western and Central Europe,
were endeavouring to teach each other theology with
the sword, the Turks, in Eastern Europe, were attempting to win their affections to the religion of Mahomet,
with the same persuasive instrument.

Literature, if it did not, like religion, lead to wars,

had considerable influence in France during the same period; and some of the characters to appear upon our stage were contributors to it. At the time of our opening Montaigne had not been dead twenty years; Malherbe was making a revolution in French poetry; and Jean Louis Guez de Balzac (a writer very different from the Honoré de Balzac of a later period), if some one truly said of him *"il écrit pour écrire,"* and not because he had anything in particular to say, was on the point of adding much to the lucidity, vivacity and grace of a national literature which had hitherto been too often diffuse, careless, obscure, clumsy and ponderous. At the same time St. Francis of Sales, if not in France yet in French, was writing in an attractive style about religious subjects; and, if there were not very many famous authors at the moment, a number of writers, subsequently very celebrated, were either lately born or were about to be born.

The most famous general living at the time of the birth of the celebrated marshal who will form the subject of this book, was Gustavus Adolphus, King of Sweden, who is considered by some authorities to have been the greatest general that ever commanded an army. Sweden, at that period, was one of the most important powers in Europe; the power of Spain, on the contrary, was on the wane, while that of the Empire was dwindling away altogether. The monarch, who bore the title of Emperor, was powerful as a King, but not as the representative of the Cæsars; and, if his kingdom was large, his Empire beyond it was even less his own than the property mortgaged beyond its value can be called his own by a bankrupt country gentleman.

One more subject needs notice by way of prelude. Much as the wars of the early part of the seventeenth century did to hamper all civil industries, in some districts bringing production and commerce almost to a standstill, the middle classes, especially among the Dutch burghers, the bourgeoisie of Paris, the citizens of London, and still more those of Strasburg and the other free cities of Germany, were gradually learning their powers, asserting their rights, and endeavouring to hint to their superiors in rank, that trade was as important a factor in politics as nobility, if not royalty, and that the shop demanded recognition, as well as the castle.

Two little boys, apparently so hopelessly delicate that their respective fathers despaired of their ever being able to maintain the military traditions of their families, were destined to become very celebrated generals, to rank among the greatest military commanders of history, and to revolutionise the sciences of strategy and tactics. These two officers were Henry, Viscount of Turenne, and Louis, Prince of Condé, commonly called The Great Condé.

It is with the first named, and by several years the first-born, of these boys that we have to do. His father, Henry de la Tour, Duke of Bouillon, was sovereign of Sedan, one of those small sovereignties which sometimes bring about great wars, especially when they are situated, as is Sedan, between large and

important countries.   As it happens, Sedan never
acted as the match for enkindling a great military
conflagration; but it served as the battlefield on which
a great nation was practically defeated rather more
than two and a half centuries later than the date at
which this story must begin, namely, on the 11th of
September, 1611, with the birth of Henry of Turenne.

The Duke of Bouillon was distinguished as a
soldier, as a diplomatist, as a student, and as the
leader of the Protestant party in France.   Turenne's
mother, Elizabeth of Nassau, daughter of William of
Nassau, Prince of Orange, and of Charlotte Bourbon-
Montpensier, was also distinguished in her way, and
likewise a very staunch Calvinist.

In his infancy Turenne had a succession of severe
illnesses.   He nearly died in teething, and he fore-
shadowed the reserved manner of his adult life by
remaining apparently dumb until he was four.   He
continued to be fragile and delicate until he was
twelve years old, and his father frequently said, in his
hearing, that he would never be strong enough to bear
the fatigues of war.   Irritated by this, the boy determined to prove the contrary by spending a night
upon the ramparts of Sedan.   One evening, when he
was at the age of ten, his tutor missed him, and, at the
end of a long and anxious search, he found the child
lying asleep upon the carriage of one of the guns of
the fortress.

This embryo general was exceedingly stupid and
equally lazy at his lessons.   Indeed his masters com-

plained that he either could not, or would not, learn
anything; whereupon his father prescribed the invari-
able severe remedy of those days for juvenile headaches,
backward development, natural bad memory, and nervousness in children.   In the seventeenth century boys
were promoted to wearing little swords almost as soon
as they are now promoted to wearing jackets and
trousers. Soon after Turenne had received this dignity,
his tutor was surprised, on approaching him with a rod,
to see the boy approaching him with a drawn sword.
Considering his weapon less suited for duelling purposes
than that of his opponent, the tutor fled to the Duke
of Bouillon and appealed for his protection, when the
Duke upheld the authority of the birch over the blade
by having the young swordsman whipped with unusual
severity.   But the blade was yet to conquer.   One
fine afternoon the boy found his tutor lying asleep on
the ground in a secluded part of the garden, and close
to him was a snake which seemed about to dart at him.
Drawing his sword, he killed the snake, an action
which woke the tutor, who, seeing his pupil sword in
hand, imagined that his last moment had arrived.
When the terrified pedagogue learned what had really
happened, he was fool enough to fall on his knees
and implore the lad's forgiveness for suspecting him of
a murderous intention.[1]

   Bewildered at finding that learning could not be

[1] *La Vie du Vicomte de Turenne.* Par M. du Buisson (G. de
Courtliz de Sandras).   A la Hague, chez Henri van Buldren,
1698.

flogged into the boy, the Duke tried the effect of banter-
ing him upon his ignorance, and of impressing upon
him that he would be even more incapacitated for
military command by his mental, than by his physical,
deficiencies. The result was as remarkable as it was
satisfactory. Although still refusing to trouble himself
about mathematics, the boy read most industriously at
such classics as described military campaigns, especially
the works of Cæsar and Quintus Curtius.

The Duke of Bouillon died when Henry of Turenne
was twelve, and was succeeded by Henry's elder
brother. But Henry's education was not neglected
after the death of his father, as his mother was a
woman of strong character and considerable ambition.

Before he was thirteen, an officer to whom he had
been belauding his favourite author, Quintus Curtius,
had the effrontery to observe that the writings of that
biographer of Alexander the Great should be regarded
rather as romance than as veracious history, at which
Turenne fired up and stoutly asserted the contrary.
His mother, much amused, signalled to the officer to
persist in the argument. Very soon the little champion
of Quintus Curtius left the room in a rage, sought a
second and sent by him a challenge to the officer. On
receiving it, the officer showed it to the Duchess.
Delighted to see so much spirit in a lad who had hitherto been looked down upon as a nervous and useless
invalid, she asked the officer to accept the challenge
and to name as the scene of the duel a rendezvous
which she suggested. When the little duellist, attended

by his second, reached it on the following morning, he found his adversary in readiness; and, to his great surprise, beside his foe stood his mother, who gravely informed him that she had come to act as second to his opponent.   She then led both the duellists into a wood where they found a table prepared with a sumptuous breakfast and her courtiers waiting to join in it. When breakfast was over, horses and hounds appeared, and the two principals hunted together instead of fighting about Quintus Curtius.   The young Turenne was well fitted to ride to hounds, for, like many boys who have been delicate, walking little he rode much, and, if an indifferent pedestrian, he became a capital horseman.

One of his biographers, Monsieur de Ramsay, says that his characteristics, as a boy, were scrupulous truthfulness, mildness of manner, a discretion beyond his years, and extraordinary humanity.[1]   In the latter respect he was a great contrast to Condé, whom Lenet "one day saw cruelly whipped in the presence of M. le Prince (his father) for having put out the eyes of a sparrow".[2] Another feature of Turenne's character was his gener-

---

[1] *The History of Henri de la Tour Viscount of Turenne, Marshal-General of France; containing the Authorities. In three Parts. London: Printed by J. Bettenham. Sold by Bettesworth & Hitch, etc.*, 1735.   It was written by Ramsay for Turenne's great-nephew, the Prince of Turenne.   With it are Turenne's own Memoirs, the Duke of York's Memoirs, and many papers bearing upon Turenne's life.   The French edition contains plans of battles, several of which are given here in reduced size.

[2] *Life of Louis, Prince of Condé.*   By Lord Mahon.

osity : most of his pocket-money found its way into the hands of the poor ; nor did this characteristic end with his boyhood, for he was noted for his liberality, his self-denial, and his charity to the end of his life.

His health improved wonderfully when he was between the ages of twelve and thirteen and, the next year, his Spartan mother thought it time that his military education should begin.   Being a rigid Cal-vinist, she would not send him into the French army, because Richelieu was reported to be preparing an attack on the Huguenots ; but her Protestant brother, Prince Maurice of Nassau, President of the United Provinces, was fighting against the Popish Spaniards, and such a war was exactly suited to the tastes of the Duchess and her son, who was as strict a Calvinist as his mother. Turenne's brother, then Duke of Bouillon, had been serving under their uncle, Prince Maurice, for some little time.

Prince Maurice took a great fancy to his younger nephew and conversed much and freely with him ; but he made the boy begin his military duties by carrying a musket in the ranks.   Three months later the Prince died and was succeeded by his brother, Henry, who by giving a company of infantry to Turenne made him a captain when barely fifteen.   The little captain was accompanied by a tutor or governor, as he was called ; for, at the siege of Bois-le-Duc, the Prince of Orange thought it necessary to reprimand Henry for unnecessarily exposing himself to danger, in disobedi-ence to "his governor".   Not long afterwards these restrictions were relaxed and Turenne was allowed to accompany his elder brother in intercepting a detachment of Spaniards, who were coming to the relief of Bois-le-Duc, when a sharp skirmish took place, in which the two brothers distinguished themselves unhurt, while the nervous governor was wounded.

Turenne's military service in Holland lasted five years, and during the greater part of that period he was employed on sieges. The time thus spent proved of great value to him, and he made the most of his opportunities of learning all about forts and fortifications. "You might see him continually with a measuring rod or a pencil in his hand," says Ramsay. "He examined and considered everything that offered, and made his remarks upon the answers he received from the officers, engineers, pioneers and even the meanest soldiers, to his questions." It was during these experiences that he learned much about the art of defending a besieged fort, knowledge which he is said to have retailed to others in his "maxims"; such as "Lay on the parapet of your ramparts great beams, stones, and fire-machines to crush or burn all who may slip into your fosse. . . . Have ready . . . all sorts of combustible stuff as oil, lime, boiling pitch, tallow, molten lead, burning sand, and everything your imagination can suggest for the annoyance of the enemy."

Much as he was interested in the arts of defending and besieging fortresses, he began to wish for a wider range of military experience; and his chance of obtaining it soon came. Richelieu was intriguing to abolish

the sovereign independence of Sedan, and was pitting
his brains against those of the Duchess of Bouillon,
who was doing all she could to frustrate the attempts
of the cardinal.   At one point of the proceedings, when
directly opposing a suggestion of Richelieu's, she sent
Turenne to Paris as a kind of hostage.

Very shortly before Turenne's arrival in Paris a
curious scene had been enacted.   The King of France
was on his knees, beside him knelt Cardinal Richelieu,
and before them stood Marie de' Medici in a towering
passion.   When Louis XIII. had been dangerously ill,
his mother had induced him to promise the dismissal
of Richelieu, whom she herself had raised to eminence,
but now wished to hurl from power.   On her son's restoration to health, she had called upon him to fulfil this
promise.   By way of reply, he had brought Richelieu
into her presence; and, kneeling side by side, the cardinal
had begged her forgiveness and the King had besought
her to grant it.   Crying with rage, the Queen-Mother
gave vent to a torrent of abuse against Richelieu,
called him a traitor to his face, and, in answer to the
supplications of her son, told him that she would never
forgive him for being the author of this unpleasant
incident.   Probably her pardon and good graces, if
granted, would have been accepted.   As they were
refused the entire position was altered; and she little
suspected that, while she looked scornfully down
upon them, she was in reality standing on her
own trial before her two judges upon their knees.
Richelieu had little trouble in persuading the King

that his mother was encouraging cabals which endangered the throne, and she barely escaped arrest by
a hurried flight to Flanders. Richelieu then became
paramount; and he had just attained to this position
when Turenne reached Paris.

Turenne, who was now nineteen, was very well received at the French Court and Richelieu put him in
command of a regiment of infantry. Neither he nor his
mother had then any scruple about his serving under the
French banner, as the arms of France were at that time
allied to those of the United Provinces, and Turenne
took part in one or two campaigns in which both armies
were engaged. But the first opportunity he had of
obtaining great military glory was in a war brought
about through the medium of a woman ; and women
had a finger in most of the disputes which led to the
wars wherein Turenne distinguished himself during
the next few years.

Charles, Duke of Lorraine, had made a marriage for political purposes only, or, to speak more
accurately, for purposes of personal aggrandisement.
He was shamefully and unconcealedly unfaithful to
his wife, who left him to implore the protection of
Louis XIII. of France. On the other hand, her
husband attached himself to the House of Austria,
which Richelieu made an excuse for seizing Nancy
and, afterwards, Lorraine.

In March, 1634, the French troops had taken
every place of importance in the enemy's country,
with the exception of La Motte, a fortress situated at

the summit of a very high rock, which was of so hard a substance as to render sapping and mining extremely difficult. After enormous labour, five mines were made, a bastion was shattered, and the general in command, Marshal de la Force, whose daughter Turenne married some years later, sent his son to attack it. He made a gallant effort but was obliged to retire. The next day the marshal sent Turenne with his regiment on a similar errand. The enemy not only kept up a very heavy fire, but rolled enormous stones over the top of the parapet. These stones, falling upon points of rock, broke into many pieces and killed or disabled numbers of Turenne's men, as they tried to scale the heights. Nothing daunted, Turenne pressed on at their head, and eventually he succeeded in effecting an entrance into the fortress, which then surrendered. A remarkable incident in this siege was that, when the governor of the fortress was killed, his brother, a Capuchin Friar, conducted the defence. We have not yet done, however, with ecclesiastical warriors. Two more will figure in the next chapter. Marshal de la Force reported so highly of Turenne in despatches that, at the age of twenty-three, he was raised by Richelieu to the rank of marechal-de-camp, or major-general.

CHAPTER II.

IT is a disputed question whether it is better to form one's ideas of the personalities of the past exclusively from the records of their doings, or to seek the help of portraiture. Most people may have observed that the representations of their own friends on canvas or in marble have been very misleading in many instances. Probably the chisel, the pencil and the brush have been the mediums of as much mendacity as the pen.

In trying to imagine the appearance of Turenne, we have the assistance of his portraits and his description by Ramsay. Unfortunately, neither enables us to picture to our minds either a very imposing or a very handsome personage. Of but medium height, broad-shouldered, and rather short-necked, he was near-sighted and he stammered. His hair was of a dark chestnut, and his heavy eyebrows, according to Ramsay, almost met, although this is not shown in all his portraits. His forehead was high and prominent; his cheek-bones were high and wide; wide, too, was his mouth; but his cheeks themselves were rather sunken, and if his jaws were not very narrow, his chin, instead of having the width said to be the characteristic of those born to command, was inclined to be pointed. His expression was a curious mixture of sternness and amiability. No one could fairly call him handsome, and his appearance was not improved by his trick of carrying his head slightly on one side. Yet his contemporary, St. Evremond, said there "was something in his countenance that discovered an inexpressible greatness of soul and mind".

In ordinary conversation he was neither fluent nor brilliant, he seemed to prefer silence to talking; and, partly perhaps from this reason, he was a patient listener. He was remarkable, we might even say distinguished, for scarcely ever talking about himself. In appearance, manner and disposition he seems to have inherited more of the characteristics of his stolid Dutch mother than those of his brilliant French father.

A most trustworthy friend and (in later years) a faithful and devoted husband, he was, both in friendship and in love, prosaically moderate. His affection took the form of good services—sometimes splendid services —to those whom he liked or loved, rather than that of rapture or rhetoric. A skilful and most persevering adversary, in warfare he felt little, if any, personal hatred towards his enemies. He was as stolid and unemotional in military as in domestic matters. There was more of cold common sense than of fervid enthusiasm in his strategy, more of logical calculation than of fire and dash in his tactics, and his calm, taciturn contemplation of the game of war was what might have been expected from a grandson of William the Silent. His social taciturnity, on the contrary, can hardly have been

a legacy from William, Prince of Orange, who was by
no means given to holding his tongue, and in fact
obtained the nickname of "the Silent" from his silence
on one particular occasion.   It is more likely that
Turenne inherited from him his strength of character,
his love of justice, his dislike of luxury, and his personal
courage.

When serving under generals who treated him
with scant courtesy, Turenne was scrupulously obedient,
obliging, good-tempered and cheerful.   When his
junior officers made mistakes, he reprimanded them
sharply in private, but endeavoured to conceal their
faults and their failures in public; and, whenever it
was possible, he gave a man who had lost his character
an opportunity of recovering it.

To private soldiers he was exceptionally considerate
and kind; he was constantly thinking and inquiring
about their wants and their comforts; and they looked
up to him as to a father as well as a commander.   He
possessed the happy power of talking familiarly to
those beneath him without the slightest loss of dignity.
His mere reproach was felt as a disgrace and as a
punishment.

By his servants he was beloved.   He always tried
to avoid giving them trouble; his personal wants were
few; he took an interest in all who served him; nor
did he ever scold them without good cause.   One
lovely morning having awakened earlier than usual, he
got up, went into his sitting-room, opened the window,
and leant out of it as far as he could reach to enjoy

the air and the scene. Only his legs remained in the room and he was in a bent position. He was meditating in profound peace, when he suddenly received a stinging blow upon the upper part of his thighs. Turning sharply round, he was confronted by one of his upper-servants, who immediately fell upon his knees and exclaimed in confusion: "Please forgive me, Monseigneur, I thought it was George".

"Well!" replied Turenne, in a gentle voice, as he fondled the injured part, "even if it had been George, there would have been no need to hit *quite* so hard." And that was the only notice which he took of the incident.[1]

Lest these pages about Turenne should be expected to consist solely of panegyric, it shall be stated that Ramsay admits nature to have "denied him that fire of genius, that liveliness of imagination, those qualities which constitute a sparkling, entertaining wit. . . . He neither said nor did anything that was useless." Such a description would, in most cases, mean that its subject was a dull companion.

Without questioning the above description as a whole, it may be open to doubt whether Ramsay was accurate in saying that he lacked imagination. Would it not be almost impossible for a successful commander-in-chief to be wanting in that quality? Could the strategist succeed unless he vividly imagined every movement which his adversary would be likely

[1] *Louis XIV. in Court and Camp.* By Col. A. C. P. Haggard, p. 79.

to make, in a given locality, under given circumstances? Again, although Turenne's strongest characteristics were truth and straightforwardness, he was a past master in the art of deceiving an enemy. And while Ramsay declared Turenne to be wanting in "entertaining wit," such a celebrated wit as Grammont said that " M. de Turenne was fond of merriment".

In the matter of food and drink, Turenne was exceedingly simple and exceptionally moderate. He ate little and was very quick over his meals. Des Maizeaux, in his notes to Bayle's *Dictionary* (vol. v., p. 35), says that the foreign officers with Turenne's armies used to praise "the good cheer of his table, but could not endure that the meals should be so short". On campaigns he sometimes shared the food of the private soldiers. While very generous, he was scrupulously economical. And he was at least as scrupulously honest. Unlike most generals of his period, he never sought to obtain wealth through his military successes ; nor did he attempt advancement by interest ; and when he died, he was rather poorer than when he had first inherited his patrimony.

In the seventeenth century the same men were frequently generals, admirals and politicians. Turenne never tried his hand as an admiral ; but although he hated politics, he was inevitably mixed up in them. Cardinal de Retz,[1] who had ample opportunities of judging, considered Turenne much more suited to be at the head of an army than of a party, as he was "not

[1] *Memoirs of Cardinal de Retz*, vol. i., p. 160.

venturesome enough for politics, although sufficiently
courageous for warfare"—a rather remarkable distinction!

Such was the man whom Richelieu made a major
general at the age of twenty-four.   It was at a moment when that very politic ecclesiastic had much upon
his mind.   He had made an alliance with the Swedes
to try to crush the Emperor Ferdinand II.; he had
made another alliance with Bernard, Duke of Saxe-
Weimar, in hope of wresting Franche-Comté from
Philip IV.; he had made others with the Dukes of
Savoy, Parma and Mantua, for the purpose of invading Milan; and he had made one more with the
United Provinces, with the agreement that he and they
should divide Flanders between them.   In short,
Richelieu now joined for the first time in the Thirty
Years' War, a war which was originally undertaken with
the object of obtaining liberty for Protestants, but was
converted by that astute diplomatist into a war for the
aggrandisement of Catholic France.

Besides the powers already described on either side,
there was a perfidious potentate who fought sometimes
on one side and sometimes on the other.   "The Duke
of Lorraine," Ramsay tells us, "although deprived of
his sovereignty by Richelieu, still kept up a small army
of between ten and twelve thousand men, which by
turns served the Empire, Spain and France.   The
money designed for the payment of his soldiers he
retained for his private use and suffered them to live
at discretion," which meant pillaging without scruple

2 *

any country in which they might happen to be at the moment. When he was fighting on one side he was generally negotiating with the other. At the time of which we are now thinking Lorraine happened to be on the side of Spain.

Cardinal Richelieu placed his main army of 20,000 infantry, 5,000 cavalry and fourteen guns under the command, not of a soldier from his youth, but of a brother cardinal, Cardinal de la Valette, a son of the Duke of Epernon, and, formerly, Archbishop of Toulouse, a see which he had resigned some years earlier. "His indifference to the wrath of Pope Urban VIII." says Dr. Ward in *The Cambridge Modern History* (iv., 367), "made him a fitting agent of the present policy of his fellow cardinal." His army advanced towards the Rhine and Turenne was one of its generals.

In 1635 La Valette, who was as indifferent a general as a bishop, advanced through Metz, joined his army with that of the Duke of Saxe-Weimar near the Rhine, and, after various manœuvres and adventures, fearlessly and imprudently established himself close to Mayence, on that river. The Imperial army was stationed about twenty-five miles to the south, at Worms, under General Galas, who, considering his forces too weak to attack La Valette, endeavoured to sever La Valette's communications by seizing Kaiserslautern, Saarbrücken and other towns, which lay on the road from Metz to Mayence, thus cutting off the convoys, which should have brought provisions to the French army. As a consequence, La Valette's soldiers were soon reduced to living on roots and herbs, and his horses on the leaves of trees and vines. Under these circumstances, retirement was inevitable, and it was conducted under exceptionally difficult conditions. In this retreat, one of the most trying and disastrous in the history of the seventeenth century, Turenne did splendid service under great disadvantages, fighting a series of rearguard actions, personally enduring severe bodily privations, and labouring to alleviate the sufferings of the troops.

At one point, when Galas was pursuing them, Turenne lay in ambush with 9,000 horse as the Imperial troops were entering a defile, and routed them with great loss; but sufficient of the enemy remained to dog the footsteps of the retreating allies. Some of Turenne's men deserted to their foes in hope of having their hunger appeased. He threw out of the waggons all baggage which could possibly be dispensed with to make room for his men who were too weak to walk; and he shared the food provided for his own personal use with the common soldiers. "In short, he showed an activity, a courage, and above all a humanity, which drew the admiration of the army and the attention of the Court."[1]

In the summer of the following year (1636) La Valette besieged Saverne, a city of Alsace about twenty miles north-west of Strasburg. On the last day of the siege Turenne was wounded in the right arm by a musket-bullet. The surgeons decided to

[1] Ramsay.

amputate, but the operation, put off, was never performed.   Later in the autumn 1636, Turenne had
not quite recovered from this wound, when he was
sent by La Valette to drive the Imperial army under
Galas, which had already sustained a heavy defeat near
Dijon, out of Franche-Comté and across the Rhine, a
service which he performed with success.

These accounts of Turenne's early military experiences will seem brief, abrupt and dry : the cause of
their brevity is the necessity of reserving space for
more detailed descriptions of his services when a commander-in-chief.

In 1637 Richelieu sent La Valette to attack
Flanders.   That general entrusted to Turenne the
task of besieging two fortresses, Landreçies, a city on
the borders, and Sobre-sur-Sambres, the strongest
castle in Hainaut.   After the capitulation of the
last named, a fortress garrisoned by 2,000 men
which surrendered in a few hours, the soldiers found
a woman of extraordinary beauty and, knowing that
Turenne was highly susceptible to female charms,
they brought her to him, thinking to please him
by giving him the choicest gem of all the booty.
He thoroughly understood their meaning; but, pretending not to do so, he commended their conduct
in bringing so dangerously beautiful a woman under
his protection.   Finding that she was married, he
sent some soldiers to find her husband.   When he
had arrived, Turenne delivered her into his hands
and told him that he owed the preservation of

the honour of his wife to the virtue and discreet behaviour of the soldiers of France then present. This story goes far to disprove the assertion that Turenne was unimaginative.

Cardinal de la Valette was now opposed by another military cardinal, the Cardinal Infant of Spain.[1] This Spanish cardinal outgeneralled the French cardinal and would have given him a serious defeat, had it not been for the presence of mind and rapid movements of a layman, Turenne, now a lieutenant-general, who obliged the Cardinal Infant to fly and, in so doing, to lose many of his men in crossing a river. Like those of 1635 and 1636, the campaign of 1637 was indecisive and unsatisfactory.

In 1638 Turenne was sent to the assistance of the Duke of Weimar, who took Breisach, after a siege of eight months, a siege in which Turenne proved the main factor of success. Breisach, a fortress on the Rhine, some forty or fifty miles south of Strasburg, was a most important place to conquer, as its retention included the submission of Alsace and protected Burgundy. Reynac, who commanded at Breisach, made a gallant defence, but that defence entailed terrible and ghastly sufferings. "Provisions became so excessively scarce," says Ramsay, "that he was obliged to post some of his soldiers in the churchyard, to prevent

---

[1] There was yet another contemporary fighting bishop. When Schomberg took Tortosa in 1648, its bishop "was found amongst the foremost killed in the breach, with a pike in his hand" (De Motteville, i., chap. xi.).

digging up the bodies of the dead;" and Ramsay
quotes Pussendorf in support of this statement. At
last Reynac had only one fort left, but it made him
master of the principal branch of the Rhine, by which
he hoped for succour; and so long as he held it, he
would not listen to terms. The Duke of Weimar
ordered Turenne to attack it. "Turenne advanced
to it at the head of 400 men, who cut down the
palisades with hatchets, entered it in three places at
once, and put all who defended it to the sword." This
may sound cruel; but it was the custom of the times,
when a fortress was obstinately defended after its
garrison had had terms offered and had refused them.
At the end of this long and tedious campaign under
Weimar, in 1638, Turenne had a serious attack of
quartan ague; and, not very long afterwards, Weimar
died.

In the winter, 1638, Turenne went to Court, where
Richelieu received him with great honour, and at that
time Richelieu was practically King of France. Of
poor Louis XIII. Madame de Motteville (*Memoirs*,
vol. i., chap. ii.) says: "He found himself reduced to
the most melancholy, most miserable life in the world;
without suite, without court, without power, and without honour. In this way several years of his life were
passed at St. Germain, where he lived like a private
person . . . amusing himself by snaring birds. . . .
Jealous of the grandeur of his minister [Richelieu]
. . . he began to hate him." Richelieu offered to
Turenne one of his nieces in marriage. This offer

opened a prospect of high military advancement as well as of wealth; but Turenne refused it because, as he told the cardinal, he was a Protestant and the lady was a Catholic, and husbands and wives were unlikely to be happy together if they were of different religions. To so staunch a Calvinist as Turenne, it must have been a great grief that, a little before this time, his elder brother, the Duke of Bouillon, to use a phrase common in this country, "went over to Rome". The apparent cause of the Duke's change of faith, was the "piety void of ostentation and free from all trifling devotions" of his wife Eleanor, who came from the family of De Bergues in Gelderland. This led him to inquire into "the doubts and difficulties which her conversation raised in his mind about Calvinism"; and he soon perceived "the absurdity of a sect whose fundamental principles, by denying freewill, by consequence make God the author of evil".[1] From a worldly point of view, Bouillon was a heavy loser by becoming a Catholic, as he thereby offended his uncle, the old Prince of Orange, who had intended to nominate him as his successor in the government of the United Provinces, and he thus lost all interests in Holland, while he had Richelieu as an enemy because, although he had changed his religion, he had not changed the republican principles which he had imbibed in that country.

If Turenne, who had no republican principles, had

[1] Ramsay.

thought only of his temporal advancement, it would have been greatly to his interest to have made his brother's change of religion an excuse for following his example and to have married the niece of Richelieu; but he was not the kind of man who would change his faith for such a reward.

An event of great importance had happened in this year of 1638. The Court party had hoped for the fall, or, at any rate, for the diminished importance of Richelieu, when the weakly Louis XIII. should die, if that King were to be succeeded by the Duke of Orleans; but in 1638 a son was born to Louis, and the courtiers had good reason for fearing that the government would be bequeathed to Richelieu during the boy's minority, in which case the power of the cardinal, instead of being decreased by the death of Louis XIII., would be rendered almost absolute.   In short, it is doubtful whether any visitor to a court was less welcome to the majority of its inmates than the royal baby who was in four years to reign as Louis XIV. and to become celebrated in history as Le Grand Monarque.

CHAPTER III.

IN our times the family affairs of a monarch never lead to a war; and, much more than this, near relationships between the royal families of two countries never prevent one; but in the seventeenth century it was far otherwise.

Louis XIII.'s sister, Marie Christine, widow of the Duke of Savoy, implored the help of her brother against her brother-in-law, Prince Thomas, and against the Cardinal of Savoy, upon whom the Emperor had bestowed the regency during the minority of the young Duke, Charles Emmanuel. In 1638 La Valette was sent by the King of France to her assistance, but he was very unsuccessful and incurred thereby the displeasure of Richelieu. So threatening indeed became the wrath of Richelieu, that, to escape from it, La Valette fled to England, where he joined the banished Queen-Mother; and he died in the following year.

It was supposed that Turenne would be appointed to La Valette's command; but his brother, the Duke of Bouillon, had just done something which offended Richelieu, who was probably also not overpleased at Turenne's refusal of his niece. Therefore, Richelieu gave the command-in-chief to Count d'Harcourt, and placed Turenne under him.

How far the successes of Count d'Harcourt were

owing to the skill and courage of Turenne may be doubtful; but Turenne's biographers claim them in every instance.   After the success known as the battle of La Route de Quiers, a place about five or six miles from Turin, in a letter to Paris Turenne said little or nothing about his own part in it; but, in reply, a friend wrote back that, according to Turenne's account, Fame must have been mistaken, "since she everywhere published that he had had the principal part in the victory".

The next spring (1640) at Casal, a town a few miles to the north of Turin, Count d'Harcourt, with 10,000 men, defeated Leganez, the Spanish general, who had 20,000; and this battle is interesting, because it is the first instance we meet with of Turenne's wonderful skill in deceiving his enemies.   At one moment of that battle, Harcourt was nearly surrounded and taken prisoner by the enemy's cavalry; but Turenne "immediately drew up all the cavalry of the army together so close in one single front that the enemy could not discern whether they were supported or not.   Deceived by this disposition, their courage failed them, and they fled to the right and to the left. Turenne pursued them till night, took twelve pieces of cannon, six mortars, and the greatest part of their baggage; 3,000 men were killed in the field of battle, 1,800 were made prisoners, great numbers were drowned in the Po, and the rest owed their safety to the night only."[1]

[1] Ramsay.

In the tactics of Turenne, deception of the enemy as to the numerical strength of his troops took a very prominent position. Among the maxims attributed to him are these :—

"If your army be small, you must give it more front and less depth ; and let the same troops pass in the sight of the enemy several times ; widen your intervals, let your drums beat and your trumpets sound out of sight of the enemy, and where you have no troops. On the contrary, if you are strong, hide part of your troops behind some cover, and let your front be narrow, by giving depth to your regiments and drawing one or more in the rear of the other." And again, "To throw terror and consternation into the enemy's country, separate your troops into several bodies as secretly as you can, to execute several enterprises at the same time. Let it be reported abroad that your troops are more numerous than they are, and to confirm this opinion let bodies of them appear in different places at the same time."[1]

Contrary to the advice of the other generals, Turenne persuaded Harcourt to besiege Turin. His opponents urged that it was rash to attack with 10,000 men a fortified town garrisoned by 12,000 men, when Leganez, who still had 15,000 men, was coming to its assistance. So also thought Leganez himself, who wrote to Prince Thomas, the commander-in-chief in Turin, that Harcourt could not possibly escape him

[1] Williamson's *Military Memoirs and Maxims of Marshal Turenne*, 1740.

this time; and that the ladies of Turin had better hire windows looking into the principal street, as soon as possible, for the day when Leganez should lead Harcourt through it as a prisoner.

The siege of Turin brought about a very curious condition of affairs, which is thus described by Napoleon in his *Memoirs* dictated to Montholon.[1] " The siege afforded an extraordinary spectacle: the citadel occupied by the French was besieged by Prince Thomas of Savoy, who was master of the city, but he was himself besieged by the French army, whilst the latter was besieged in its lines of countervallation by the Spanish army under the command of the Marquis de Leganez."

Turenne was with that portion of the French army which was besieging Prince Thomas; and not with the portion which was besieged in the citadel.   In the course of a skirmish he was wounded in the shoulder by a musket-bullet.   Both the French in the citadel and the troops of Prince Thomas in the city were so short of provisions as to be nearly starving.   " It is asserted, that the town was supplied for some time by Francesco Zignoni Bergamesco, an Engineer, who filled several large bombs with meal, and threw them into the town over Count d'Harcourt's camp: but the

---

[1] *Memoirs of the History of France During the Reign of Napoleon Dictated by the Emperor at St. Helena to the Generals who Shared his Captivity and Published from the Original Manuscripts Corrected by Himself.*   Historical Miscellanies, vol. iii. Dictated to the Comte de Montholon.   London: Printed for Henry Colburn & Co., etc., 1823.   Copious quotations from this work will be found in these pages.

French having the benefit of such as fell by the way, this expedient was laid aside, which became almost as advantageous to the besiegers as to the besieged."[1]

The French besieged in the citadel fared much better; for Turenne, although still suffering from his wound, fought his way through ambuscades laid by Leganez, and conducted a convoy of provisions into the citadel. The result was that on the 17th of September, while the French in the citadel were able to withstand their besiegers, Prince Thomas, in the city, was forced by sheer want of food to capitulate. Leganez then retreated across the Po, and Marie Christine, Duchess of Savoy, re-entered Turin.

Count d'Harcourt remained in France during the early part of the Italian campaign of 1641, and left in command Turenne, who took Montecalvo and besieged Yvrée. This year, while Turenne was serving Richelieu in Piedmont, his brother, the Duke of Bouillon, was quarrelling with that cardinal. He, the Duke of Guise, and the Comte de Soissons, issued a manifesto throughout France, signing themselves "The Princes of Peace". In this manifesto they abused Richelieu and all his works. As a reply Richelieu sent an army of 10,000 men towards Sedan, in opposition to which Bouillon enlisted the assistance of the Imperial army. There was one great battle, in which the King's army was defeated; but soon afterwards the Imperial troops were withdrawn and Bouillon would have been in diffi-

[1] Ramsay. See also *L'histoire de la Republ. de Venise.* By Nani, tom. iv., lib. xi.

culties if the King of France had not granted him a pardon. In the course of the battle Soissons was found dead among his own guards, without having fought. "It is probable that he had unfortunately killed himself in attempting to raise the visor of his helmet with the end of his pistol,"[1] an action which one could scarcely imagine possible except on the stage of a theatre devoted to burlesque and broad farce.

For the details of the long and complicated dispute which followed, there is no room in these pages; but it may be stated that the Duke was arrested, in 1642, for being implicated in the plot of the Marquis of Cinq-Mars, who instigated Gaston, Duke of Orleans, to rebel and made a secret treaty with Spain for military assistance in that rebellion. Cinq-Mars was executed; but Bouillon, although he had joined in the conspiracy, had had nothing to do with the secret treaty with Spain. The Duchess of Bouillon announced that, if her husband were executed, she would immediately deliver up Sedan to the Spanish troops; and the Prince of Orange, the Landgrave of Hesse, and Turenne interceded for the Duke to such purpose that he was liberated and given certain large estates in France, on condition that he retired to the town of Turenne with the loss of his little sovereignty, and that the King's troops should occupy Sedan, which then became French territory.

The year 1642 was very eventful to France, for Cardinal Richelieu died in the course of it; and five months later died also his King, Louis XIII. When

[1] Ramsay.

this wretched King was told that his case was hopeless, he thanked his informant for "that good news, and assured him that he had never felt such joy in life, as he received in hearing that he was to lose it" (*Memoirs of Madame de Motteville*, vol. i., chap. ii.). The little new King, Louis XIV., was then only four and a half years old; and his mother, Queen Anne of Austria, was left Regent during his minority. Her regency was destined to be beset by many troubles, as we shall find in due time; but, for the present, we must turn our attention from France to Italy.

Prince Thomas of Savoy, not being treated by the Spaniards as he desired, openly broke away from them and took up the cause of his sister-in-law, the Duchess of Savoy. Upon this, Anne of Austria appointed him general of the army of the King of France in Italy; but being suspicious of his good faith, she made it a condition that he should have Turenne to advise him. Prince Thomas, being in bad health, was only too glad to have the assistance of Turenne, and very soon left the command of the army entirely in his hands.

That most straightforward of men, but most insidious of opponents in a campaign, Henry, Viscount of Turenne, succeeded in his Italian campaign of 1643 almost entirely by deceitfulness. His object was to drive the Spaniards out of Piedmont, and specially to oust them from Trino, a fortress on the Po, about thirty miles east of Turin; and he achieved that object as follows.

There are three towns forming a triangle. The

3

first of these is Trino, the second is Alessandria, which
is about thirty miles to the south-east of Trino; and
the third is Asti, a place famous—or according
to the opinion of some critics infamous—for the
wine bearing its name, about twenty miles to the
south of Trino, and about twenty-five to the west of
Alessandria.   In order to induce the Spaniards to
leave Piedmont, Turenne made a great demonstration
as if he intended to carry the war into the Duchy of
Milan.   He marched to Alessandria and pretended to
invest it; but he purposely left sufficient intervals in his
investment to allow the enemy to bring succours into
the town.   Completely deceived, the Spaniards withdrew half the garrison from Trino and threw it into
Alessandria.   As soon as the Spaniards had done this,
Turenne, who had everything in readiness, hurried back
with all his troops to Trino, quickly carried the out-
works and besieged it.   The Spaniards followed him
and tried to throw troops into Trino, as they had
succeeded in throwing them into Alessandria, by leading them between Turenne's lines; but against this
contingency Turenne had carefully provided.   Failing
to relieve Trino, the Spaniards adopted Turenne's
own stratagem and endeavoured to draw him away
from Trino by besieging Asti.   Turenne, however,
had foreseen the possibility of this danger and had
stored Asti with everything that could be necessary for
withstanding a siege.   He took Trino in six weeks;
and shortly after he had done so, Queen Anne of
Austria sent him the staff of a Marshal of France.

Turenne was no gambler, and he is reputed to have said: "Prevent gaming among the troops as much as possible. Soldiers have often deserted when they have lost their pay and are indebted to their fellow-soldiers, of which gaming is frequently the cause." But during the siege of Trino, one evening when that well-known gamester, Count Grammont, was visiting him, he proposed some play to entertain him. Grammont said that, when he visited friends, he did not consider it civil to take their money away with him, or prudent to leave his own behind. "You will find neither deep play nor much money here," replied Turenne; "but let each one of us stake a horse." A number of officers joined in the game, which resulted in Grammont winning fifteen horses, one of which he insisted on returning "to pay for the cards".[1]

Turenne was then (in 1643) thirty-two and he had served "an apprenticeship to the profession of arms," as Ramsay calls it, during seventeen years—one as a private, four as a captain, four as a colonel, three as a major-general, and five as a lieutenant-general. His own descriptions of the lessons which he had learned from the different masters of the art of war, under whom he had served, may be worth quoting. From his uncle, Henry, Prince of Orange, he learned "How to choose a camp with advantage and how to attack a town; to form a project as long as might be before he carried it out, to turn it over frequently in his thoughts,

---

[1] *Memoirs of the Court of Charles II.* By Count Grammont. Bohn's ed., 1846, pp. 54-55.

3 *

and to let nothing appear till the very moment of its execution ; to avoid ostentation, to fill his mind with elevated sentiments, and to have a more ardent zeal for the interests of his country than for his own glory ".

Of the Duke of Saxe-Weimar, he said "that he was a general who, with nothing, did everything, and yet was never vain of his successes; that, when misfortune befel him, instead of wasting time in complaints, he concentrated his whole attention upon getting out of it ; that he preferred to be unjustly blamed to excusing himself by laying the blame on others, even justly ; that when he committed a fault he tried to repair it instead of making apologies ; and, lastly, that he wished to be loved rather than to be feared by his soldiers ".

From Cardinal de la Valette he learned that to be popular with and trusted by his army on a campaign, "a general must renounce the delicacies, the gallantries, and the witty conversations of Court life, and live the same life as his officers, without ceremony or affectation ". As to Count d'Harcourt, he was a standing confirmation of the great maxim of Cæsar, " That, of all military virtues, diligence and expedition are the most essential, and that they seldom fail to be rewarded with success when accompanied by prudence and circumspection ".

By this time Turenne had obtained that reputation for extraordinary courage which he never lost; but the writer of these pages, in his endeavour to tell the whole truth, admits that he has found one, though only one,

account of nervousness in Turenne. The story is told
by Cardinal de Retz in the first book of his *Memoirs*.

Turenne, De Retz, the Bishop of Lisieux, three
ladies and two other men were driving back to Paris
in one of the gigantic coaches of the period, from an
entertainment at St. Cloud, very early in the morning.
Suddenly the coach stopped, and, when asked the cause,
the coachman replied: "Will you have me drive over
all the devils in hell which I see here before me?"
And, surely enough, in the dim light, weird black
figures could be seen moving slowly forward along the
road. The footmen all hid behind the coach "quaking
with fear. Madame de Choisie's shrieks made M. de
Turenne get out of the coach. . . . I took one of the
footmen's swords, which I drew, and went to join M.
de Turenne on the other side. I found him looking
steadfastly on something which I could not see."

Now both Turenne and De Retz were short-sighted.
De Retz could not see the mysterious objects at all, and
Turenne could only see them so dimly as to make
them appear still more mysterious and supernatural.
" M. de Turenne, who had drawn the little sword he
wore by his side, after he had looked about a little,
turned to me and said with the same air with which
he would have given the enemy battle: 'Let us go
towards them!' 'Towards whom?' I asked. . . .
'Why,' said he, 'towards those devils, for they may
really be devils for ought I know.'" De Retz now
saw what looked liked "a long procession of black
sprights, the sight of which," he says, "put me at first

owing to the skill and courage of Turenne may be doubtful; but Turenne's biographers claim them in every instance. After the success known as the battle of La Route de Quiers, a place about five or six miles from Turin, in a letter to Paris Turenne said little or nothing about his own part in it; but, in reply, a friend wrote back that, according to Turenne's account, Fame must have been mistaken, "since she everywhere published that he had had the principal part in the victory".

The next spring (1640) at Casal, a town a few miles to the north of Turin, Count d'Harcourt, with 10,000 men, defeated Leganez, the Spanish general, who had 20,000; and this battle is interesting, because it is the first instance we meet with of Turenne's wonderful skill in deceiving his enemies. At one moment of that battle, Harcourt was nearly surrounded and taken prisoner by the enemy's cavalry; but Turenne "immediately drew up all the cavalry of the army together so close in one single front that the enemy could not discern whether they were supported or not. Deceived by this disposition, their courage failed them, and they fled to the right and to the left. Turenne pursued them till night, took twelve pieces of cannon, six mortars, and the greatest part of their baggage; 3,000 men were killed in the field of battle, 1,800 were made prisoners, great numbers were drowned in the Po, and the rest owed their safety to the night only."[1]

[1] Ramsay.

In the tactics of Turenne, deception of the enemy as to the numerical strength of his troops took a very prominent position.   Among the maxims attributed to him are these :—

"If your army be small, you must give it more front and less depth ; and let the same troops pass in the sight of the enemy several times ; widen your intervals, let your drums beat and your trumpets sound out of sight of the enemy, and where you have no troops.   On the contrary, if you are strong, hide part of your troops behind some cover, and let your front be narrow, by giving depth to your regiments and drawing one or more in the rear of the other."   And again, "To throw terror and consternation into the enemy's country, separate your troops into several bodies as secretly as you can, to execute several enter- prises at the same time.   Let it be reported abroad that your troops are more numerous than they are, and to confirm this opinion let bodies of them appear in different places at the same time."[1]

Contrary to the advice of the other generals, Turenne persuaded Harcourt to besiege Turin.   His opponents urged that it was rash to attack with 10,000 men a fortified town garrisoned by 12,000 men, when Leganez, who still had 15,000 men, was coming to its assistance.   So also thought Leganez himself, who wrote to Prince Thomas, the commander-in-chief in Turin, that Harcourt could not possibly escape him

[1] Williamson's *Military Memoirs and Maxims of Marshal Turenne*, 1740.

ing-pan of the musket—and those of the match-lock, in
which the powder was set on fire by the fall of a hammer
upon a match in the priming-pan. A few years after
Turenne had become a field-marshal, both these locks
were superseded by the snaphaunce, an early form of
the flint-and-steel lock. When Turenne himself carried
a musket, the barrel was four feet long, or nearly double
the length of that at present in use in our own army.
The petronel, or poictrinal, was a heavy pistol, the
stock of which rested upon the right of a horseman's
breast when fired. The hargobusiers carried a carbine
three feet three inches in length. English dragoons
were armed with a dragon, a carbine with a barrel
sixteen inches long; but the French dragoons seem to
have been mounted infantry and carried long carbines.
The cuirassiers, or pistoliers, carried two carbines, with
barrels more than two feet in length.[1]

The rests to stick into the ground for the purpose
of placing the musket on their forked tops, known as
sweyn feathers, had probably fallen into disuse early in
Turenne's military career; but the Swedish army,
which was at one time allied to the French and fought
beside Turenne's, introduced a rest with sharp metal
spikes on the top of the forks, and, when its base was
thrust into the ground and the spikes sloped towards
the enemy, it served as a kind of fixed bayonet. But
the bayonet itself, in the form of a dagger with a hilt

[1] See Markham's *The Souldier's Accidence* (1645), Meyrick's
Critical Inquiry into Ancient Armour and *A Brief Treatise of War*
by W. T. (1649), *Harleian MS.*, No. 6000.

fitting into the muzzle of the musket, was introduced into the French army four years before the death of Turenne.[1]

It is doubtful to what extent cartridges came into use in Turenne's time; although the *Pallas Armata*, a book written towards the end of the lifetime of Turenne, says: "Horsemen should always have the charges of their pistols in patrons (boxes), the powder made up compactly in paper and the ball tied to it with a piece of packthread". But the usual practice of musketeers during most of Turenne's life was to carry the charges of powder in bandoleers hanging on a belt passed over one shoulder. Of these, Harford, in his *Military Discipline* (printed in 1680), says that they were dangerous because he had often seen them take fire, especially when a matchlock was used; "and when they take fire," he adds, "they commonly wound and kill him who wears them and those near him; for likely, if one bandoleer takes fire, all the rest do in that collar". And in recommending the use of cartridges, which were then just coming into use, he shows what the difficulties of musketeers must have been in at least many of the wars of Turenne. "Whoever loads his musket with cartridges, is sure the bullet will not drop out, though he takes his aim under breast high, for the paper of the cartridge keeps it in, whereas those soldiers which on service take their bullets out of their mouths (which is the nimblest way) or out of their pouches,

[1] Meyrick's *Critical Inquiry*, vol. iii., p. 118.

which is slow, seldom put any paper, tow, or grass, to ram the bullet in; whereby if they fire above breast high, the bullet passes over the head of the enemy; and if they aim low, the bullet drops out ere the musket is fired; and 'tis to this that I attribute the little execution I have seen musketeers do in time of fight, though they fired at great battalions, and those also reasonable near." One would imagine that the aim of a marksman would not be very steady or accurate if he had his mouth full of bullets; but it was a common practice, and, when describing the most honourable conditions of a capitulation, Turenne is stated to have said that the troops should be allowed "to march out, with arms and baggage, drums beating, colours flying, lighted matches, *ball in mouth*," etc.

In his splendid standard work, *The History of the British Army*, Mr. Fortescue says[1] that Gustavus Adolphus "encouraged the use of cartridges," and, as he died in 1632, and Turenne was a good deal in company with the Swedish army, it is probable that they were adopted in the French army also.

In the middle of the seventeenth century infantry were divided into musketeers and pikemen. Markham, in his *Souldier's Accidence*, says that pikes should be of ash-wood, "well headed with steel, and armed with plates downward, at least four feet," and that the length of the pike ought to be fifteen feet, "besides the head"; but Mr. Fortescue says that in the continental armies, about the time of Turenne's great campaigns,

[1] Vol. i., p. 181.

the pikes had been cut down, from fifteen or even eighteen feet, to eleven feet. Besides the pike, favourite weapons with the defenders in sieges were scythes— "scythes set in long staffs to reverse," of which Turenne said : " Scythes are of great use to cut off the enemy as they mount, overset their ladders, and tumble them into the fosse, when it is easy to fire on them ".

In France, says Meyrick,[1] the pay of the pikemen "was somewhat greater than that of the musketeers," and the tallest and strongest men were chosen for that service. They also carried swords. Vauban, says Napoleon, in his dictated *Memoirs*, effected the abolition of the pike ; and Vauban served with Turenne ; but he was too young a soldier to have brought about its complete abolition in Turenne's time. Pikemen wore an open helmet, armour on the breast, the back and the front of the thighs ; strong buff or leather coats, and very large leather gauntlets. Musketeers wore no armour except a "pot-helmet"—a sort of steel, flat-brimmed, bowler hat—but they had strong leathern coats, supposed to be nearly sword proof, and, like the pikemen, they carried swords.

Popular as was the pike, in the earlier wars which we are about to consider, its near relative, the lance, as a weapon for cavalry, had gone out of fashion. This is the more extraordinary, because the knights of old had jousted with it, and it had been the chief weapon of cavalry in the middle ages. No cavalry seem to

[1] *Critical Inquiry*, vol. iii., p. 122.

have used the lance in the wars of Turenne; yet, whereas the pike was in its decadence in Turenne's later wars, the lance had its second birth in the following century, owing to the renown of the Cossack and the Polish Lancers, and, as everybody knows, it is still used by modern cavalry.

The proportion of cavalry to infantry, in the seventeenth century, was enormous. Napoleon says: "At least one half of an army, at this period, was composed of cavalry. . . . At present four-fifths of every army are infantry." The most honourable kind were the pistoliers, or cuirassiers, even the troopers in many such regiments being entirely of gentle birth. They wore armour as low as the knee and carried so-called pistols and swords. The second class of cavalry were carbineers, or hargobusiers, and the troopers were supposed to be of the yeoman class. They, too, wore armour and they carried carbines much longer than the rifles of the present day, as well as swords. The third class of cavalry consisted of dragoons, men of a lower type and practically mounted infantry, who were armed with "dragons," or, more usually in the French army, with carbines and short swords. They wore no armour except helmets, but they had strong buff coats. Turenne was a great advocate of dragoons; although they were not used in any great numbers in the French army until the second half of the seventeenth century. "Cavalry," says Lord Wolseley (*Life of Marlborough*, vol. i., p. 91), were "mounted on big, clumsy 'war-horses'"; but the horses of dragoons, "the mounted infantry of to-day," were "small and light—seldom above fourteen and a half hands high ".

In that century cavalry were put to uses unknown to them in our times. When an attack was to be made upon fortifications, or entrenchments, the infantry were followed by squadrons of cavalry loaded with fascines and hurdles. When a particularly rapid march was to be made, a foot-soldier mounted behind every trooper. Cavalry horses, therefore, were sometimes loaded with bundles of sticks, and sometimes had two men on their backs.

Cartridges, and even shells of some sort, were used by the French artillery, even in the reign of Henry IV., the predecessor of Louis XIII. In his reign, says Colonel Chesney,[1] "improved missiles, such as tin cases filled with steel bolts or darts, also canvas cartridges filled with small balls, and hollow shot filled with combustible materials," were in use. Bombs are said to have been invented by Cosimo and Francis de' Medici[2] early in the sixteenth century, although they were supposed for many years to be more dangerous to friends than to foes ; but, as we have already seen, they were used in the time of Turenne. According to General Williamson, Turenne recommended that upon the bastions of fortified cities should be placed "mortars to throw stones with, and cannons loaded with grape-shot or pieces of old iron ".

[1] *Observations on the Past and Present State of Fire Arms* (1852), p. 67.
[2] Napier's *Florentine History*, vol. v., p. 262.

As to cartridges for cannon, Mr. Fortescue says that while they were undoubtedly used, it was more common to load the guns with loose powder in a ladle, and, on the title-page of a French history of Turenne,[1] there is an engraving of a gun being fired with a tremendous puff of smoke from the touch-hole, while large powder barrels are standing close to it.[2] Mr. Fortescue says that a gun's crew consisted of a gunner, his mate, and an odd man, one of whose duties was to cover up the powder barrel before the gun was fired, lest a spark should ignite its contents.   The rolling out of the missile was a contingency which embarrassed gunners as much as musketeers.   " Military writers," says Mr. Fortescue, "generally agreed that cannon should be posted on an eminence, since a ball travels with greater force downhill than uphill.   On the other hand, it was objected even to this simple rule that if guns were pointed downhill there was always a risk of the shot rolling out of the muzzle."   The gunners of those days evidently experienced the same difficulties which used to try our tempers as boys, when the peas we used to put into our little spring-cannons would persist in rolling out, unless we gave the guns such an elevation that they sent the peas higher than the heads of our tin enemies.

A very important addition was made to guns in

[1] *La Vie du Vicomte de Turenne.*   Par M. du Buisson (1695).
[2] Col. C. H. Owen, in his *Principles and Practice of Modern Artillery* (1831), p. 301, says much the same as Mr. Fortescue as to cartridges having been in use in the seventeenth century, but the ladle and loose powder having been more usual.

PICTURE OF A BATTLE.

From the Title-page of Du Buisson's *Vie du Vicomte Turenne*, 1695.

France, about 1650, in the elevating screw, and French
guns were greatly improved and superior to those of
other nations in the second half of the seventeenth
century. Possibly this may have had something to do
with Turenne's successes. The guns of the seventeenth
century were generally 4-pounders or 6-pounders, and
were drawn either by the heavy horses of the country
or by bullocks. When a reverse occurred and a hasty
retreat had to be made, the guns were generally
abandoned. Sometimes, however, very much heavier
guns were used. Most of Tilly's were 24-pounders
and required twenty transport horses. Turenne also
recommends 24-pounders "to batter in the breach,"
as siege guns, but he says, "You must have small and
great cannon, but most small, because they are more
easily removed from place to place than the great".
For sudden surprises, he even advises "small pieces of
artillery, mounted on very light carriages, and drawn by
one horse each ".[1]

In the reign of Louis XIV.[2] a battery of artillery
consisted of four guns. It was accompanied by a cart
of tools drawn by four horses; three carts of powder;
eight carts each carrying fifty round-shot, ten cartridges
and six packets of wicks; five carts each carrying

[1] Williamson's *Maxims of Turenne*.
[2] *Maximes et Instructions sur l'art Militaire. Supplement à
l'Histoire Militaire de Louis le Grand.* Par M. le Marquis de
Quincy. Mariette, Paris, 1726, tom. vii., 2e partie. See also
Turenne et l'Armée Francaise en 1674. Par le Captaine Cordier
(1895).

powder and three barrels of lead. There were also two "chariots" for officers of artillery, who appear not to have ridden, but to have driven. For a battery of four guns with its carts 118 horses in all were used— when they were available—and these horses were all for draught; none of them being for riding purposes.

Turenne is said to have recommended that, in some cases, cannon should be charged "with old nails, bolts, pieces of iron chains, old iron, and chain-bullets".

An implement of war much used in the seventeenth century was the petard. The following description of one is said to be by Turenne: "The petard is a sort of brass pot, very thick in metal, they are generally 6 inches thick at the mouth, 10 at the bottom, and about 10 wide, their weight is about 60 lb. They have a touch-hole, and you load them with good powder. Your petard is strongly fixed to a piece of oak plank, 2 feet broad, 2½ or 3 feet thick or more. This plank is strongly fixed to a gate, drawbridge or the like to burn them open. They are likewise used to open palisades, or throw down a wall that is sapped." [1]

Tactics, during the career of Turenne, varied and developed considerably. The order of battle commonly consisted of two lines and a reserve. There was a body of cavalry on either flank, the infantry were in

---

[1] "Let it work: for 'tis the sport to have the engineer hoist with his own petard; and it shall go hard, but I will delve one yard below their mines, and blow them at the moon" (*Hamlet*, act iii., scene iv.).

the centre and the artillery were generally placed in front of the centre of the first line. The intervals between the battalions and squadrons were equal to their fronts; and the battalions and squadrons of the second line and the reserve covered the intervals in the line in front of them.

An action was generally opened by the artillery. Then the cavalry on the wings charged the cavalry opposed to them. If, after a successful charge, the cavalry could be collected, it attacked the flanks of the infantry; but too often it got out of hand and amused itself by pillaging the camp and baggage of the enemy. When cavalry attacked infantry it galloped to within firing-range—but a short distance with the arms of the period—and fired from the saddle.[1] Then it advanced with the sword. The companies of pikemen were in line, from six to ten deep or more, and between these companies of pikemen stood the musketeers. When the cavalry were advancing the musketeers fired, and then ran to the rear of the pikemen to reload. The pikemen received the cavalry by sloping their pikes and resting the butts of them against their right feet. Pikemen were very carefully drilled and, as they stood in close order, they presented a formidable front to cavalry. These tactics, however, were sometimes modified, especially in the Swedish army; and it

[1] In the background of the equestrian portrait of Turenne, given as an illustration later in this book, troopers may be observed galloping to the front, carrying, not swords, but carbines in their hands, ready to fire. The officers are carrying swords.

4

gradually became more common to place larger groups of musketeers between the companies of pikemen.

It was in strategy that Turenne was chiefly remarkable, in comparison with the other great generals of his period. A soldier who lived in his days said that he should like to be with Condé at the end of a battle and with Turenne at the end of a campaign. Battles and sieges had been, and still were, considered the main part of war; but Turenne thought marches, countermarches, and manœuvres at least as important. He said, "It is a great mistake to waste men in taking a town when the same expenditure of soldiers will gain a province".

The conditions of those times presented many difficulties to a strategist. Roads were very bad, very few, and very far between; as a consequence of their rarity, the enemy was pretty safe from attack, except from perhaps one or two well-known lines of communication. A general, therefore, could rarely surprise his enemy.

Roads frequently ran along the sides of rivers, and the important bridges across those rivers were generally commanded by fortified towns. One of these fortified towns on a line of communication could not be left behind neglectfully, lest the garrison should cut off, or carry off, the convoys; therefore, if they could not be taken, forces had to be left to invest them. Not only were the roads very bad, being mere tracks, undrained, and with stones thrown into them, but worse still was the ground on either side through which they passed.

Scarcely anywhere was there agricultural drainage, and, near the rivers, the roads often ran through bogs, quagmires and morasses.

Very little land was cultivated, except close to the towns or villages. Even in times of peace an isolated farm would have been pillaged by robbers. In consequence of the scarcity of tillage, an army had to carry nearly everything with it. This stood much in the way of any division of forces and, as a result, in the way of many strategical operations. On the other hand, a general was not obliged to weaken his force by dividing it in order to feed it, and he therefore always had it with him, under his own eyes, under his immediate command, and ready for action at any moment. But when, as often happened, an army had consumed the provisions which it had been carrying, all this was changed and it had to divide and forage as best it could.

In fortifications, as in other military matters, there were important developments in the seventeenth century. Errard, of Bois-le-Duc, had been the chief authority on fortifications in France at the beginning of that century, and in 1629 Antoine de Ville published his treatise in which the system of Errard was developed and improved. But in 1645 Comte de Pagan, an author who had written works upon astronomy and mathematics, brought out a book in which he demonstrated that fortifications were at that time planned too much upon abstract mathematical principles and venerable custom, and not enough upon practical experience and the necessities of modern arms. Unfortunately

4 *

this eminent engineer, after serving at twenty·five sieges and gaining a great reputation, became blind at the age of thirty-eight.   But an engineer of at least equal ability was in readiness to work upon Pagan's principles and to develop, if not to perfect, his system. Sébastien le Prestre de Vauban, who was born in 1633 and had shown extraordinary geometrical talent as a boy, conducted fifty-three sieges, and took part in a great number of battles.   He combined experience with theory; as the inventor of parallels in sieges he became one of the most distinguished engineers of all history, and he left behind him twelve folio manuscript volumes recording both his principles and his practice.   In the later campaigns of Turenne, Vauban played an important part; and he revolutionised the art of fortification to such an extraordinary extent that, whereas before he had established his system, a period including all the earlier campaigns of Turenne, the advantage in a siege lay with the defence, it afterwards rested with the attack, provided that the attack was conducted with adequate means and on scientific principles.

In accounts of the wars of the seventeenth century, a reader might naturally be surprised at the wholesale returns of prisoners to their own countries and even to their own armies; but, in those times, a large capture of prisoners was a great embarrassment, on account of the difficulty in feeding them.   For this reason it was usual to take from them their arms and their equipments—very valuable things when little

machinery had been invented for making such things [1]—
and then to set them free.   For the same reason, when
an enemy suffered defeat the slaughter may possibly
have been continued rather longer than in more modern
battles.   " Putting-to-the-sword "—a prettier expression
than "killing the prisoners "—occasionally comes in for
casual mention in the history of seventeenth century
warfare.

[1] " The Arsenal at Woolwich or the factories at Essen probably
turn out more military armaments in the course of a week, than
did the sword makers of Toledo or the armourers of Mons in the
course of a century, at the time which we are considering "
(*Turenne.*   By H. M. Hozier, p. 53).

CHAPTER V.

IF the princes and the courtiers imagined their troubles to be ended by the death of Richelieu, or that Richelieu was the only ambitious ecclesiastic in France, they were mightily mistaken; for, if six was the quantity represented by Cardinal Richelieu, that represented by Cardinal Mazarin may be roughly estimated at half a dozen. Voltaire couples them together thus in his *Henriade* (vii., 327 *seq.*):—

> Richelieu, Mazarin, ministres immortels,
> Jusqu' au trône élevés de l'ombre des autels,
> Enfants de la fortune et de la politique,
> Marcheront à grand pas au pouvoir despotique,
> Richelieu, grand, sublime, implacable enemi :
> Mazarin, souple, adroit, et dangereux ami ;
>
> Tous deux haïs du peuple, et tous deux admirés ;
> Enfins, par leurs efforts, ou par leurs industrie,
> Utiles à leurs rois, cruels à la patrie.

When Turenne returned to Paris in the autumn of 1643 Queen Anne of Austria was Regent ; Gaston, Duke of Orleans, was Lieutenant-General of the Kingdom, and the direction of the Government was under a council, consisting of the Prince of Condé, Cardinal Mazarin, Seguier the Chancellor, and two

others. The Queen had always had the support of
what may be called the old Court party, and, through
her, that party hoped to be paramount for a long lease,
as the King was only four and a half years old. The
Court party tolerated, even encouraged, Mazarin, because he was necessary for putting foreign affairs on a
satisfactory footing; but, that done, they intended him
to sink into a subordinate position. During the last
illness of her husband the Queen had entrusted her
children to the charge of the Duke of Beaufort, the
youngest son of the Duke of Vendôme.   The confidence thus shown to him had led the courtiers to
suppose that he would be the Queen's chosen adviser
and minister on the death of the King.   For some
time after that event the Queen apparently showed
equal favour to Beaufort and to Mazarin.   Beaufort
used to spend much of his time by her side; meanwhile
Mazarin, who was determined to be supreme, was
quietly biding his time.

At a moment when everything seemed to promise
profound peace at Court an absurdly trivial incident
led to very serious consequences, consequences with
an important bearing upon the future of Turenne. A
reception was being held at the house of a great
Duchess, when a girl noticed a small piece of paper
lying upon the floor. Having picked it up and—of
course—read it, she found it to be an unaddressed and
unsigned love-letter. Of so harmless a thing she
thought it fair to make a little fun, so she showed it
to her friends. Out of mere fun, again, her friends

suggested possible names for the writer and the receiver. The story of this little incident was repeated, and repeated again; so also were the names, until it came to be said that the letter had actually and indeed been written and received by the persons named, but named only in jest. One of these persons happened to be a Princess of the blood royal and she appealed to the Queen, maintaining that the great Duchess, who was reported to have spread the calumny, had committed the crime of *lèse-majesté*. The Duchess was made to repudiate the scandal, in words written out for her on a piece of paper fastened upon the back of her fan; but she did so in a tone of such scornful derision that her reparation was an aggravation of her offence; and ultimately she was banished from Paris on account of it. As a consequence, the Court became divided into two parties, one of which sided with the exiled Duchess, the other with the calumniated Princess. Very soon men became as violent partisans on either side as the women who had brought about the feud. And thus it happened that a little bit of unsigned and undirected writing had led to a joke, the joke had led to a personal quarrel, the personal quarrel had led to a Court scandal, the Court scandal had developed into an affair of State; and the Court itself received a shake from which it may be said never to have recovered until Louis XIV. had grown old enough to take the reins of Government into his own hands after the death of Mazarin. Obviously, the gunpowder had been lying waiting for ignition, and the flame from the

scrap of paper had caused the explosion.   One faction
was headed by Beaufort and the other by Condé, who
was at that time still Duke of Enghien.   As a matter
of fact, however, the man who had most control over
the party opposed to that of Beaufort was Mazarin,
who had begun by attempting, or at least by pretending to attempt, to act as peacemaker between the rival
factions.   The two ladies at their heads were both
very beautiful; one was the Duchess of Montbazon,
the alleged scandal-monger, whom De Retz describes
as extremely beautiful but wanting in modesty, little
to be trusted in her amours and not at all in general
affairs; the other was the Princess of Condé, mother
of the object of the scandal.   Of this Princess Madame
de Motteville says that, even when more than fifty, she
was fair and white, with eyes blue and beautiful, and
that her manner was most charming when she was
pleased; but quite the contrary when she was vexed.
The quarrels among these princes and princesses,
dukes and duchesses, weakened the Court and eventually resulted in civil wars, in which Turenne was
destined to take a very prominent part.

The Queen was not inclined to place herself entirely
at the bidding of either rival faction; nor could she
endure to be hampered by the indecision and delays
of the council prescribed by her late husband; and
she gradually placed the government of the country to
all intents and purposes under the control of one man,
and that man Cardinal Giulio Mazarin.

This ecclesiastic, who was forty-one at the date of

the opening of this chapter, after studying law in Rome
and in Spain, had become a soldier in the papal army.
He was next employed on several diplomatic missions
by the Roman Curia, and eventually he became an
ecclesiastic, though never a priest.[1]   He was so useful
a servant to the Holy See, in foreign affairs, that Pope
Urban VIII. made him a cardinal in 1641.   He was
employed a good deal in France, where he acquired the
friendship of Richelieu, who, on his deathbed, recommended him to Louis XIII. as his successor.   Concerning the piety of these two cardinals, another
cardinal, Cardinal de Retz, who was well acquainted
with both Richelieu and Mazarin, said that Richelieu's
"stock of religion was sufficient for this world," but that
Mazarin "turned religion into a jest".[2]

Mazarin was ambitious, avaricious and unscrupu-
lous.   He looked upon men and women as mere tools,
and he was an adept at playing them against each other.
He followed Richelieu's policy of weakening the powers
of the great nobles of France, and among these one of
the earliest to whom he applied this process was
Turenne's brother, the Duke of Bouillon.   Instead of
carrying out the agreement of his predecessor, he
made all sorts of difficulties about the estates which had
been promised to the Duke in place of Sedan ; and,

---

[1] This has been questioned; but on weak grounds, namely
that it was said that he gave a certain lady the last sacraments;
but this may merely have meant that he was present at her deathbed and directed that they should be administered.

[2] *Memoirs of the Cardinal de Retz*, vol. i., pp. 73-74.

CARDINAL MAZARIN.

when Bouillon exhibited considerable impatience and resentment, Mazarin proposed, in open council, to arrest him. On hearing of this, Bouillon went to Rome, where, to Mazarin's great annoyance, he was received with royal honours and was offered the post of general-issimo of the troops of the Church. Mazarin, thinking that it was dangerous to leave Bouillon's brother so near him, in command of a French army, summoned Turenne from Italy to Paris, a recall which turned out much to Turenne's military advancement, although that had been far from the intention of Mazarin in ordering it.

One of the armies of the allies of France, that of the Duke of Saxe-Weimar, met with a disastrous defeat on the 24th and 25th of November, 1643, at Dütlingen. Its commander-in-chief was taken prisoner by General von Mercy, and 7,000 of its soldiers were lost. This was a heavy blow to France. Mazarin then ordered Turenne to go towards the Rhine, to collect the scattered remnants of the defeated army and to endeavour to defend the banks of the river from the Dukes of Bavaria and Lorraine, who had united against France now that they observed her to be in an awkward predicament.

It went against the grain with Mazarin to entrust an important command to the brother of a man he had done his best to ruin, but Turenne was undoubtedly the best marshal upon whom he could lay his hand at the moment; and it went equally against the grain with Turenne to accept an appointment from the greatest enemy of his house; but he was above all things a soldier, and a command in the great war between France and her allies against the Empire promised splendid opportunities of brilliant service.

The Empire is a term the significance of which has changed so often, and it is one which will be so frequently used in these pages, that it may not be superfluous to remind readers of its signification during the particular period dealt with. Nominally, from first to last, the Empire claimed to be the Roman Empire founded by Julius Cæsar and Augustus ; actually it was something widely different. In A.D. 395 the Roman Empire was divided between two brothers, one of them becoming Emperor of the East and the other Emperor of the West. After various subsequent changes, divisions and subdivisions, the Frankish King, Charlemagne, was elected Emperor of the Western Empire in the year 800 and was crowned in Rome by Pope Leo III. For many ages afterwards, there was again one Emperor in the West and another in the East, each claiming to be the true Roman Emperor. It was not until nearly another 800 years had passed that various marriages resulted in reuniting several portions of the mutilated Empire under the dominion of one ruler, who was crowned Emperor by Pope Clement VII. at Bologna. Then the Empire, in spite of having been robbed of much territory in the East by the inroads of the Turks, once more became the greatest power in Europe under the Emperor, Charles V., only ninety-eight years before the birth of Turenne.

The Empire had changed greatly during the half

century which passed between the abdication of Charles V. and the birth of Turenne. Proud as Charles V. had been of the restoration of the Empire, he himself effected its final destruction; for he granted all his German possessions, except the Netherlands, to his brother Ferdinand, who divided those possessions at his death between his three sons. Charles's son, Philip II., inherited Spain and the Netherlands from his father, but the title of Emperor went to his uncle and the Austrian branch of the House of Hapsburg.

During the life of Charles V. Europe had been disturbed by the religious revolution known as the Reformation, a revolution which led to many complicated wars; and, when Turenne first entered the army, the nominal Emperor was Ferdinand II., who was also nominally supreme over a large part of Germany, but in reality only over Austria, Bohemia, Silesia and Hungary. A war—the well-known Thirty Years' War—was raging in Europe between Catholics and Protestants—we might almost use the word "nominally" once more—about religion; the Emperor with Spain and the Catholic Princes of Germany forming an alliance against the United Provinces, the Protestant Princes of Germany—some of them Princes of the Empire itself—Denmark and Sweden.

The farce of calling this a religious war became broadest when Cardinal Richelieu allied Catholic France to the Protestant League. Turenne, a Protestant, fought in the Catholic army of France, on the Protestant side, in the latter part of this war. After the Peace (of

Westphalia) which followed it, the Empire, says Mr. James Bryce (*Ency. Brit.*, viii., 181), "was no Empire at all, but a federation of very numerous principalities, some large, some very small, united under the presidency of a head who bore the title of Emperor, but enjoyed scarcely any actual power, and represented in a Diet which was now not so much a national parliament as a standing congress of envoys and officials". It was against the Empire in this latter, and last, condition that Turenne fought some of his most important battles. At the time, however, with which we are dealing in the present chapter, the Thirty Years' War was still in progress.

Turenne reached Alsace in December, 1644, collected the scattered forces and marched them into winter quarters among the mountains of Lorraine. His army was in want of everything; but, at a time when most of the great men of France were selling their smallest services at high prices, Turenne, with his own and borrowed money, remounted 5,000 cavalry and clothed 4,000 infantry, before he had received any remittances from the Government.

Early in the spring of 1644 Turenne crossed the Rhine at Breisach, surprised Gaspard von Mercy, a brother of General von Mercy, near the source of the Danube in the Black Forest, and defeated him, taking prisoners 400 of the 2,000 men that Gaspard von Mercy had with him. Then he returned to, and occupied, Breisach, a frontier town on the right bank of the Rhine, then regarded as the key of Germany on the West; but now only remarkable for its magnificent minster.

Turenne also occupied Freiburg, a town fifteen miles to the east of Breisach. For some reason, which is not very clear, he then returned to the west of the Rhine. For this he is criticised by Napoleon, who says : " The marshal should have encamped under Freiburg, which would have hindered Mercy from besieging that place ".

In May, Turenne, being with his army at Colmar in Alsace, about a dozen miles to the west of Breisach, received intelligence that Mercy had laid siege to Freiburg, where Turenne had left a garrison of 600 or 700 men. On hearing of the siege, Turenne immediately gave orders that his army should cross the Rhine and spend the night at Breisach. With some reinforcements which he had received, he had now about 10,000 men, half infantry, half cavalry, and fifteen or twenty guns, a large proportion of artillery for the times.[1] If Turenne had made a mistake in retreating to the west of the Rhine, Mercy made another in not sending scouts to watch for the first sign of Turenne's recrossing that river, and the French army was well on its way from Breisach to Freiburg, on the following day, before Mercy was aware of it.

When he was some six miles distant from Freiburg, Turenne observed the Bavarian army drawn up on a plain in order of battle. The mountains of the Black Forest, which rise above Freiburg, form a

[1] The usual proportion then was one gun to 1,000 men.

semicircle half round this plain; on another side of it
was some marshy ground, and the only available
entrance to the plain before Freiburg was very narrow.
Mercy's position was very strong; but Turenne noticed
that one mountain commanding the plain had not yet
been defended, and he at once ordered two regiments,
about 1,500 men in all, to seize that position. This
movement of Turenne's, unnoticed by Mercy until its
object had been almost accomplished, was observed
by him only just in time to order fifteen or twenty
musketeers, who were on guard on his side of the
hill, to run up to the top of it and make a demonstration. This handful of Bavarians reached the crest
before the French and fired a volley at them. Turenne's
men, believing the hill to be undefended, were so surprised at receiving this fire that they imagined a large
body of the enemy's troops to be awaiting them on the
other side of the hill. They hesitated and then went
alongside the hill instead of ascending it. This gave
the Bavarian musketeers time to reload and fire again,
which confirmed the French in their mistake; and, to
their shame be it spoken, they ran, some 1,500 men
being thus put to flight by fifteen or twenty. This
disgraceful flight was led by two young ensigns who
came running down the hill, colours in hand, and
Turenne degraded them immediately on their return.

So good an opportunity of seizing an advantageous
position being lost, Turenne was obliged to remain for
some time encamped about four and a half miles from
Freiburg, as he was not strong enough in numbers to

Condé.

... and, although he kept harassing
... mishes, he was unable to re-
... to his intense chagrin, capitulated.
... that "with so considerable an
... that of Mercy, he might have
... to defend Freiburg. He should
... tion to intercept the enemy's

... was experiencing ... unfortunate
... another French general
... forth. This was Louis de
... n, who was to succeed his
... ther as Prince of Condé. As
... of Condé, he will be so
... res. Madame de Motteville
... his portrait: His eyes were
... city; his nose was aquiline,
... from being very large and
... but in his countenance gener-
... great and haughty, somewhat
... He was not very tall; but his
... well proportioned. He danced
... expression, and the air, and a
... dress, however, Mademoiselle
... him "the most slovenly man in

... him at great length, among
... of him: "Fiercely resolute in
... neither the lives of his soldiers

... de Motteville, vol. iii., p. 526 (ed. 1723).

attack the enemy; and, although he kept harassing
Mercy's troops with skirmishes, he was unable to relieve Freiburg, which, to his intense chagrin, capitulated.
Napoleon, however, says that "with so considerable an
army, although inferior to that of Mercy, he might have
done more than he did to defend Freiburg. He should
at least have taken a position to intercept the enemy's
convoys."

While Turenne was experiencing "unfortunate
occurrences" in the south, another French general
was victorious in the north. This was Louis de
Bourbon, Duke of Enghien, who was to succeed his
father a couple of years later as Prince of Condé. As
he is best known by the name of Condé, he will be so
styled throughout these pages. Madame de Motteville
has presented us with his portrait:[1] "His eyes were
very blue and full of vivacity; his nose was aquiline,
his mouth very disagreeable from being very large and
his teeth too prominent: but in his countenance generally there was something great and haughty, somewhat
resembling an eagle. He was not very tall; but his
figure was perfectly well proportioned. He danced
well, had an agreeable expression, a noble air, and a
fine head." As to his dress, however, Mademoiselle
de Montpensier calls him "the most slovenly man in
the world".

Ramsay described him at great length, among
other things saying of him: "Fiercely resolute in
command, he husbanded neither the lives of his soldiers

---

[1] *Memoirs of Madame de Motteville*, vol. iii., p. 526 (ed. 1723).

nor his own; and, in every engagement intrepid to
excess, seemed always determined to conquer or to die.
He had an understanding sublime and profound, was
eloquent, improved by letters, acquainted with the
principal beauties of all the sciences that qualify for
conversation, the cabinet and the field." A marvellous sentence!

Intellectually, he was probably superior to Turenne;
but he was without Turenne's kindness of heart. He
was dissolute, cruel to his wife, and a revengeful enemy.
Even when a young man of twenty-six, Condé was
neglectful of his dress and personal appearance; and
he allowed his hair to grow long and to hang as it
would, unkempt. Judging from his picture, Turenne
also never had his hair cut; and another celebrated
contemporary warrior, Count Schomberg, was notorious
for his long, uneven, and flowing locks. In those times
it seems to have been considered the mark of a valiant
soldier to waste no time at the hairdresser's, in contrast to the custom at present prevailing among many
officers of having their heads shorn like those of felons
undergoing penal servitude.

St. Evremond, in his *Parallel between the Prince
of Condé and M. de Turenne*, wrote during their life-
times: " You will find in the Prince of Condé strength
of genius, height of courage, a quick instinct, and ready
judgment. M. de Turenne has the advantages of cool
blood, great capacity and confirmed valour. The
activity of the former carries him further than is necessary, to the end that he may not omit anything that

may be of use: the latter is as active as he ought to be, forgets nothing that is of use, and does nothing that is superfluous. M. de Turenne prefers the public good to anything else. The Prince has more regard for the orders of the Court. In the course of an affair, the Prince's conduct is spoken of with most advantage; but when the affair is over, the fruits of what M. de Turenne has done are of a longer duration."

No apology is needed for saying so much about a man whose life was destined to be linked to such a large extent with that of Turenne, sometimes as an ally, sometimes as an opponent; but generally, though not always, as a personal friend.

While Turenne was confronting Mercy, Condé achieved a brilliant victory over the Spanish army, at the battle of Rocroi in France, a place very near the borders of the Spanish Netherlands. He showed great courage on this occasion. When he had put on his body-armour, on the morning of the battle, he refused to wear a helmet, and put on instead a hat with large white plumes, so that it might serve as a rallying point. When certain that the victory was won, he "threw himself on his knees at the head of his army, to return thanks to the God of battles" (*Memoirs of Mlle. de Montpensier*, vol. i., p. 74, footnote). To be quite candid, he was not always so devout. Rocroi was a most important battle, and, for the time, it completely broke down the power of the supposed invincible army of Spain. After several other successes, he was ordered to march south to the assistance of Turenne.

5 *

Shortly after his victory at Rocroi, Condé, we learn from St. Evremond,[1] sent to ask Turenne how he would advise him to conduct the remainder of his campaign in Flanders. "Make few sieges," replied Turenne, "and give many battles. When once you have made your army superior to that of your enemy, by the number and quality of your troops, which you have very nearly done already by the battle of Rocroi; when you are master of the open country, villages will be of as much service as the fortified towns; but it is thought much more honourable to take a fortress. . . . If the King of Spain had spent as much in money and men in forming armies, as he has spent in making sieges and fortresses, he would now be the most powerful monarch in the world."

When Condé joined Turenne, he was only twenty-three, while Turenne was thirty-three; but he was given precedence over Turenne, on account of his rank, and he became commander-in-chief. He had brought with him 6,000 infantry and 3,000 cavalry, so he now had about 19,000 men under his command. The two armies effected a junction between Breisach and Freiburg.

Freiburg stands at the mouth of the Valley of Hell (Höllenthal) near the foot of the Schlossberg, one of the principal heights of the mountain range of the Black Forest; and in this situation, rendered so beautiful by nature, there rises, to a height of nearly 400 feet, the spire of one of the finest Gothic churches

[1] *Works*, vol. iii., p. 2.

in Germany.   Mercy was encamped in a very strong
position near the town, partly on the plain and partly
upon the slopes commanding it.

Ought an enemy in such a position to be attacked?
Condé, who had 19,000 men against Mercy's 15,000,
thought that, with his superior force, an attack was
justifiable.   Napoleon was of the contrary opinion.
"The Prince of Condé," said Napoleon, "infringed one
of the maxims of mountain warfare: *never to attack
troops which occupy good positions in the mountains, but
to dislodge them by occupying camps on their flanks or
in their rear.*"   Turenne was probably of Napoleon's
opinion.   Never liking to blame others, he says nothing
of this in his own account; but Lord Mahon, in his well-
considered *Life of Condé* (p. 30), thinks there is
sufficient evidence that his hero acted, in this case,
against the advice of Turenne.

Condé ordered Turenne, on the 3rd of August, to BATTLE OF
start at daybreak, to make a détour through the woods, FREIBURG, 3rd August, and to attack Mercy on the flank.   He calculated that 1644.
it would take Turenne till three hours before sunset (*i.e.,*
till about 4.45 P.M.) to do this; and he arranged to
make a frontal attack himself just when Turenne would
make his flank attacks and thus strike at Mercy from
different quarters simultaneously.

Turenne was able to deliver his attack at about the
time agreed upon.[1]   He had to traverse a large half-

---

[1] Turenne's advance may be observed on the right-hand side
of the accompanying plan.   The position of the fallen fir-trees
may also be seen.   Condé's first attack may be seen on the right
of the plan.   It is entitled "Armée du Duc d'Anguien".

circle through the dense woods by a narrow valley, or defile, the exit from which the enemy had blocked with fallen fir-trees. He succeeded in driving the enemy beyond the wood, but, as he could not get his cavalry to the front, he dared not advance upon the plain against the enemy's combined horse and foot. Nor, on their part, did the enemy venture to advance over the open against Turenne's musketeers and pikemen, who were standing with their backs to the wood. Both armies remained, firing at each other, at a distance of about forty paces, until it became dark; and, for that matter, even in the dark.

Condé had begun his attack about the same time as Turenne. He also could only use his infantry, as he had to climb a hill covered with a vineyard, having four-foot walls, at short intervals, to support the terraces on which grew the vines. Having dismounted, and leading his men on foot, he was at first repulsed with the loss of a great many men; but, renewing the attack, he succeeded after a battle of three hours in forcing the barricades and pouring his men into the enemy's trenches; by nightfall he had inflicted a loss of 3,000 men upon his enemy and had taken the hill with the exception of a palisaded fort. This was a most brilliant performance and a prodigy of valour on the part of Condé; but it did not lead to anything decisive.

The losses on either side were very heavy. Turenne estimated those of the Bavarians as greater than those of the French; but in such a desperate frontal

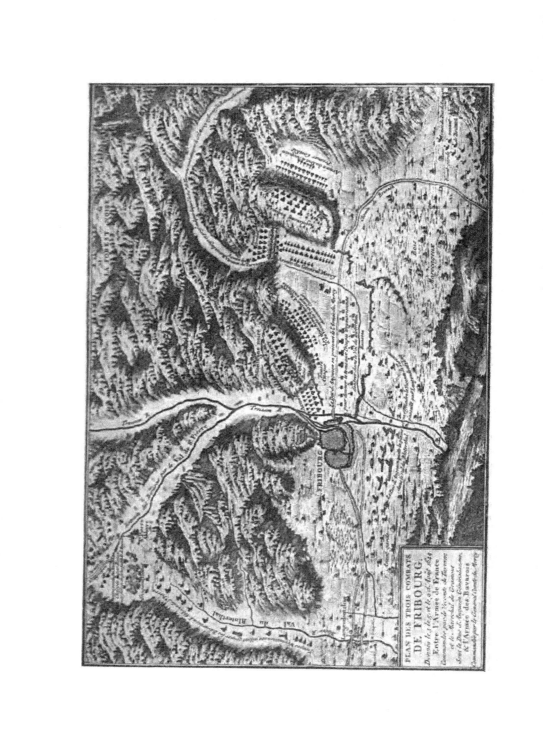

PLAN DES TROIS COMBATS
DE FRIBOURG,
Donnée les 3 5 et 6 d'Aoust 1644
Entre l'Armée de France
Commandée par le Vicomte de Turenne
et le Duc d'Enguien Généralissime
Sous le Duc d'Enguien Généralissime
& l'Armée des Bavarois
Commandée par le Général Comte de Mercy

attack as that of Condé, his losses are likely to have been enormous.

Where Turenne was placed the firing did not end with the day. All through the night the darkness, which was increased by an almost continuous rain, was intermittently illumined by flashes from the muskets on either side. Such firing would seem to have been objectless; but Turenne's troops and those of the enemy were very close to each other; and the Bavarians were endeavouring to conceal a retreat under cover of their fire, which the French punctually enough returned. Even in the deep gloom a shot was occasionally effective at the short distance. It was a restless, wearying, ghastly night, following a battle that had lasted for seven hours.

CHAPTER VI.

THE nights are short in August, and, when the sun rose at about half-past four on the morning of the 4th, Turenne and Condé, from their different positions, saw that the Bavarians had withdrawn from the plain on to the spurs of the Black Mountains. The plain being now open to them, Turenne and Condé rode down to it, met, and held a council of war.

Turenne says "'tis certain" that, if Condé had there and then attacked the Bavarians, "he would have found them in great confusion ; but the foot of the King's army was so dispirited by fighting the whole night, and by the great number of officers and soldiers killed or wounded, that they were not in a condition to undertake any considerable action". Napoleon is disinclined to accept this excuse. "As the Prince of Condé meant to attack," says he, "he should have attacked on the 4th, in the hope that Mercy would not have had time to secure his new position."

As it was, the French army rested on the 4th, while Turenne and Condé examined the position of the enemy. Early on the morning of the 5th Condé began his attack, but by that time Mercy had entrenched himself.[1] Some skirmishing having proved unsatisfactory, the two generals suspended hostilities for a time, in

[1] See near the middle of the plan.

order to ride to some rising ground and inquire into the truth of a report, which proved to be groundless, that the main body of the Bavarian army was retiring.

During their absence, owing to some error or, says Turenne, "perhaps to raise his own character in the world by some little action," the officer in command of Condé's infantry attacked without orders. This upset all the plans that had been made for the battle by Condé and Turenne, who, when they heard the sound of firing, galloped back as fast as they could, only to find everything in confusion. They both did their best to mend matters; but, as the Marquis de la Moussaye says in his account of the battle, "in vain did the generals tell" their men "of the disorder which was seen in the Bavarian camp; in vain did they press them, threaten them, drag to the fight. When once a soldier is seized with fear, he no longer either sees his general's example, or hears his orders." At the end of two hours' fighting, the French army had failed in its attack and had lost 3,000 men. The enemy had also suffered severely.

"Had Condé taken up a position commanding the Val de Saint-Pierre," says Napoleon, "Mercy would have been immediately compelled to take the offensive side, which he could not do with an inferior army. . . . He would therefore have been obliged to pass the Black Mountains to regain Würtemberg, and to abandon the fortress of Freiburg, which would have been left to itself."

After the battle of the 4th both armies rested for two or three days and within sight of each other, "in a camp," we are informed by Ramsay, "covered with blood, heaps of dead and dying. This moving sight affected the compassionate Viscount; he visited in person the field of battle, and caused the wounded, without distinction of friends and enemies, to be taken up and carried to Breisach. In the heat of action, humanity was ever in him the basis of heroism."

Condé now determined to do what Napoleon says he ought to have done before, namely, to occupy the valleys in his enemy's rear, with the hope of intercepting his communications and cutting off his retreat. As soon as Mercy perceived that Condé was about to adopt this strategy, he began to retire as fast as he could through the long and very narrow valleys which led through the Black Forest back to Würtemberg. In fact he got away before Condé had time to intercept him. But the whole of an army cannot retire more rapidly than the pace at which its slowest unit can travel, while an army in pursuit can send cavalry at a gallop to threaten its line of retreat. This was done by Turenne, who hurried round with his cavalry up the valley of Bloterthal,[1] which joins the valley of St. Pierre, near the abbey of that name, where Mercy was obliged to fight a severe rearguard action. This he did with tolerable success; but the French cavalry kept harassing the Bavarian army as it passed on through the narrow valley; and, at last, in order to escape from it Mercy abandoned his guns and his baggage, took to the mountains and escaped. Condé and Turenne made an effort to pursue him, but with little result.

[1] See extreme left of the plan.

"Thus ended the famous action of Freiburg, in which the Bavarians lost between 8,000 and 9,000 men, with their artillery, and almost all their horses: the loss of the French was also very great: but as Mercy had been forced to decamp, the honour of victory was given to the Duke d'Enghien."[1] Very true! But it is curious that this French historian should give the number of the Bavarian loss, which it would be difficult for him to ascertain accurately, yet should be silent as to the number of the French casualties, which he probably knew. It has been stated that the French loss was 9,000 and the German 8,000, which is not unlikely. Ramsay admits that Mercy made an orderly and honourable retreat under great difficulties.

Having driven the enemy out of the Marquisate of Baden into Würtemberg, Condé went back to the Rhine, and, in opposition to the general advice of his staff, but at the urgent request of Turenne, he did not besiege and retake Freiburg. Instead of doing so, he went to Breisach, sent supplies from there with all his guns down the Rhine in boats, and started with his army along the right bank of it by land, in order to secure the complete command of that river through the Lower Palatinate. The French army marched along the frontier of the Marquisate of Baden, and besieged Philippsburg, a fortress about eighty miles north of Strasburg, at that time in the hands of the Germans. This was a comparatively new fortress of the Empire, having been built at the beginning of the Thirty Years' War.

[1] Ramsay

While the siege of Philippsburg was going on, a
bridge was made across the Rhine, and a force was
sent to the left of the river to occupy Spires, which was
found ungarrisoned. Spires, which is only about eight
miles north of Philippsburg, had fallen greatly in
importance since the days when it had been the
residence of Charlemagne and the seat of the Germanic
Diet; but it was still the Imperial Chamber, such as
that chamber then was; and its enormous Romanesque
cathedral, with its tall twin towers, gave it a dignity
which it still possesses.

Philippsburg capitulated, with the honours of war,
in less than three weeks, on which Turenne at once
started north and, by forced marches, occupied Worms,
Oppenheim, Mayence, and other towns on the Rhine
nearly as far down the river as Coblentz, only meeting
with opposition at Landau, a fortress which was taken
and retaken no less than eight times during the Thirty
Years' War. It now fell in a few days. Condé, with
the help of Turenne, was thus victorious over the
Bavarian army; and except in the dashing operations
before Freiburg, he succeeded rather by rapid marches
and judicious strategy, than by brilliant tactics or
remarkable battles.

The opportunity so wisely and so promptly seized,
of carrying guns and provisions down the Rhine by
boats, which enabled the French army to accomplish
the march to Philippsburg in so short a time, contributed largely to the success of the campaign. At
the important city of Mayence the good-will of the

inhabitants, who obliged the Duke of Lorraine with
his army to withdraw from it, was another piece of
luck for the French army.   Dr. A. W. Ward, in *The
Cambridge Modern History* (iv., 389), says : "The
readiness with which the population . . . submitted to
French control was attributable not only to the skill
with which Enghien, with Turenne's aid, carried out
the comprehensive plan of operations long cherished in
vain by Guébriant, but also to the wise humanity that
characterised their proceedings.   'If,' Grotius wrote
about this time to Oxentierna, 'the French continue by
their acts to show that they have come to make themselves not masters, but protectors of German liberty,
they will also be able to allure other German States
to their side.'"   France, by this campaign, became
mistress of the Rhine from Breisach almost to Coblentz,
as well as of the Lower Palatinate and all the country
between the Rhine and the Moselle.   So much having
been accomplished, Condé, leaving a few of his regiments of infantry with Turenne at Philippsburg, returned to France with the rest of his army.

As soon as Condé had gone, Mercy, who by this
time had recruited his army, came near the Rhine
between Heidelberg and Mannheim, towns within ten
miles of each other.   Mannheim, then a fortress and
the capital of the Lower Palatinate, was occupied by
Mercy, who made pretence of building a bridge there,
in the hope of inducing Turenne to withdraw his
troops from Philippsburg, but without avail.

Soon afterwards it was reported to Turenne that

the Duke of Lorraine was coming to join his army to Mercy's, and that, on his way, he was besieging Bacharach, a town on the Rhine about half-way between Mayence and Coblentz. Turenne at once left Mayence accompanied by only 500 men, halted within about ten miles of Bacharach, and then ostentatiously sent men to mark out a very large camp, near that town, within sight of the enemy. This quite took in Lorraine who, deceived into the belief that Turenne was approaching with a body of troops large enough to fill such an immense camp, raised the siege of Bacharach in a hurry, and retired beyond the Moselle.

After taking the then important castle of Kreuznach, a fortress about a dozen miles from the Rhine, south of Bingen, Turenne had command of all the important positions on or near the Rhine, between Breisach and Coblentz, with the single exception of Mannheim; and, having reinforced his garrisons, "he placed himself in such a manner between the enemy's two generals [Mercy and Lorraine], that they could not join again all the rest of the winter; and in order to watch them the more narrowly, instead of going to Court, he retired to Spires".[1]

Of all this Napoleon says: "Turenne's conduct after the departure of the Prince of Condé was skilful; but he was indeed wonderfully seconded by local circumstances. The armies of Bavaria and Lorraine were separated by the Rhine and by mountains, and their junction was a difficult operation."

[1] Ramsay.

CHAPTER VII.

In some of Turenne's campaigns, even in some of his longest and his most successful campaigns, there was scarcely any fighting; but in that of 1645 there were to be two remarkable battles.

After wintering at Spires, Turenne heard, early in March, 1645, that Mercy had weakened his army by sending 4,000 of his men to the assistance of the Imperialists, who had been defeated by the Swedes in Bohemia. This made Turenne in a hurry to attack him; and, having crossed the Rhine on a bridge of boats, with 5,000 cavalry, 6,000 infantry and fifteen guns, he advanced steadily after Mercy who, with little more than 6,000 men, was obliged to retire before Turenne's superior force. Turenne, or some of his troops, marched from his base at Spires, unmolested, over considerable distances, some of his cavalry going as far as Nuremberg; and he finally took up his quarters at Marienthal or Mergentheim, a small town on the Tauber, about fifteen miles to the west-north-west of Rottenburg and about twenty-seven miles to the south-west of Würzburg. Mergentheim is now one of the minor German watering-places, frequented in the summer for its saline chalybeate springs; but in histories

the place is more often called Marienthal or Mariendal.
Turenne chose it for his headquarters, because it
bordered on the dominions of the Landgravine of Hesse-
Cassel, who was allied to France against the House of
Austria; and he hoped to effect a junction with her
army, thereby making up in some measure for the reinforcements he had sought in vain from Mazarin. For
some miles round Marienthal he quartered his regiments in cantonments among the neighbouring villages.

Both his men and his horses were wearied out by
their long marches, and he determined to give them a
rest. Unfortunately, the grass had not yet made its
full spring growth and there was soon a want of forage.
His cavalry officers begged to be allowed to disperse
with their men and horses in search of fodder and, if
possible, to purchase remounts. He did not at all like
this proposal; but it was reported—the report having
been purposely spread by Mercy—that the enemy was
fully thirty miles off, that his forces were divided, and
that each portion was fortifying its position at some
distance from the others. This report put a rather
different complexion upon the situation, yet Turenne
"blames his own too easy compliance" in even listening
to the suggestions of his officers. He states that at
last he "unadvisedly resolved" to let them go, sending
a general with four or five regiments to Rottenburg,
and keeping with him at Marienthal his infantry and
his guns. In fact, Turenne was taken in by the report
of the division of Mercy's forces.

It was seldom that Turenne hesitated or showed

indecision; but, the very day after he had allowed his
cavalry to leave his quarters in search of forage and
remounts, he heartily wished that he had refused to
give them that permission; he sent messages to order
them to return, and he appointed as a rendezvous
Herbsthausen, a place about six miles from Marienthal,
probably because he thought that would be the point
at which they could most rapidly reassemble.   In the
course of the day vague rumours came in to the effect
that Mercy's troops were on the move.   Meanwhile
Turenne's cavalry were returning but slowly.

At about two o'clock on the following morning, the
2nd of May, intelligence was received that Mercy
was approaching with his whole army.   Turenne immediately sent off the Swedish General, Rosen, with a
strong force to Herbsthausen, the rallying point at
which he had ordered his troops to assemble from their
various cantonments, where, moreover, he hoped that
such of his horse as had not already returned to the
cantonments, might concentrate in the course of the
early morning.   When Turenne arrived there himself
he found 3,000 of his infantry and a portion[1] of his
cavalry on the ground.   In front of Turenne was a
wood, and rather more than a mile farther on was
another and a much larger wood.   From that wood
the forces of the enemy were already emerging.

---

[1] "Unluckily," says Turenne, "a great many of the troopers
having caused their horses to be blooded, on account of the season,
the regiments could not mount a horse-back soon enough to come
to the battle."

6

The report which Turenne had received at two
o'clock that morning had not prepared him for so early
an appearance of the enemy. He ordered Rosen to
draw up such cavalry as had arrived, which was rather
more than half of what he had at first brought to
Marienthal, on the near side of the nearest wood. Instead of obeying this order, Rosen, says Turenne,
"passed the wood, which might be five or six hundred
paces across, and sent for the cavalry to come and join
him on the other side of the wood; which surely he
never would have done had he thought that the enemy's
army was so near; for 'tis certain, had the cavalry joined
him on this (the near) side of the wood, the King's army
might have joined him without fighting ".

This action on the part of Rosen had the effect of
forcing a battle upon Turenne under very disadvan-
tageous circumstances. He rode through the nearer
wood and there found Rosen drawing up his cavalry
in order of battle, while the enemy was approaching
from the further wood and was then less than a
mile away. There was no time to be lost. Turenne
sent his infantry to take up their position in a small
wood, which lay to the right, and considerably to the
front of that taken up by his cavalry, and sent Rosen
to command it, while he placed himself at the head of
the cavalry on the left.

Mercy opened the battle with a cannonade, which
did Turenne's troops little damage, although he had
no guns ready to reply to it. According to the plan
of the battle given here and taken from the 1749

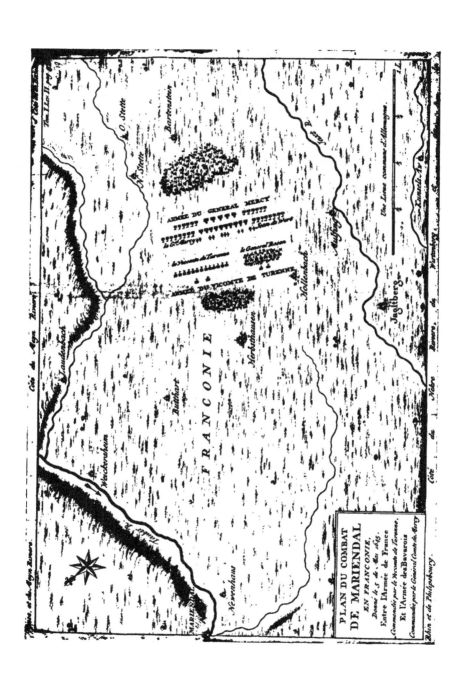

PLAN DU COMBAT DE MARIENDAL
EN FRANCONIE,
Donné le 5 de Mai 1645.
Entre l'Armée de France
Commandée par le Vicomte de Turenne,
Et l'Armée des Bavarois
Commandée par le General Comte de Mercy.

edition of Ramsay's *Vie de Turenne*, Mercy had eleven guns in position. Against at least seven of these guns, cavalry were advancing over an open plain; yet their fire, we are told, had "little effect". Mercy then led his infantry to attack Turenne's infantry in the small wood on Turenne's right. At the same time Turenne led a charge of his cavalry against the Bavarian horse on his own left, broke up the first line, captured some guns, took twelve standards and then advanced to attack the second line.

While Turenne was thus successful on his left, his fortunes were not so prosperous on his right; for his infantry, in the little wood, seeing themselves greatly outnumbered by the Bavarian infantry, simply ran away. Rosen was taken prisoner, and it must be remembered—for we shall have to refer to this farther on—that he had been the primary cause of the disaster.

Mercy's cavalry on his left, led by John de Wert, a general whom we shall meet again in subsequent battles, galloped round the small wood and, wheeling to their right, attacked Turenne's cavalry in the rear, as they were in the act of charging the second line of the Bavarian cavalry on Mercy's right. Being thus attacked on both front and rear, there was nothing left for Turenne to do but to order a retreat, and it was only with the greatest difficulty that he escaped being taken prisoner himself.

Unflurried by his narrow escape, he calmly considered his next proceeding. If he fell back upon the

Rhine he feared that Mercy might capture some of
the fortresses upon it then in French hands. Partly
for this reason, and partly in hope of obtaining fresh
troops from its landgravine, he gave orders to his
generals to rally his beaten forces as best they could,
and concentrate in Hesse. Then, with the couple of
regiments that remained, he covered the rear of the
retreat, often turning to repulse the Bavarians, who
harassed him nearly all the way until he reached the
frontiers of Hesse, where he joined the remnants of
his defeated army, having lost five-sixths of his infantry, 1,200 to 1,300 horse,[1] and all his guns and
baggage.

Upon this disastrous reverse Napoleon, as might
be expected, has something to say: "Turenne having
contracted his cantonments to the space of three leagues
round his headquarters, his position was not dangerous;
it is not, therefore, to his position that the loss of the
battle of Marienthal is to be attributed. It was doubtless unnecessary to go into quarters of refreshment in
so rich a country, where it was so easy to collect great
magazines. But his real error was the rallying point
he fixed for his army; he should not have selected
Herbsthausen, because that village was situated at the
advanced posts by which the enemy was approaching;
but Mergentheim (Marienthal) behind the Tauber,
where the army would have been in junction four hours
earlier, and where Mercy would have found the French
army covered by a river and in position. It is one of

[1] Turenne himself gives these numbers.

the most important rules in war, and rarely violated
with impunity, to collect one's cantonments on the point
most distant and best sheltered from the enemy."

Turenne himself attributed his defeat to his weakness in yielding to the requests of Rosen and the
Germans for permission to disperse in search of provisions and remounts. St. Evremond says that "he
never forgot Rosen's importunity in asking quarters and
his own too great easiness in granting them". But,
beyond this, it is quite clear that the actual battle was
forced upon Turenne, under very unfavourable conditions, by Rosen.

When Turenne had entered Hesse with the remains
of his army, the landgravine,[1] who up to then had
wished to take no active part in the war, perceived the
imminent danger of Mercy entering her territories to
complete the destruction of Turenne, and, for that
reason, she gladly joined her troops to those of Turenne.
Most opportunely for Turenne again, a few days later
Count Königsmark joined him with the Swedish army.
The result was that, in little more than a week after his
defeat, he was at the head of 15,000 men, or an army
nearly a third larger than that with which he had first
reached Marienthal. And, more than this, he received
the welcome news that Condé was on the road to join
him with 8,000 men. Although Mercy had been reinforced by an Austrian division of 4,000 men, the
French army, augmented by Condé and with its

---

[1] The Landgravine of Hesse was a cousin of Turenne, being a
granddaughter of William I., Prince of Orange.

Swedish and Hessian allies, was now much stronger than his.

Turenne felt that he was not being fairly treated by Mazarin. When he had implored him for reinforcements, none had been sent; now that reinforcements were being sent, Condé was sent with them to supersede Turenne in the command.

Mercy retired before the superior force which Condé brought against him; but, just as everything was going well, Count Königsmark imagined himself slighted by Condé and went away in a huff, taking the Swedish army with him, and mounting an infantry soldier on horseback, behind each of his troopers, for the sake of rapid expedition. Condé thus lost 4,000 men at one swoop; but he pretended not to care and he sent a message to wish Count Königsmark a pleasant journey, which made that general more angry than ever.

The French and Hessian armies were unopposed until they reached Rothenburg, a town just within the Bavarian frontier, but that place was attacked and carried in a night, and it happily proved rich in provisions for the large body of troops which then entered it. In a few days Condé proceeded to besiege Dinkelsbühl, a town also within the frontier of Bavaria, about twenty-five miles farther south. But he raised the siege in order to pursue Mercy when he heard that Mercy's army was only half a dozen miles off, on its retreat towards Nördlingen, another frontier town very strongly fortified, about eighteen miles still farther to the south-south-east. The French army started soon after midnight, and Condé and Mercy marched side by side, in the dark, without knowing it, until the day broke, when they discovered their propinquity. There was a river between them, and they both mounted their guns and opened fire. A very heavy and effective cannonade continued throughout the day, each side suffering severely, and Turenne admits that the French lost more men by it than the Bavarians. An engagement, in the open, conducted entirely by artillery, was a very exceptional affair in those times.

When night came on, both armies were again on the march. Condé hurried towards Nördlingen in hopes of intercepting Mercy; but, in the morning, he found that Mercy, by a skilful march, aided probably by a better knowledge of the country, had got there first and had already occupied a very strong position at the rear of the town. Mercy's position protected the town itself, and at the same time commanded the road to Donauwörth, another fortified town, twenty miles to the south-east, on the river Danube.[1]

The army under the command of Condé consisted of 17,000 men, that under Mercy of 14,000, and the number of guns was nearly equal on either side. But Mercy had the stronger position. He had drawn up his main forces on rising ground strengthened by entrenchments. On the edge of the plain, in his immedi-

BATTLE OF NÖRDLIN-GEN, 3rd August, 1645

---

[1] A religious riot at this town had been the immediate cause of the Thirty Years' Wars. Donauwörth was afterwards carried by storm by the troops of Marlborough a few days before the battle of Blenheim.

ate front, but a little in advance of his centre, was the village of Allerheim, in which he had placed three or four regiments and had loopholed the walls of the houses. Musketeers were posted in the church tower and behind gravestones in the churchyard. On either side of his main position were two hills. That on his right was called Weinberg, and here he had placed several guns and the cavalry under the command of the famous General Glein of the Imperial army. The hill on his left was surmounted by the château or castle of Allerheim, and on this eminence he had posted artillery and a strong body of cavalry. On the great plain of Nördlingen before him, the French army was advancing, in extended order, on the opposite side of the village of Allerheim, which became the central point of the subsequent action.

After discovering the position of the enemy, Condé had held a council of war. Turenne suggested—and it will be seen later that Napoleon thought he rightly suggested—that an attack upon Mercy, when he held such a splendid position, would expose the French army to almost certain defeat. Condé, on the contrary, was determined to attack; and, as he was in supreme command, the final decision lay with him. He proposed to begin by leaving the enemy's centre alone, and by attacking the hills on both his flanks with cavalry. Turenne objected that it would be dangerous to proceed against the flanks, without first attacking the enemy's infantry in the centre. On this point Condé yielded to the advice of Turenne.

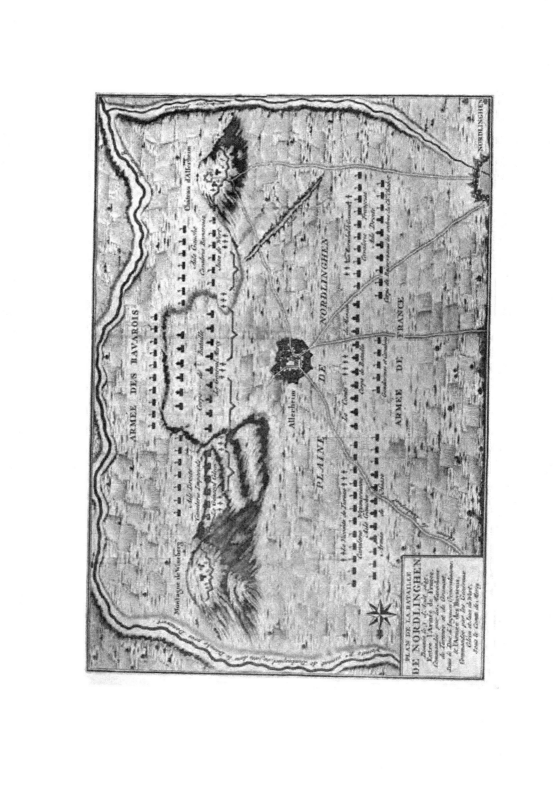

PLAN DE LA BATAILLE DE NORDLINGHEN

The French army had entered the great plain about midday on that 3rd of August; but the troops were not extended in fighting order until after four o'clock and the actual battle did not begin much before five. It is remarkable that several of the battles, in which Turenne was engaged, did not begin until late in the afternoon. The action was opened by the French artillery, which was sent forward to batter the village of Allerheim; but, as Turenne says, artillery already posted in entrenchments have enormous advantages over guns drawn to the front on an open plain by horses; and, in the artillery duel which followed, the Bavarians naturally had much the best of it.

The village was next attacked by the French infantry and a terrific struggle followed. Here, again, the cover from behind which the Bavarian musketeers were firing gave them a great advantage, and the French loss was much the heaviest; but their attack was magnificent. Condé, who moved about from one part of the battlefield to another, frequently went into the village to encourage his men; while, on the opposite side of the village, Mercy was close at hand during a great part of the action. "God," exclaimed Mercy, "has turned the heads of the French; they will soon be routed." Yet they held on, after wavering several times, and so obstinate was the fight, between musketeers and pikemen on both sides, that it looked as if the issue of the battlefield was to be decided at the village. Each commander-in-chief was growing anxious, and each was determined to finish off the contest quickly in his own favour. At about the same time both Condé and Mercy rode into the thick of the conflict to encourage their men. According to Ramsay, Condé's clothes were "shot through in many places"; a horse fell under him; he mounted another and that also was soon wounded. He himself received a contusion on the thigh; but in vain was he implored to retire for the purpose of having his injury examined and relieved. Mercy was no less in the thick of the fighting, and he had been exhibiting marvellous courage when a musket-ball struck him and ended his life; and although nearly the whole of the French infantry that had attacked the village had been killed, wounded or dispersed before he fell, the loss of this splendid commander spread dire discouragement among the troops which had hitherto been fighting so courageously under his skilful direction and fearless personal leadership.

The struggle at the village had lasted an hour, and it was not far from six o'clock when Condé ordered the French cavalry, on his right, to charge the Bavarian cavalry on the enemy's left. Although Marshal de Grammont did all in his power to induce them to make a successful attack, he failed in doing so; they were soon routed and he was taken prisoner.[1]

[1] This was not the frivolous courtier, Count Philibert de Grammont; but his valiant elder brother, Field-Marshal the Duke of Grammont. A curious incident occurred after he had been taken prisoner. A captain was taking him to General Mercy, not knowing that Mercy had been killed. They were met by a page of Mercy's, a boy of fifteen. The lad was enraged at the death of his master and was determined to be revenged upon the first

Having now neither centre nor right, Condé rode to Turenne, who was in command of the left, and at once granted his urgent request to be allowed to attack. As Turenne advanced up the hill, the enemy fired first with round-shot, and then, he says, "with cartridge-shot," which was probably some form of case-shot suitable for short ranges. One of these shot glanced across the cuirass on his breast and another wounded his horse. He was leading, not French, but German cavalry; and, although it wavered once, it returned to the charge and behaved splendidly. The indefatigable Condé came up at the head of a reserve of Hessian horse, and when Turenne's Weimarian cavalry, which were again almost overpowered, saw the Hessians coming to their support, they made a desperate effort, and, in conjunction with the Hessians, broke the Bavarian and Imperialist ranks, captured the guns on the hill, and took General Glein prisoner. Turenne then changed front, turning to his own right, and attacked the Bavarian centre on its right flank, with a result which will presently appear.

Meanwhile, no less complete than the success of the French left had been the defeat and utter rout of the French right. The Bavarian cavalry pursued the French all the way back to their camp; and it was

Frenchman he met. Snatching one of Grammont's pistols from its holster, he held it to his head and tried to fire it. Fortunately Grammont had already discharged it in the battle. The Germans wanted to punish the boy very severely; but Grammont begged him off (*Memoires du Maréchal le Duc de Grammont*, p. 262).

getting near sunset when John de Wert,[1] who was in command of the victorious left wing, discovered that things were going badly with his own army, on his right.   Leaving a couple of regiments to harass the flying Frenchmen, he led back the rest of his cavalry to the hill from which he had started, the hill on which stood the château.   Thence he turned towards the Bavarian right with the object of attacking Turenne.

But he was a little too late!   After routing the Bavarian right, Turenne had pressed on to the village of Allerheim, where some of the Bavarian infantry, taken by surprise and unaware that a body of their own cavalry, under John de Wert, was hurrying to their assistance, came out of the village, in the twilight, without their arms and surrendered.

Then darkness came on and the fighting ceased. It is a question which of the two armies was in the worse plight.   Turenne himself estimates the French loss as greater than the Bavarian.   Both armies had lost their right; the French army had also lost the whole, and the Bavarian army a part, of its centre. But in the night John de Wert, who was now in command of the Bavarian army, finding his troops discouraged by the death of Mercy, and being uncertain of the position of the enemy, retreated with his army to Donauwörth, leaving twelve or fifteen guns in the hands of Condé.

In Turenne and Condé, two splendid and gener-

[1] John de Wert was the son of a peasant and rose to the rank of general solely by merit.

ous-minded generals fought side by side on that terrible field of Nördlingen.   When Condé had received a letter from the Queen of Sweden thanking him for avenging the defeat which the Swedish army had suffered on the same battlefield eleven years earlier, he told her, in his reply, that the credit of the victory was due less to himself than to the skill and the courage of Turenne.

CHAPTER VIII.

THE glory of war, and even the glory of victory, soon begins to lose something of its dazzling brilliance when submitted to capable and cold-blooded criticism.

Napoleon analyses the conduct of the battle of Nördlingen at considerable length. Condé, says he, was wrong "in attacking Mercy in his camp with an army composed almost entirely of cavalry, and with so little artillery". (In his account of the relative forces at the beginning of the battle, however, he says: "The number of pieces of artillery was nearly equal on both sides".) Nevertheless, he admits the attack on the village of Allerheim to have been "a grand affair". It was but natural, he continues, that Condé should fail in his attack upon Allerheim with "all its houses, as well as the church and cemetery, embattled and defended by an infantry superior to the French, not only in number but in quality. Had it not been for Mercy's death, the Bavarians would have remained masters of the field of battle."

Again he says: "Notwithstanding the death of Mercy, the Bavarians would still have gained the victory if John de Wert, on his return from pursuing the right wing of the French, had advanced against

Turenne, not by first resuming his former position, and thus traversing two sides of the triangle, but by crossing the plain diagonally, leaving Allerheim on his right, and falling on the rear of the cavalry of Weimar, which was then engaged with Glein's Austrian troops. By this plan he would have succeeded; but he was not daring enough. The angle he made retarded his movement only half an hour, but the fortune of battles frequently depends on the slightest accident."

In spite both of the death of Mercy and of the mistake of De Wert, Napoleon thinks that the Bavarians would "still have conquered, if the infantry posted at the village of Allerheim had not, although victorious, capitulated. The capitulation accepted or proposed by these troops is a new proof that a body of troops in line ought never to capitulate during a battle." In those times, he says, it was a generally received principle that troops in the field might capitulate when surrounded, "thus assimilating themselves . . . to the garrison of a fortress". No general can wage war with success "if the officers are allowed to capitulate on the field, and to lay down their arms according to the terms of a contract favourable to the individuals of the corps constructing it, but injurious to the army. Such conduct ought to be . . . punished with death. . . . Of the generals and officers, one in ten ought to suffer, of the sub-officers, one in fifty, and of the men, one in a thousand." He says that the general who has been chiefly guilty of the capitulation ought in any case to suffer death.

Napoleon gives the credit of saving the day to the obstinacy and extraordinary intrepidity of Condé, and neither to the skill nor to the courage of Turenne ; for it was Condé "who directed all the movements of" the left " wing and is entitled to all the glory of the success. Ordinary minds will say that he ought to have made use of the wing which remained untouched, for the purpose of securing his retreat, and not to have hazarded the remainder of his forces; but with such principles, a general is sure to miss every opportunity of success, and to be constantly beaten. . . . The glory and honour of his country's arms is the first duty to which a general who gives battle ought to attend, the safety and preservation of his men is but the second : their safety and preservation is, in fact, to be found in that daring obstinacy itself; for even had the Prince commenced a retreat with Turenne's corps, he would have lost nearly all his men before he could have reached the Rhine. . . . If he did wrong in giving battle to Mercy in the position he occupied, he did right in never yielding to despair while he had brave men under his colours."

The French avoidance of defeat at Nördlingen, for that is all it can truthfully be called, although it prevented a terrible disaster, was poor in its results. Condé was soon afterwards taken ill and had to retire to France, and no reinforcements were sent to Turenne, whose army had suffered greater losses than that of the enemy. The Bavarian troops, on the contrary, were reinforced by the Archduke Leopold with 5,000

horse.   Before this superior force Turenne was obliged
to retreat, and he mounted each foot-soldier on a horse
behind a trooper to enable his army to march more
rapidly ; for he was pursued by the Archduke, who
retook Nördlingen and two or three other towns which
had been captured by Condé.

Turenne retreated to Philippsburg ; but, even there,
he would not have been safe, as there was no bridge
over which to cross the Rhine and the Archduke was
close at his heels, if there had not been a wide space
between the fortress and the river.   Upon that space
he was happily able to entrench himself, while boats
were sent for from farther down the river, and when
they came he made a bridge with them.

This, says Napoleon, "ought to be a lesson for
engineers, not only with respect to fortified places, but
also for that of *têtes-de-pont :* they should leave a space
between the fortified place and the river, so that an
army might draw up and rally between the fortified
place and the bridge, without entering the fortress,
which would place it in jeopardy ".

A month or two later the Archduke and his army
were summoned to Bohemia.   Then Turenne was able
to cross the Rhine without danger of molestation ; and
he made the march of 120 miles in a very hard frost to
Trèves, on the German side of the borders of Luxemburg, and Trèves speedily capitulated.   There he re-
instated the elector, an ally of France, who had been
driven out of it a dozen years earlier.

This was a particularly adroit move on the part of

Turenne, as it secured Trèves to the alliance of France and prevented the roving Duke of Lorraine from making use of it as winter quarters for his army. It also made the Moselle a boundary for the allies, and Turenne immediately set to work to put all the fortresses on that river in a state of defence. Having completed these works, he returned to Paris early in February, 1646.

At Court, Mazarin, who was at that time practically Regent of France, gave Turenne an excellent reception and offered him the Duchy of Château-Thierry. As this duchy, which was only some forty miles west-north-west of Paris, was one of the estates which had been promised to Bouillon in exchange for Sedan, before the rupture between that Duke and Mazarin had broken off all negotiations between them, it would seem that the diplomatic cardinal intended at the same time to reward Turenne for his services and to make a breach between him and his brother. In this amiable scheme Mazarin was defeated, as Turenne saw through it and refused the offer, stating that he could accept nothing until the exchanges promised to his brother were completed.

Having disposed of his personal affairs, Turenne urged upon Mazarin the importance of the union of the French and Swedish armies. Little progress, he assured him, could be made with the war in Germany so long as the allied armies were working apart, and without any concerted and systematic action.

To enter fully into the tangle of continental politics,

in the spring of 1646, would unduly extend the present volume. That there was a tangle may be inferred from a few lines which shall be quoted from Ramsay:[1] "The Catholics were treating with the Protestants and endeavouring to unite with them, in order to continue a war, which at first had been wholly undertaken in defence of [the Protestant] religion. The Swedes caballed with the Emperor against France their ally: France hearkened to the Duke of Bavaria, in order to hinder the Swedes from carrying their conquests too far in Germany: Spain supported the Elector of Brandenburg, the head of the Calvinist league: and the Dutch sought the friendship of the Spaniards, their old enemies."

Respecting this "confusion of views," as Ramsay presently calls them, all we have to bear in mind for the moment is that Mazarin was listening to the overtures of Bavaria, and that, although he wished to give the Imperialists what Wellington used to call "a damned good drubbing," he feared that, if the House of Austria were to be completely crushed, Protestantism might reign throughout the whole of Central Europe; and a preponderance of Protestantism would have interfered with his own political designs. These double motives of the cardinal proved vexatious to Turenne on more than one occasion.

In the beginning of April, 1646, Turenne returned to his army, which he removed from Trèves to near Mayence. When there, he sent to inform the com-

---

[1] Vol. ii., p. 120.

mander-in-chief of the Swedish army, General Wrangel,[1] that he intended to cross the Rhine, by a bridge of boats, at Bacharach, and join his own to the Swedish army in Hesse-Nassau.   To his great annoyance, just as he was starting to put this design into execution, he received an order from Mazarin to give up all idea of it, because the Duke of Bavaria had promised not to join his army to that of the Emperor,[2] on condition that the French army did not join that of Sweden, or cross the Rhine.   Instead of crossing the Rhine, Turenne was commanded to turn to the West, to leave Germany and to besiege Luxemburg.

Turenne felt certain that the Duke of Bavaria was hoodwinking Mazarin, and that to besiege Luxemburg would be a fatal mistake at such a moment; therefore he obeyed the order not to cross the Rhine, but he made excuses for remaining in Germany instead of proceeding to Luxemburg.

While Mazarin was fulfilling his share of the bargain, it was far otherwise with the Duke of Bavaria, and while the French and Swedish armies were still wide apart, that perfidious Duke had joined his forces to those of the Emperor.   In the face of this direct breach of contract what was Turenne to do?   He was not long in deciding.   Without waiting for orders from

[1] Wrangel had just taken the place of General Torstenson, who had been obliged to relinquish his command owing to a very severe attack of gout.

[2] The Emperor at that time was Ferdinand III., who had married the Infanta of Spain, to whom Charles I. of England had paid court in 1623.

Mazarin, he started at once to join his army to that
of Sweden; and, as a flood had destroyed his bridge
of boats at Bacharach, and he learned that no bridge
across the Rhine nearer than Wesel was open to him,
he determined to make the long march of 150 miles to
that place, which is within 100 miles of the mouth of
the Rhine.   When he reached Wesel he had considerable trouble in obtaining leave from the Dutch to cross
the river.   Having at last obtained that permission and
transferred his troops to the right bank of the Rhine,
he made a second lengthy march, in a south-easterly
direction, to join his army to that of Wrangel, near
Friedburg, a fortified town in Hesse-Darmstadt, of which
the walls and a fine, tall, round tower are still standing,
about a dozen miles to the north of Frankfurt.   Altogether, Turenne's march from Trèves, by Wesel, to
Friedburg, was about 320 miles, and it was made in
very little more than a month.

The combined Imperial and Bavarian armies had
already approached the Swedish army; but, although
greatly outnumbering it, they dared not do more than
encompass it, because Wrangel's position was very
strong and admirably entrenched.   On the arrival of
Turenne, they withdrew to a considerable distance.
The French and Swedish allies numbered 10,000
horse, 6,000 or 7,000 foot, and 60 guns; the Imperial
and the Bavarian allies numbered 14,000 horse, 10,000
foot and rather more than 50 guns.

We are now at the beginning of a long campaign
which will require a chapter to itself.

CHAPTER IX.

THE campaign of the united forces of Turenne and Wrangel (August, 1646) consisted of a series of strategical marches rather than of battles.

Turenne and Wrangel got on well together; but not so the two great generals opposed to them. When the rival armies were within easy reach of each other, the Bavarian general urged an immediate attack upon the French and Swedish allies, on the ground that the Bavarian and Imperialist armies outnumbered those of France and Sweden in the proportion of nearly, if not quite, three to two. The Archduke Leopold, on the contrary, was busily engaged in entrenching his position, his favourite occupation when on a campaign, and he refused to move until he had finished his works; in fact, we are told by Ramsay that, "so far from offering battle, he employed himself day and night in making deeper the entrenchments of his camp, in which he was almost buried already".

Wrangel and Turenne had now a difficult and an intricate position to consider. It was almost the middle of August. If they fell back towards the Rhine they would find themselves in a country already laid waste

by wars. On the other hand, if they assumed the
offensive they would be fighting at a serious disadvantage in numbers. Finally they decided to take
advantage of the enemy's delay, to leave them behind,
buried in their own trenches, and to make a bold dash
for the very heart of Bavaria.

The difference between wintering in a devastated
and in an undevastated country was greater in those
days than we, who live in times of rapid transport of
supplies, can readily imagine. Nor did this difference
only affect a general and his plans in respect to his
army at the moment; for "such a difference," says
Turenne, "proves a great advantage in the next campaign, because new soldiers will readily come to serve
in armies that are in plentiful countries".

The rivers of the country through which they intended to pass were very favourable to their projects.
Roads in those times usually followed water-courses,
and certain tributaries of the Rhine on the one hand,
and of the Danube on the other, flowed through
the valleys leading by the shortest route to Munich,
the capital of the Duke of Bavaria's kingdom, a city
nearly 200 miles to the south-east of Friedburg. If
the allies could but make good their way along this
route and garrison the fortresses which they would
have to capture and leave in their rear, the Bavarian
and Imperialist armies would have to go a long way
round to get at them.

The plan of Turenne and Wrangel was to leave
Friedburg and reach the river Main by one of its

tributaries, not very far from Frankfurt, then to go up the valley of the Main to where the river Tauber runs into it, and after that to go up the valley of the Tauber almost to the top of the watershed, which is there not a very high one. They proposed next to cross over the watershed and to go down one of the tributaries of the Danube, until they reached that river; to go up the Danube to where the Lech flows into it; then to go up the Lech and seize its fortresses, and finally to strike across the country to Munich. It was a very bold venture; but circumstances assisted the strategic skill of the French and the Swedish generals.

To begin with, the Archduke could not be persuaded by the Bavarian general to start at once so as to intercept Turenne and Wrangel. He was much too busy digging! The French and Swedish armies started at two o'clock in the morning and had actually to pass within sight of the enemy; but, says Turenne, his foes "seemed to be irresolute, and only put themselves under arms. De Wert, however, had been sent on to defend a pass, but apparently without sufficient strength;" for, brave as he was, he retired "towards the main body of the enemy's army". Turenne and Wrangel marched twenty-seven miles that day. The hesitation and seeming want of courage on the part of the Archduke Leopold is almost inexplicable.

The chief difficulties that Turenne and Wrangel had to face were the fortresses lying on their route; for, unless they could be taken, success would be next to impossible. The inhabitants of the country through which they passed knew that the large united armies of Bavaria and the Empire were in the north-west, with the object of defending their own nations, and of crushing the French and the Swedes; when, therefore, the Swedes and the French, very obviously uncrushed, appeared in view, they not unnaturally inferred that the Imperial and Bavarian armies must have been conquered in a great battle and, acting upon this inference, they fled in all directions.

Of course the suspicion of the defeat of the armies of the Empire and Bavaria was rapidly developed by rumour from suspicion into fact; and the report being carried from one garrison to another, they, in most cases, either surrendered at once or made only a feeble and brief resistance.

When the Duke of Bavaria, at Munich, heard what had happened, he was terribly frightened and furiously angry. He ordered all his valuables to be packed up immediately and removed to a distance; and he sent to reproach the Archduke Leopold for allowing the enemy to pass him, practically unopposed and entirely unpursued, into the richest plains of Bavaria. Forgetting his own perfidy to France, he assumed an air of virtuous indignation at what he regarded as the perfidy of the Archduke, who had rewarded him for breaking his word to Mazarin and joining his army to that of the Empire, by permitting the troops of the outraged Mazarin to punish him for his breach of faith by plundering his dominions.

In respect to this question of plunder, the reader ought to impress upon his memory that the fact that, if Ramsay is to be believed, "the booty might have been inestimable," and that "the Viscount might have demanded for himself alone, 100,000 crowns per month, without doing anything contrary to the usages of war : but with an unparalleled disinterestedness, he only took out of the enemy's magazines what was sufficient to subsist his army". It will be important to remember this when, farther on, we meet with accusations against Turenne of inflicting cruel devastation, as a punishment for some infamous ill-treatment of his own soldiers.

The allies successfully carried out their programme described above, so far as it included reaching the Danube, where the Lech flows into it. Near that point stands Rain, now an insignificant town, but then one of the important fortresses of Bavaria. This place was besieged by Wrangel, while Turenne sent the Marquis de Beauvau with 500 horse to demand the surrender of Augsburg, another fortress twenty miles due south of Rain and also on the Lech. There being scarcely any garrison in Augsburg, the Marquis de Beauvau was immediately admitted, without his men, and the citizens began to make terms with him for the surrender. Augsburg stood on a high and commanding position at the junction of the rivers Lech and Wertach. Besides being an important fortress, it was the chief point of commerce between Northern Europe and the Levant. In its trade and in its merchant nobility it was almost a rival to Venice About the time when

Turenne was approaching it, one Augsburg family, originally descended from a weaver, numbered no less than forty-seven counts and countesses of the Empire among its five branches.

Now Wrangel was particularly anxious that the French should not take exclusive possession of Augsburg, partly on the ground that it had once been captured by the great Gustavus Adolphus of Sweden, and partly on account of its importance; therefore he sent to Turenne, who had started for Augsburg, urging him to return at once to his assistance at Rain, as he was in urgent need of support. On receiving this message, Turenne recalled De Beauvau from Augsburg and hurried to support Wrangel in the siege of Rain, which capitulated in a few days.

Meanwhile the Bavarian General Royer had come from Meiningen, a fortress forty miles to the south-west near the frontier of Würtemberg, and had strengthened the garrison of Augsburg by from 1,200 to 1,500 men. News of this reached Turenne, who, from Wrangel's frequent mention of the former capture of Augsburg by Gustavus Adolphus, had by this time perceived his object and recognised his own mistake in retiring from Augsburg at Wrangel's request, a mistake for which he is severely criticised by Napoleon.

After the capture of Rain, both Turenne and Wrangel hurried to Augsburg, in order to besiege it and cut their trenches before the arrival of the united Imperial and Bavarian armies, which they expected to appear in about a week. It was well that they were prepared against an attack from these armies in their rear; for the Duke of Bavaria had told the Archduke that unless he raised the siege of Augsburg, he himself would forsake the Imperial alliance and join his army to those of France and Sweden; and, with this fear before his eyes, the Archduke was bestirring himself.

In due course the Bavarian and Imperial armies, which had come from Friedburg by Bamberg and Nuremberg, a route much to the east of the short cut taken by the French and Swedes, appeared before Augsburg. As we have seen, their armies had been half as large again as those of the French and the Swedes, even at Friedburg. Since then they had been reinforced *en route*, while the French and the Swedes had been obliged to leave some of their troops behind them, for the purpose of garrisoning the fortresses which protected their rear on their march. For all his numerical strength, the Archduke's ardour began to cool, now that he was getting so near his enemy. Prudence having by this time taken the place of valour, he decided to wait until the French and Swedish armies had consumed their provisions, and then to drive them into Franconia, *i.e.* the district which they had already traversed and devastated on their march to the Danube, a district in which it would be impossible for them to remain for want of food. When they should have left it in search of supplies, he flattered himself that he would be able to recover the fortresses taken by the French and the Swedes, without any serious fighting, and thus rob them of all the fruits of their campaign.

On the appearance of forces so greatly outnumbering their own, Turenne and Wrangel thought it prudent to raise the siege of Augsburg and retire to Lauingen, a town on the Danube thirty miles to the north-west. Their plan of campaign from the first had been some-what hazardous ; and now that the middle of November was approaching, in spite of their successes things began to have a very ugly look. They were in an enemy's country, they were greatly outnumbered, they were more than 150 miles from the nearest friendly boundaries, their communications were practically cut, as the Imperial army on its way to Augsburg had passed behind them ; or, to be more accurate, they had no communications to be cut. Their troops "were weak and fatigued," wanting "horses, arms and clothes,"[1] and winter was now setting in, with unusual severity, the ground being already covered with snow.

To realise what follows, we may imagine an ill-shaped square of territory, with Rain on the north-east, Ulm on the north-west, Meiningen on the south-west, and Landsberg on the south-east, with the river Lech flowing towards the north from Landsberg to near Rain, the Danube flowing towards the south-west from near Rain to Ulm, and the river Iller flowing towards the Danube in the north from Meiningen to Ulm. The side of our square from Landsberg to Rain, that is the eastern side, is the longest, and the four sides vary in length from something over thirty to a little over forty miles. Augsburg, it may be observed, lies

[1] Ramsay.

about half-way between Landsberg and Rain, and Lauingen about half-way between Rain and Ulm.

The Imperial and Bavarian generals, apparently thinking that Turenne and Wrangel had marched to the north-west with the object of making their way through the rich country still farther to the west, marched westward themselves to intercept them and to prevent them from obtaining supplies from either Ulm or Meiningen.

Both Turenne and Wrangel, contrary to the advice of most of their staff, advanced westwards over the snow-covered roads towards the enemy; either, says Turenne, "to fight them, or when in sight of them to consider what to do". When they did come within sight of them, near Meiningen, and, saw them at a distance of three miles in a very strong position, with marshes in their front, Turenne and Wrangel decided not to fight them, especially as the Archduke, as usual, had been busy entrenching himself, but "to consider what to do". This they did to some purpose!

They had ascertained that, although the richest country lay to the west of our square, the enemy had a very large stock of provisions at Landsberg, and had only left 100 horse as a garrison for that town, never dreaming that the French and Swedes, in the face of greatly superior forces, would dare to advance still farther to the south-east, direct into their enemy's country and in an opposite direction to their own line of retreat. Turenne and Wrangel, therefore, determined to deceive the Archduke by affecting to make Ulm their objective, while they seized Landsberg and all its stores.

Turenne left 2,000 horse facing west, ostentatiously drawn up within sight of the enemy, as if he was preparing to give battle, while he hurriedly marched away to the east in the direction of Landsberg.   He and Wrangel thus made the whole march to within a few miles of that town before the Archduke, who was doubtless still digging, had · realised that they had started.   The march had been a very rapid one; and when Turenne had advanced his infantry as far, over the distance of some thirty miles, as it was possible in one day, he sent on sufficient horse to the river Lech, to cross the bridge, which happily was not broken, and to call upon the little garrison of 100 men at Landsberg to surrender.   Tired as were their troops after their long march, Turenne and Wrangel had them on foot again before the night was over; and during the day following they got their whole army with its baggage safely across the Lech, cut off all danger of pursuit by the enemy at the bridge, and possessed themselves of the ample store of provisions at Landsberg.

There was yet another important step to be taken, which Turenne took as soon as he was able, and this was to send 3,000 horse to the gates of Munich, which was then occupied by the Duke of Bavaria.   The route to Munich was a continuation of our imaginary straight line from Meiningen to Landsberg, Landsberg being half-way between Meiningen and Munich.   " 'Tis affirmed," says Turenne, "that nothing ever provoked the Duke of Bavaria to such a degree, or excited him so much to make peace, as to see the army of the confederates, in the beginning of winter, send parties to the gates of Munich, and to have no news of the Imperial army or his own, for which he had been at so great an expense, and which he believed, as it was true, much superior to ours."

And peace he made! Although the Imperial and Bavarian armies still largely outnumbered the French and Swedish, which, moreover, were in an enemy's country, the Duke of Bavaria recalled his troops and left the Archduke Leopold, whom he refused even to see, to take care of himself. The Archduke then retired and marched eastwards with his army.

From the contents of this chapter—it may be added from the contents of the whole of this book—it may be observed that Turenne endeavoured to succeed in his campaigns rather by strategic marches than by great battles. He is reported to have said: "The cause of general battles is either the hope of victory, the necessity to relieve a place besieged, the want of provisions, such an ardour and courage in your troops as cannot easily be restrained, a considerable reinforcement known to be on its march to join the enemy in the near future, which would make their numbers much superior to yours, some happy conjuncture which the enemy's movements may give you, such as the passing of a river, or the weakening or separation of their forces. The occasions which oblige you to avoid a battle are, when there is little to be got and a great deal to be lost by it, when

you are weaker than the enemy, when the enemy is
very strongly posted, when your troops are separated,
when there is any misunderstanding among your
superior officers, when you perceive fear or consternation
among your soldiers, or when you suspect their fidelity,
or, in short, when you think you can waste the enemy
by delays."

Of the latter part of this campaign, Napoleon said :
" The manœuvres by which the Archduke was dislodged
from his camp between Meiningen and Landsberg, display great boldness, sagacity and genius : they are fertile
in grand results, and ought to be studied by all military
men ".[1]

[1] Two cardinal generals have already been mentioned. During the year in which Turenne's last described campaign took
place, a third cardinal was given command of an army. This
was Cardinal Michel Mazarin, who was sent by his brother, Cardinal
Jules Mazarin, to besiege Lerida, an attempt in which he failed.

CHAPTER X.

THERE is probably no disappointment more keen, or
more vexatious, than to be robbed of the fruit of a
hardly-earned victory; and great was Turenne's chagrin, when he was forbidden by Mazarin to reap the
reward of the campaign of 1646 by conquering the
Imperial army in 1647, a task which he believed
would have been easy, now that it was weakened by
the withdrawal of the whole of the Bavarian army.
Worse still, orders came from Mazarin that Turenne
was to proceed with all his troops to Flanders, as a
large French force had been taken away from there to
proceed against the Spaniards in Catalonia.

Turenne had two special objections to leaving
Bavaria for Flanders. The first was that he still
thoroughly distrusted the Duke, or, as he was more
often called, the Elector, of Bavaria, who, he felt persuaded, would not hesitate to break his promises and
rejoin the Emperor if he should think it to his interest
to do so. The second was his strong suspicion that, if
he were to start for Flanders, his German or Weimarian
cavalry, which had fought so valiantly for him at
Nördlingen, would refuse to follow him because their
pay was five or six months in arrear. He sent to im-

plore Mazarin for these arrears; but Mazarin replied
by saying that one month's pay was all that he could
possibly send for them at the moment.

The event proved the reasonableness of Turenne's
fears. With the exception of one regiment, the German horse flatly refused to go to Flanders until they
were paid their full arrears. Rosen, who had only
lately been a prisoner of war, had been made Lieutenant-General of the Horse at the request of Turenne.
Instead of being grateful to Turenne for this appointment, Rosen felt ill-disposed towards him; because he
supposed that Turenne must despise him for having
been the cause of the disaster at Marienthal, the only
battle in which Turenne had ever been defeated.
Galled at this imagined contempt, Rosen took a dislike to him, and secretly encouraged the German
cavalry in their refusal to move until they were paid
their arrears. Turenne, however, had no suspicion of
the disloyalty of Rosen. Still believing that, if he put a
bold face on it, the German cavalry would follow him,
he started with his infantry for Flanders, taking Rosen
with him. When, after the first day's march, the
German horse did not appear, Turenne sent Rosen
back to command them to come at once. After
further marches, not only were they still absent, but M.
de Traci, another French officer, whom Turenne had
sent with Rosen, returned and told him that although
Rosen was pretending to be forcibly detained by the
mutinous Germans, there were grave grounds for suspecting his loyalty. All the French forces, including

8 *

the German cavalry, were on the west of the Rhine; but De Traci informed Turenne that Rosen was about to lead the German horse across the river into Germany.

Then Turenne, sending on the rest of his forces towards Flanders, made a march of twenty-seven miles in one day with five regiments of cavalry and 3,000 infantry; and, to the astonishment of the Germans, he caught them just as they were crossing the Rhine at Strasburg.

So unexpected had been the appearance of Turenne with his troops that the German cavalry were thrown into confusion. " Rosen, who was thunderstruck at the sight" of Turenne, "not knowing what to do, and perhaps imagining that he could yet conceal his unfaithfulness from him, said to him: 'You see how they drag me along with them'. These words and Rosen's countenance, convinced Turenne that he was betraying him; but nevertheless, he thought it necessary to dissemble his resentment. He might lawfully have fallen on the mutineers; their conduct deserved an exemplary punishment; his troops were superior in number, and there was so great confusion among theirs that he could have put them all to the sword. But Turenne, who was the father of the soldiery, could not resolve to sacrifice so many brave men, who had served the King so well, and might still be useful to him."[1]

Through their officers, the men professed a desire to return to their duty; but in practice they still held aloof and asked for their arrears of pay. Most of the officers

[1] Ramsay.

renewed their loyalty to Turenne, but among the exceptions was Rosen, who secretly continued to foment discord among the men. Turenne was persuaded—it is difficult to understand why—to allow all the German cavalry to cross over to the German, or eastern, side of the Rhine. Days passed without any definite submission on the part of the Germans, and as very urgent orders arrived that Turenne should send all his troops into Flanders, he sent thither all but one of the French regiments of horse which he had with him, and also all his forces which were already at Saverne. The orders which he had received to lead his army to Flanders in person he thought himself justified in disregarding, as he was convinced that, were he to do so, all his Weimarian cavalry would immediately go over to the enemy. He was determined to arrest Rosen; but, with his reduced forces, it was necessary to await an exceptionally favourable opportunity of doing so. For this purpose he took up his quarters with Rosen and rarely allowed him out of his sight.

After waiting nearly a month on the banks of the Rhine, Turenne heard one night that the German cavalry were mounting their horses to march towards the north. This was a great relief to his mind; for his chief fear had been lest they should march to the east and join either the Imperial army or that of Bavaria, which he shrewdly suspected might be on the point of renewing its alliance with the Empire.

The German cavalry no longer obeyed their officers and had elected others from their own ranks.

Ignoring all this, Turenne rode at their head as if he was still general in command, keeping with him the deposed officers as his staff, and never allowing Rosen to be out of his sight. "He sent before him the quarter-masters to mark out their camp; did all the offices of a general as usual, as if there had been no revolt; and not one of the new leaders durst retain the least shadow of authority in his presence." After marching thus for two days, the leading mutineers came again to demand their six months' pay. Turenne told them that, if they would recross to the west of the Rhine, he would give them one month's pay, and the rest as soon as he could obtain it from the Court of France; but that he could not possibly give it to them until he had got it himself. At this the mutineers looked very sulky, and he suspected from the expression of their faces that they had some idea of arresting him; but he pretended to be quite at his ease and ordered them to return to their quarters, which they did.

Rosen, being exceedingly anxious to get rid of Turenne, endeavoured to persuade him to leave troops with which he declared that general's personal liberty to be in serious peril; but Turenne took no notice of his warning and again marched at the head of the rebels on the following day. In the afternoon they arrived at Ettlingen, a town about twenty miles from Philippsburg. Turenne, Rosen, and the officers with them, stayed in the town, and the troops encamped outside it. As soon as he had arrived, Turenne sent one of the trustworthy men, whom he had with him, to gallop off to Philippsburg, which was garrisoned by French troops, and to order 100 musketeers to come to him at once. When they arrived very early the next morning he made them arrest Rosen and quietly carry him off as a prisoner to Philippsburg. As soon as they had got safely out of reach, he sent to the rebel camp to inform its occupants of what he had done, and to order them no longer to consider Rosen their commander. Upon this, all the officers, down to the corporals, submitted themselves to Turenne and promised their unqualified obedience, as also did two entire regiments of the mutineers. The rest of the German cavalry, to the number of 1,500, elected fresh officers from their own ranks and galloped away towards the valley of the Tauber. As soon as he heard of this, Turenne pursued them with the two regiments that had returned to their duty.

After two days' march Turenne came up with them in a narrow valley of the Tauber, and, in leading the attack on their rear, he was very nearly taken prisoner; but, shortly afterwards, the mutineers, although outnumbering their loyal fellow-soldiers, lost heart and turned tail. Turenne pursued them, killed 300 of them and made as many prisoners. The eight or nine hundred that escaped, instead of going over to the Imperialists, joined the Swedish army.

All the prisoners were condemned by Turenne to be hanged. As they were being marched off to execution before him, an old trooper looked him steadily in

the face, and baring his breast, which bore the marks
of sword-cuts, said: "General, don't stain the glory of
your noble actions, by causing an old soldier who is
covered with scars, and has a thousand times braved
death under your standards, to die by the hands of the
common hangman".

What followed shall be described by Ramsay:
"The Viscount was softened, forgave him and all the
rest, and incorporated them in his own troops, to which
he then returned. The Court did justice to his merit;
all the world admired his courage, prudence and
humanity. He had, in a very delicate and important
conjuncture, dissembled the most just resentment; paid
court to his inferiors, without lessening his authority;
chastised particular persons, without losing the confidence of the body; made himself respected by the
rebels at the same time that he put himself in their
power; then punished some and pardoned others, as
prudence required; and at last brought back the
greatest part of them to their duty." Never, perhaps,
in his whole life did Turenne show greater tact.

With the cavalry now regained, Turenne went
to Luxemburg and joined his army, which he had
already sent on. He received orders from Paris to
remain there. It was then September and he employed
his time in taking several "sorry castles" as he calls
them. Having heard that Turenne was showing a
bold front in that quarter, the Emperor sent a large
portion of his forces to resist him. This weakened the
Imperial army, which was opposed to the Swedes in

Hesse, and the Swedish army began to drive it towards the south-east. Then the Duke of Bavaria did exactly what Turenne had expected him to do, by once more breaking faith with France and sending his army to join that of the Emperor. The Duke, however, with an air of injured innocence, pretended that, although he was fighting the Swedes who were allies of France, he was still maintaining his treaty with France. Thus reinforced, the Imperial army was enabled to retake some of the fortresses which Turenne and Wrangel had captured in the campaign of the previous year, and to besiege Worms. Turenne then received orders to go to the Palatinate with his army, where he obliged the Imperialists to raise that siege.

About the middle of December Turenne received further orders to send a formal declaration of war to the Duke of Bavaria, on the ground of that Duke's breach of his treaty. Turenne brought 4,000 cavalry, 4,000 infantry and twenty guns to the assistance of the Swedes, whereupon the Imperialist and Bavarian armies retired to Ingolstadt, a place on the Danube, a little more than twenty miles to the east of Rain, a town which, as we have seen, had been besieged not long before by Turenne and Wrangel.

In February, 1648, having got remounts for his cavalry from Switzerland, Turenne marched with the Swedes through Franconia, a devastated country—devastated to some extent by Turenne's own troops—in which it was very difficult to find provisions for men or horses. For the first time Turenne and

Wrangel now disagreed as to their plan of campaign. Wrangel proposed to make a dash at the Upper Palatinate, while Turenne objected that such a step would take them too far away from Swabia, the only district upon which they could depend for provisions. Neither general would give way. Turenne made no quarrel; but, while Wrangel started to carry out his design, he waited quietly where he was, feeling assured that the Swedish army, unsupported by the French, would not be strong enough to cope with the united armies of the Emperor and the Duke of Bavaria. And he was right in his supposition; for, as he had anticipated, Wrangel and his army presently came back again.

While the French and Swedish armies were on the north of the Danube, the Imperial and Bavarian armies were on the south of it. Turenne, with some difficulty, persuaded Wrangel to march with him to Lauingen, a town on the Danube, which it will be remembered lay about half-way between Rain and Ulm.

A reconnoitring party of 3,000 horse, which had crossed the Danube to the south, having sent back a report that the enemy was encamped about four or five miles off, Turenne took his infantry over the river very secretly during the night. Early the next morning, the enemy, ignorant of the proximity of the French, moved leisurely away, and Turenne came up with their rear-guard at a place called Zusmershausen, on the road to Augsburg. General Melander, who had taken the place of the Archduke Leopold as commander-in-chief of the Imperial army in the south while the Archduke commanded the Imperial army in Flanders, came galloping back with supports, and made a stubborn resistance. While showing splendid courage he was killed and his troops were repulsed; but they succeeded in crossing the river Lech and fought a most creditable rearguard action during the retreat, under the command of Montecuculi, a general with whom we shall have a good deal to do in later pages.

After this battle the French and Swedish troops manœuvred about Bavaria. Turenne was the first French general to place the colours of France on the banks of the river Inn. The Duke of Bavaria, who was now seventy-eight, fled with his wife and family to the Archbishop of Salzburg for protection. A city almost within sight of Munich surrendered; and the Swedish General Königsmark surprised and captured Prague with the assistance of some French troops. The absence of these troops temporarily weakened Turenne, opposite to whom the Imperial and Bavarian armies were drawn up for a month, but never dared to attack him. Wrangel, however, came in for what it is now the fashion to call "an unfortunate incident," in which he lost some standards, a great many officers and men, and 700 or 800 horses, near Munich. For all that, the French and Swedish armies were practically masters of the enemy's country. "Such," says Ramsay, "was the irruption into Bavaria, in which the enemy were pursued from city to city, from post to post, from river to river, without intermission, for four months together; during which the whole country was exposed to the fury of the soldiers as far as the gates of Munich, Ingolstadt, Ratisbon, and Prague; and in which, nevertheless, no considerable action happened, but only a few convoys taken, and some parties defeated." One of these parties, however, as has just been mentioned, was of considerable size.

Turenne went into winter quarters at Lauingen. He was contemplating a campaign, with Vienna as its objective, for the following year, when a message was brought to him announcing the Peace of Westphalia, which meant the end of the Thirty Years' War. It was indeed high time that that long war should be finished. Every march and countermarch, such as those of Turenne already described, entailed the devastation of a large tract of country. It is stated that, in Bohemia alone, 29,000 villages were destroyed. So great was the agricultural ruin that, for more than a generation after the Peace of Westphalia, a third of Northern Germany was left entirely uncultivated. As to the depletion of population in consequence of the war, it is said that that of the Empire was reduced by two-thirds, owing to the slaughter in battles, disease, famine, and emigration for the purpose of escaping from those evils.[1]

This peace was brought about to a large extent by the masterly strategy of Turenne —it cannot be strictly said by his victories; for there were scarcely any great battles in the campaigns of either 1646 or 1648. It

[1] See *The Cambridge Modern History*, iv., 417-19.

was also partly due to the victories of Condé in Flanders.
The gains of France by its terms were very great.
They included the acknowledgment of her right to the
three Lotharingian Bishoprics (Metz, Toul and Verdun)
and also to the possessions hitherto held by the House
of Austria in Alsace; although Strasburg and some
other places were to remain independent.   Her ally,
Sweden, received considerable territories in Northern
Germany.

From this time that nation has little to do with
the story of Turenne; but few of the bye-paths beset-
ting that story offer a greater temptation to wander
from it than the reign of Sweden's monarch during
the time when Turenne was serving its interests con-
jointly with those of France.   That temptation shall
be resisted beyond the giving of a few quotations from
a letter from the Duke of Guise to a friend about
Queen Christina, shortly after her abdication.   "She
has a plump waist and large hips . . . one shoulder is
higher than the other . . . eyes very fine and full of
fire; her complexion, in spite of a few pits of small-
pox, is bright and handsome."   [She wears] "a man's
wig; thick and high on the forehead, very bushy on
the sides. . . . The body of her gown laced up behind,
crookedly, is made something like our doublets; her
chemise sticks out all round above her petticoat, which
she wears ill-fashioned and not over straight.   She is
always much powdered, with quantities of pomatum,
and she never wears any gloves.   She is shod like a
man, and she has the tone of voice and nearly all the

actions of a man. She affects to play the amazon. She has fully as much glorification and pride as her father, the great Gustavus, ever had. She is very civil and very cajoling, speaks eight languages, principally French as if she were born in Paris. She knows more than our Academy with the Sorbonne added; understands painting admirably, as she does all other things, and knows more about the intrigues of our Court than I do. In short, she is a very extraordinary woman."

Mazarin was very glad to make peace. He had wished to lessen the power of Austria and had done so; he had desired to put it out of Austria's power to send troops to the assistance of Spain in Flanders, and that object he had also attained; but he was anxious not to crush the power of Austria altogether. Spain did not join in the Peace of Westphalia, and a war with Spain alone was as much as Mazarin cared for in the way of fighting at one time. Again, he was somewhat embarrassed by a separate peace, which the Dutch had just made with Spain on their own account. But Mazarin had yet another grave cause for making peace with the enemies of France, in that serious internal troubles were disturbing his own country, and likely to give him quite enough to do without any fighting beyond its borders. Those internal troubles will form the subject of the next chapter.

CHAPTER XI.

THE Thirty Years' War was now at an end, and another was to begin, a war described by Michelet as a "burlesque war," a "war of children, with a child's nickname," a war "comic in its origin, its events, its principles"; yet, he might well have added, exceedingly tragic in the bloodshed which accompanied it.

Towards the end of the first half of the seventeenth century an anti-monarchical spirit was asserting itself throughout the greater part of Europe. At the end of 1648 the reduction of the powers of Austria and Spain, in which France herself had lent a hand, had demonstrated that the greatest of kingdoms might possibly crumble; two republics, those of the United Provinces and Switzerland, had been freed altogether from royal control. There had been insurrections, either successful or unsuccessful, in Genoa, Naples and Sicily; there had been riots in Moscow; in England the King was a prisoner about to be tried for his life, and a Commonwealth was on the eve of its establishment.

The political conditions in France were very exceptional and peculiarly favourable to an outbreak of the revolutionary epidemic with which the European atmosphere was impregnated. The King was a minor ; a single minister, and he a foreigner, was ruling and even oppressing the country with a rod of iron, while one of his creatures, also a foreigner, was, or at least was supposed to be, plundering its resources for his own and his employer's personal benefit. .

The Parliament had ventured to dismiss this corrupt financier, and Mazarin replied to this disgrace of his servant by arresting four leading members of that Parliament. The chief instigator of the popular movement against Mazarin, in Paris, was its coadjutor-bishop, Paul de Gondi, better known by his later title of Cardinal de Retz, the name by which it would seem most convenient to speak of him from the first in these pages. De Retz has not been described as a saint by historians; but, to give him his due, he distributed immense sums among the poor of Paris. Ramsay describes him thus : "Ambitious without measure, and courageous even to rashness, he knew no restraint, and was fearless of danger. To gain his point, he made use of gallantry and politics, vice and virtue, religion and the passions." Yet the same author admits "that virtue rectified, in the latter part of his life, all his vicious inclinations". This appears to have been the case ; but, judging from his own account of his dispositions, even when a bishop, he must have been utterly unsuited for the priesthood, and he had fought three duels before he was ordained.

On the arrest of the four members of Parliament all Paris was in an uproar, and the mob raised bar-

CARDINAL DE RETZ.

ricades and threatened the soldiers.   De Retz, in the
character of a peacemaker, obtained the release of the
imprisoned members, and it was at first supposed that
the disturbance was quelled.   The street row was con-
temptuously spoken of as the War of the Sling, a
scornful comparison with the fights of the gutter-boys
of Paris, who used little slings for the purpose of throwing stones at each other.   But this War of the Sling,
or, to use the French word, the War of the Fronde,
was destined to become something very much more
than mere child's play.

Into the details of the Wars of the Fronde it is
unnecessary to inquire here, except so far as they have
a bearing upon the life of Turenne   Early in 1649,
just after the King of England had been put to death
by his Parliament, relations between the Parliament of
France and the Court of France were greatly strained.
The Court and Mazarin were at St. Germains; the
Parliament was supreme in Paris.   Mazarin then
decided upon a very bold step.   He blockaded Paris!
Having seized all the places in the vicinity whence
provisions could be obtained, he invested the city with
6,000 or 7,000 men, hoping thus to starve it into
submission.

Meanwhile Turenne was wintering in Swabia with
his army.   As his conduct on hearing of the events in
Paris has been much and very unfavourably criticised,
we must consider the condition of affairs as it probably
appeared to him.   He wished to be loyal to the King,
he wished to be loyal to the Queen-Mother; but he

doubtless asked himself whether to allow their misguided minister to ruin their country and endanger the throne would be an act of loyalty to either.

Mazarin's virtual dictatorship was something very different from the regency and council of assistance which the late King had willed to protect the minority of his son. It was possible, perhaps easy, to represent Mazarin as a traitor to the throne. It was true that the Queen - Regent authorised and endorsed all his actions, and that she trusted him implicitly. But his enemies protested that he had maliciously deceived a gentle and credulous lady, and had infamously obtained a pernicious influence over her.

It is not likely that Turenne was predisposed in favour of Mazarin. He had little reason for being so. That cardinal had ill-used his brother, had tried to bribe Turenne himself by offering him estates that should have been his brother's, had failed again and again to send him reinforcements when they were most urgently needed, and had robbed him of the fruits of victory through a fear of entirely destroying the power of the House of Austria.

Turenne's brother, the Duke of Bouillon, had joined the party which regarded Mazarin as a traitor in disguise, and his siege of Paris as an act of high treason against the young King. Mazarin, the Queen, and Condé were all afraid that Turenne, the best general of France, would side with his brother, and each wrote to him, pretending to feel assured of his loyalty, while they deplored the defection of Bouillon.

In a long letter to Turenne, Mazarin said: "Nothing is so true, as that the esteem and passion I have for you and all things in which your interest is concerned, are carried to as high a pitch as they can possibly be for any person". He reminded Turenne that he had offered him his niece, whom the King of Poland had wanted to marry; and he added that Turenne would receive a grant for the government of Alsace, and despatches for two bailiwicks which he named.

In reply, Turenne thanked the cardinal for his offers, and said that, being a Protestant, he did not wish to marry a Catholic. Besides, this was not "a season for him to think of his private interests". In another letter to Mazarin he candidly stated that "he looked upon the blockade of Paris as a very bold step during a minority: that he could not approve of it; and that, if the cardinal continued to use the people with so much severity, he must not expect he would be any longer his friend". In obedience to the orders which he had received, he was about to bring his troops back to Paris, but, on his arrival at that city, "he would not favour either the rebellion of the Parliament, or the injustice of the Prime Minister".

Upon receipt of this letter, Mazarin sent to the troops of Turenne, ordering them no longer to acknowledge him as their general, and, in order to insure their loyalty, he sent 3,000 crowns to be distributed among them, with a promise that their pay, which was six months in arrear, should be immediately given to them. Turenne, "after divesting himself of

9 *

the generalship . . . retired with fifteen or twenty of
his friends into Holland, to reside there till the troubles
should be pacified ".   Madame de Motteville has something to say concerning this affair, which probably
ought to be taken *cum grano salis*.   She declares that,
when Turenne found himself deserted by his troops,
he was "confounded and repentant"; that Condé received a letter from him in which, "unhappy and
humiliated, he asked pardon for his fault, and entreated
the Prince to continue his protection and to obtain
from the Minister [Mazarin] forgiveness and absolution
for his crime".   Such action sounds very unlike what
one would expect from Turenne, and the story may
have been mere Court gossip.

Not very long after Turenne had gone to Holland,
the members of the Fronde, chiefly owing to the successes of the Government troops under Condé, became
anxious for peace, for which the Government was little
less desirous.   By the treaty which followed, the
cardinal and the Parliament retained their power, the
former over the Court, the latter over the people.
The Duke of Bouillon was to receive an equivalent
for the sovereignty of Sedan, and both he and Turenne,
for their descendants as well as for themselves, received
the rank of princes descended from a sovereign house.
Turenne then returned to Paris, and met with a most
gracious reception at Court.

Condé was now a personage of very great importance and influence, not only as a distinguished general,
but also as a grandee ; for he had by this time become

Prince of Condé, owing to the recent death of his father—a very different man from the son. "Besides the bad reputation he [the father] had acquired in his youth, he was avaricious and unlucky in war. That is the mildest term one can use about a Prince said not to be valiant." Moreover, "he was in no wise agreeable to look upon" (De Motteville, vol. i., chap. ix.). Now to Condé was the merit due of bringing the Fronde into submission, if to submission on very liberal terms, and he thought and demanded that his merit should be suitably rewarded. His own and Mazarin's estimates of that merit and its suitable rewards varied greatly, and considerable friction between them was the consequence.

At last Condé, whose temper was none of the longest, insulted Mazarin in public. Mazarin completely controlled his own resentment, which for that reason increased in intensity. The denunciations of Mazarin by the disappointed Condé, both in private and in public, became as virulent as had been those of the Fronde. In his rage against Mazarin, Condé sought the friendship of the conspirators in the late or, as it was subsequently called, the Old Fronde, by no means always with success. For several months, during the second half of 1649, Condé on one side and Mazarin on the other, both having enlisted several members of the Old Fronde to their separate interests, intrigued and plotted for each other's ruin. Presently they had an open quarrel, and a climax was reached in January, 1650, when Mazarin arrested Condé, his brother, the Prince of Conti, and the Duke of Longueville, the two latter being princes who had taken an active part in the Old Fronde; and he sent all three as prisoners to the castle of Vincennes.[1] This action on the part of Mazarin, instead of ending his troubles, increased them; for it made a split in the royal family and the nobility of France, and eventually brought to birth a New Fronde far more powerful than the old.

The New Fronde was anything rather than a revolutionary mob. It included the next heir to the throne, Gaston, Duke of Orleans, uncle to the King, Louis, Prince of Condé, who was also of the blood royal, his brother, the Prince of Conti, and Henry of Orleans, Duke of Longueville, a descendant of the famous Bastard of Orleans who had fought by the side of Joan of Arc. Next to the princes of the legitimate blood royal, the Duke of Longueville was the most powerful personage in France, and he was married to a sister of the Prince of Condé. Three of these four great men were now in prison; but the larger proportion of the princes and nobles of France advocated their

---

[1] Dr. Guy Patin wrote: "Of the three princes who are prisoners, M. de Longueville is very melancholy and never utters a word; M. le Prince de Conti weeps and hardly leaves his bed; M. le Prince de Condé sings, hears Mass in the morning, reads Italian books, dines and plays at battledore and shuttlecock. A few days ago, M. le Prince de Conti entreated some one to bring him a work entitled *The Imitation of Christ*, that he might console himself by reading it. The Prince de Condé exclaimed, 'And for me, Sir, I entreat you to send me the Imitation of M. de Beaufort, so that I may be able to escape from hence, as he did two years ago'" (*Life of Condé*, by Lord Mahon (1845), p. 95).

cause, and chose to consider the young King and the
Queen-Mother as practically prisoners in the hands of
the detested Italian, Mazarin. Among other noble
adherents to the Fronde, of whom we shall hear again,
were the Duke of Beaufort, the Duke of Nemours, and
the Duc de la Rochefoucauld, the author of the celebrated *Maxims*. In addition to these, was the Duke
of Lorraine, except when he thought it more to his
interest to take, or to pretend to take, the other side.

But the Fronde, in its fresh phase, was not made
up only of princes and dukes; for duchesses and
princesses played almost as important a part in it.
In an earlier chapter it was observed that an insignificant incident had led to a split among the ladies of the
Court, and that this split subsequently proved a factor
of some force in civil wars. It is true that, at the
point which we have now reached, some of the partisans
had changed sides; that the lady who had begun the
quarrel on one side was now the leader on the other,
and that the great ladies changed from one faction to
another just as their convenience, their tempers, or
their love-affairs happened to prompt them; but the
fact remained that ever since the apparently ridiculous
thin end of the wedge of discord had been jestingly
inserted into the highest society of France, the ladies
of the blood royal, accompanied by their satellites, both
male and female, had been cleft into two parties, one
siding with the Queen and the cardinal, the other with
anything or anybody, whether Fronde, hostile nation,
or aught else that happened to be opposed to the

Queen and cardinal. The inner circle of either party usually met at the house of one of its duchesses; and at least one important political meeting was held at the bedside of a princess shortly after the birth of one of her children.

Ramsay shall tell us what Turenne did under the new conditions. "Touched with the misfortunes of Condé, persuaded that in preventing the sacrifice of a hero of the blood of France, he should do service to his country; prepossessed with the false notion that war might be made against the cardinal without fighting against the King, and with several other maxims which were authorised at that time, upon the specious pretence of the public good, he gave way to the impulses of his generous nature, and resolved to set the princes at liberty, whatever might be the consequence. His motives were the less to be suspected, as Condé, so far from courting his friendship, before his imprisonment, had very much neglected it, and had concealed from him all his secret machinations against the Court. The viscount judged that it would be mean in him to abandon the prince, and fancying himself no more than a generous friend, became an undutiful subject."

That astute Frondeur, the coadjutor-bishop, afterwards Cardinal de Retz, was far less certain than Ramsay as to the motives of Turenne in joining his party. In a letter[1] to a friend he says: I own "that to this day I am at a loss about the motives that put him upon acting in that manner". Probably the truth

[1] *Memoirs of De Retz*, vol. i., p. 215.

is that Turenne persuaded himself, as did other Frondeurs who were attached to the Queen and the young
King, that the then present dispute was a personal
quarrel between Condé and Mazarin, to which the
King and Queen were neutral.

Turenne's great act of conspiracy took place at
Stenay, a town belonging to Condé, situated on the
river Meuse, a dozen miles from the present frontier
of Belgium.   At that time it was an important fortress ;
but four years afterwards Louis XIV. had its fortifications destroyed.   Turenne's co-conspirators, at that
place, were the Archduke Leopold, a brother of the
Emperor Ferdinand III., and Madame de Longueville,
a lady who is not unlikely to have been attractive to
Turenne, if the description of her, by her contemporary,
Madame de Motteville, is not exaggerated.   Her
beauty, she says, was more in her colouring than her
features.   " Her eyes were not large but fine, soft, and
their blue was beautiful—it was like that of the tur-
quoise.   Poets could only compare to lilies and roses
the beautiful carnation of her complexion ; and her fair
and sunny hair, accompanying so many other beauties,
made her less resemble woman than angel, according
as our weak nature has pictured one to our minds."

In the *Bibliothèque Nationale of France* (vol. 3855)
may be found nineteen folios consisting of a " Traité en
original de Madame de Longueville et du Maréchal de
Turenne avec Monsieur l'Archiduc Léopold.   Stenay.
30 Avril, 1650."   This was practically an alliance for
a war against the King of France, by which it was

agreed that Spain should put 3,000 infantry and 2,000 cavalry under the command of Turenne. Historians have been divided in opinion upon the question whether Turenne was induced to join in this treaty by Madame de Longueville.

It is a question, again, whether Turenne was in love with her. Very likely he may have been, and without knowing it; for his contemporary, St. Evremond, says : " M. de Turenne was not incapable of love : his nature was not of that severe and rugged kind which no sentiments of tenderness can soften : he even loved more than he thought he did, concealing as much as possible from himself a passion which others might easily discover ".

Several great ladies, as we have seen, were intriguing in politics at the time of the wars of the Fronde : Madame de Bouillon, Madame de Montbazon, Madame de Chevreuse and her two daughters, Mademoiselle de Chevreuse and the Princess Palatine ; but none of them are generally supposed to have been more intriguing or more active than Madame de Longueville.

It is to be hoped that there is more scandal than truth in something about Turenne which Des Maizeaux says, in the notes to his edition of Bayle's *Dictionary* (iii., 265); but it shall be given so that readers may judge for themselves. Some of the intriguing ladies, he states, were guilty of immoralities which are "almost unavoidable to those women who concern themselves with civil wars. They want the confidence of the party-leaders ; it is necessary that those gentlemen should

assist them with their swords and politics; but they
do nothing gratis, and they know how to improve the
opportunity. Such is the condition of a lady who
desires to have the direction of state-revolutions. It
is said that the Marshal de Turenne, though a very
wise man, could not resist the impetuosity of the
torrent, and required also such personal services from
the ladies during the civil war. I thought it might be
the first and the last time he was talked of on account
of his gallantry; but I have been informed by a person,
who knew it well, that he frequently used that trade."

De Retz does not seem to have esteemed either the
activity or the powers of intrigue possessed by Madame
de Longueville quite so highly as did other people.
Fully admitting her "great store of wit," he says:
"Her capacity, which has not been helped by her
laziness, could never reach so far as affairs. . . . She
had a languishing air, which touched the heart more
than the vivacity of women more beautiful than she
was." And he states that her gallantries ranked first
in her mind, her politics only second. As to Turenne,
the woman who De Retz thought had most power over
his mind and actions was his sister, "an old maid,"
whom Madame de Bouillon "hated entirely" and used
to call "Turenne's governess".

If Turenne was ever in love with Madame de
Longueville, any affection she may have felt for him
must have been very temporary; for the chief object
of her passion was the Duc de la Rochefoucauld. If
anything is wanting in the portrait which he has given

us of himself in his *Maxims*, the required touches have been added by De Retz. " He never was fit for any manner of affairs, and I cannot tell why, for he had qualities which would have supplied, in any other, those which he wanted. . . . He never was fit for war, though an excellent soldier; neither was he ever a good courtier, though he had always an inclination to be so. He never was a good party-man, though all his life long engaged in parties. . . . He had done much better to have known himself, and to have been content to pass, as he might have done, for the politest and finest gentleman that appeared in that age."

Even if Madame de Longueville had not been in love with Rochefoucauld, it is improbable that Turenne could have gained her affection; for his biographer, Du Buisson, says that, at the time of which we are speaking, she was also in love for the moment with Comte de Moussaye, the Governor of Stenay.

In his endeavours to raise troops for the release of the captive princes, among the regiments which had served under him in Germany, Turenne was only partially successful. The few he obtained met with a reverse from the King's troops under the Marquis of Ferté-Senneterre, and, to avoid complete defeat, Turenne asked for assistance from the Spaniards, who immediately sent him 1,500 cavalry and some companies of infantry.

In vain did Turenne write to implore the Queen to enable him to return to his allegiance, which he heartily desired, by liberating the three princes. His only hope remaining of delivering them was by an alliance with the Spaniards, and it is but fair to say that, in his treaty with them, he endeavoured, as much as possible, to protect the interests of France. In June, 1650, he took command of the Spanish army of 17,000 or 18,000 men, but the Archduke, uneasy at the idea of the soldiers of Spain being commanded by a Frenchman, came from Brussels and personally superseded him as commander-in-chief. The Archduke took Rethel, Château-Porcein and Neufchâtel; while Turenne, with 4,000 men, defeated the Marquis of Hocquincourt at Fismes. After this victory Turenne had intended to march on to Vincennes to set the three princes at liberty; but finding that they had been removed, he rejoined the Spanish army. That army, after taking Mouzon, retired into winter quarters in Flanders in November; but Turenne remained on the French frontier with 8,000 men.

While he was doing his best to organise the relief of the princes, Turenne was infuriated by a report that the leaders of the Fronde were being bribed by Mazarin. In his anger he sent placards, signed with his name, to be fixed in conspicuous places in Paris. "It is your task, people of Paris," he wrote, "to solicit your pretended tribunes, who are at last become Mazarin's missionaries and protectors; who have for a long time made a plaything of you and of your fortunes; and have sometimes stirred you up, sometimes slackened you, sometimes pushed you on, sometimes kept you back, as they were moved to it either by caprice, or the different success of their ambition."

De Retz, who was obviously in Turenne's mind when he published this effusion, chose to treat the matter as a joke in a letter to Turenne which he describes as "sufficiently wanton, though upon so serious a subject. It began with these words : ' It well becomes you, cursed Spaniard, to call us tribunes of the people '. The end of it was no less wanton. I bantered him upon account of a young wench in the street called Des-petits Champs, whom he loved with all his heart. The middle part was more solid, and took notice of our good intentions towards a peace."

The King's forces had meanwhile been successful in Bordeaux, and before the middle of December Marshal du Plessis Praslin, with 16,000 men, besieged and took Rethel, a fortified town on the Aisne, in Ardennes, about eighty miles north-east of Paris and about thirty from the present frontier of Belgium. Turenne had left 1,300 men in Rethel, and when he heard that it was besieged he made forced marches for four days to succour it; but he arrived too late as it had just capitulated.

Contrary to the opinion of Napoleon, the *Mémoires du Maréchal du Plessis* (p. 417) blame Turenne for not immediately attacking. They state that Du Plessis felt certain he would do so; that there was a hill on Turenne's left, upon which he might have placed guns, and that Turenne's whole position would have had great advantages over that of Du Plessis.

The next day Turenne began to retire; but in no extra hurry. Napoleon says: "Finding his object unattainable . . . he ought to have marched at least seven leagues that day; he would not, in that case, have been overtaken by the French army, or been compelled to give battle to a superior army. But he marched only four leagues". Du Plessis, on the contrary, marched all day and during part of the night, and early on the following morning he arrived within a short distance of Turenne. The two armies were posted on the opposite sides of a valley.

For some time a thick December fog prevented BATTLE OF either general from ascertaining the exact position of RETHEL, the other, and made any movement dangerous. When ber, 1650. it cleared, Turenne, who was largely outnumbered and therefore wished to avoid an action, moved on along the hillside; while Du Plessis, who was anxious to force an action upon him, kept parallel with him on the opposite side of the valley. They marched thus, within cannon-shot of each other, for three miles; and then, at twelve o'clock, Du Plessis, fearing lest Turenne might escape him, descended into the valley to attack him on its opposite side. His forces were double those of Turenne, although Du Plessis' memoirs assert that while he was very much stronger than Turenne in infantry he was weaker in cavalry; but Turenne, observing that only a part of the infantry of Du Plessis had yet reached the plain, thought that by a rapid movement of his whole force against it he might overwhelm it before the remainder could come up to its support. With this hope, he accepted battle, descended into the plain, and charged the enemy with all his cavalry. To accomplish this, he attacked with what was, in proportion to his own numbers, a very extended front, which left him no men to form a reserve in support of his flanks.

In these tactics he was probably acting upon a principle which he is said to have laid down in these words: "It is not always necessary to fight in two lines, with a corps de reserve; for if the enemy be more numerous than you, and the ground open so that they may outflank you, care must be taken to extend your front (though you fight in one line) equal to the front of the enemy". We shall see presently what Napoleon thought on this subject.

Turenne led his left with success, and his artillery fire with "cartouches"—some early form of canister or case-shot—was very effective; but his right was broken by the Marquis d'Hocquincourt, who completely routed it, and then charged Turenne's flank just as that general was beginning to get the best of Du Plessis' right. After a long and sanguinary battle the troops of Turenne were utterly defeated.

Although Du Plessis got the better of Turenne in this battle, he was very inferior to him as a general. Possibly Du Plessis may have been one of those whom Turenne had in his mind when he said: "A blockhead has sometimes perplexed me more than an able general".

Turenne himself was taken prisoner—a very serious

matter, as he was liable to be executed for high treason! Happily, however, although his horse was shot in five places, he contrived to escape from his captors, killing some of them in a hand-to-hand fight. After many adventures, he reached Montmédy and from thence he went to Bois-le-Duc, where he was able to rally about a quarter of his defeated troops. Then he returned to Stenay and the charming Madame de Longueville.

Of this action Napoleon says: "When Du Plessis descended into the plain and drew up in line, Turenne might still have avoided the battle by accelerating his movement. He formed no reserve in the rear of his wings, which was the cause of his overthrow. When once broken, his cavalry could not rally: he would have had a better chance of success with a less extended order of battle."

As to Turenne's own opinion of the action, when asked by an indiscreet youth, long afterwards, how he happened to lose it, he only replied: " By my own fault!"

Cardinal Mazarin was present at the capitulation of Rethel, and he watched the retreat of Turenne from one of its church towers. He had brought up reinforcements to Du Plessis, which no doubt contributed to that general's victory; but Mazarin, on this ground, very unjustly claimed all the glory of the victory over Turenne. Probably the temptation to a clergyman to represent himself as having overcome in battle the greatest general of the age was more than

10

the not impeccable Mazarin had the moral courage to withstand. But, in addition to any desire that he may have entertained to shine as a conqueror, he had another object in view, in relation to the army, which is well described by Madame de Motteville. " Seeing that he was hated by the grandees of the kingdom, and by the people, he tried to preserve for himself the goodwill of the soldiery. His principle was to go to the army as often as he could, and always to carry money to it, taking care to provide the soldiers with all their little necessaries."

CHAPTER XII.

"FORTUNE," wrote Rochefoucauld, "so capriciously ruled the events of the battle of Rethel, that M. de Turenne, who had just lost it, became thereby necessary to the Spaniards and obtained the entire command of their army; and, on the other hand, the cardinal, who claimed for himself all the glory of this action, renewed in every breast the disgust and fear of his ascendency."

Even those members of the Old Fronde whom Mazarin had won to his side became alarmed at the increase of his power, and this alarm was intensified when a report was spread about that he was going to purchase the support of Condé, by making private terms with him, and liberating him, with his brother and Longueville. Among those most disturbed in mind was the coadjutor-bishop, not yet a cardinal, who was infuriated against Mazarin for refusing to recommend him for the cardinalate at Rome.

Ramsay thus describes the unrest which then succeeded. "Instantly all the coadjutor's turbulence rouses itself: he revives the cabals, excites the cardinal's enemies, and sets the intriguing Court ladies at work. The Princess Palatine treats with the Frondeurs about the princes; the Duchess of Montbazon is promised a hundred thousand crowns; the Duchess of Chevreuse is flattered with the hopes of marrying her daughter to the Prince of Conti; and, lastly, the Prelate brings over the Duke of Orleans, the Parliament and the people, and prevails with them to demand unanimously the destruction of the Prime Minister, jointly with the delivery of the princes."

On hearing of this, Mazarin took fright and left Paris. Shortly afterwards the Queen determined to go after him; but all the gates of Paris were guarded, and she found herself practically a prisoner in the Palais Royal. The surveillance kept over her by order of the Duke of Orleans was so strict and so annoying, that, according to Omer Talon, neither she nor the little King went outside the Palais Royal from the 10th of February till the 7th of March.

The aristocratic Frondeurs now publicly insulted men of their own position who were known to be loyal to the Queen. A party of noblemen, attached to the Court, were having supper in a garden, when Beaufort, who was followed by a strong body of his friends, all armed, came in, went up to their table, and seizing one corner of the table-cloth, pulled it until all the plates and dishes fell upon their laps, bespattering their fine clothes with sauces and gravy; a very sad affair if they were wearing the sky-blue or primrose-coloured satin breeches, trimmed with lace, which are to be seen in the pictures of that period. As to the Parisian mob, it did not even respect ladies connected with the

Court. Madame de Motteville and her sister were
chased down the Rue St. Honoré; and when they
went for refuge into the Church of St. Roch and knelt
before the high altar, although high mass was being
sung there, the howling crowd followed them and
surrounded them, calling them Mazarines and declaring
that they ought to be killed. It was with difficulty
that the curé was able to rescue the ladies from the
hands of the mob, by a private door.

Such pressure was put upon the Queen that she
was obliged to consent to the liberation of the princes
without consulting Mazarin. But news of her consent
was privately conveyed to him, and he instantly set out
for Havre, where the princes were at that time imprisoned, with the object of liberating them himself,
hoping by that means to win their gratitude and favour.
In this hope he was totally disappointed, although, says
Mademoiselle de Montpensier, he went so far as to kiss
Condé's boot; and he found it prudent to leave France
and retire to a place near Cologne, while the three
princes went in triumph to Paris.

In the spring of 1651 the Queen made an "act of
oblivion and general pardon, with regard to all who
took up arms for the three princes". The Crown tried
to obtain popularity by distributing dukedoms and
other titles, and it awarded "lands and lordships, with
all their appurtenances, dependencies, and appendages
to the Duke of Bouillon". Turenne, also, was to
be pardoned and to be welcomed to Paris. But he
felt that he could not, "with any decency, leave the

Spaniards," until "France had offered Spain such
conditions of peace as were just and reasonable".
Conditions of such a nature Turenne succeeded in
persuading the Court to offer to Spain ; but, instead of
accepting them, Spain, on her own part, was so unjust
and so unreasonable that Turenne, feeling he had done
all that in honour could be expected of him for the
Spaniards, thanked them for the help they had given
him in his recent battles, bid them farewell and went to
the French Court, at which he was cordially welcomed.

Everybody was to be forgiven and there was to be
peace for evermore.   The Queen was to welcome her
recent rebels in person.   Madame de Motteville was an
eyewitness of these gracious receptions.   The Duke
of Longueville "did not have the boldness to speak at
all.   He turned pale, then red, and that was the whole
of his harangue."   As to his wife's reception, "the
whole visit, so stiffly carried on, only served to increase
the Queen's resentment against the princess," and
"confirmed Madame de Longueville in the evil intentions she retained in her heart against the Queen".
When the Duke of Chevreuse, who was eighty years
old and very deaf, told the Queen that his daughter
had improved in beauty, she "shouted with all her
might that he had too much love for beauty and that
he ought to begin to love heaven and virtue."   When
he asked permission for his wife to remain in Paris,
the Queen replied "that she could not allow her to
remain in a city still full of rebellion".   The Queen
received Turenne's brother "rather coldly".   When

the Duke of Beaufort had arrived in Paris, he "fell
ill of so violent a colic" that he imagined he had
been purposely poisoned.   The disloyal people of Paris
went to gaze upon their hero in his agony, "and the
crowd was so great that it was necessary to open all
the doors of his chamber, raise the curtains of his bed,
and expose him to the sight of the populace.   This
great concourse, and the flattery of a few friends, made
him finally irreconcilable."   The hitherto loyal Condé,
on the other hand, was listening to the suggestions of
his sister and his family that he should enter into "their
schemes for the purpose of making himself master of
the Court, instead of being, as they said he was, the
cardinal's valet".   A peace of this kind, forgiveness of
this kind, and loyalty of this kind, was not likely to be
very lasting.

Condé, who never lost an opportunity of increasing
his own power and properties, least of all by want of
asking, suggested to Turenne that now was his opportunity also for asking favours from the Court; but
Turenne replied that the only favour he desired was
that his troops should have comfortable quarters.

Turenne, indeed, never asked favours for himself,
or was fond of asking them for others.   When those
serving him did their duty he was pleased; but he did
not invariably place the same value upon their services
that they did; and he was diametrically opposed to that
—to use a word of modern slang—"teapotting" spirit
which gives honours and rewards for simple fulfilments
of duty.   "Improving with pleasure," says St. Evre-

mond, "the merits of the most submissive, he looks with displeasure on those industrious persons who endeavour to gain a reputation under him, and to be raised by the Ministry."

The Queen, being afraid that the projected marriage between the Prince of Conti[1] and Mademoiselle de Chevreuse might increase the power of the Fronde, persuaded Conti's brother, the Prince of Condé, by bribing him with the government of Guienne, to have the engagement broken off. This infuriated De Retz, who was a great friend of Madame de Chevreuse, a lady described by Madame de Montbazon as "an old woman more mischievous than the devil," with a daughter "yet sillier in proportion"; and he bitterly accused Condé of breaking his promise. "The Queen, who hated them both," says Ramsay, "hoped that their feuds and divisions would prove their mutual ruin." Condé now aspired to step into the place of Mazarin and, like him, to act as sole counsellor to the King. The Queen, who was longing to get Mazarin restored to power, refused with horror an offer of Hocquincourt's to assassinate Condé, and consulted De Retz, who advised the milder measure of putting a stop to his pretensions by arresting him a second time.

---

[1] Of the Prince of Conti De Retz says : "This head of a party was a cypher that only multiplied because he was a prince of the blood. As for his private character, malice did in him what weakness did in the Duke of Orleans. It drowned all the other qualities, which besides were but mean, and had all of them a mixture too of weakness."

Condé heard of this sinister advice, withdrew from Paris in the greatest indignation, and determined to make himself master of the Court and the King's person by force of arms. To this end he negotiated with the Spaniards, and tried to obtain the support of all the dukes who had joined the Fronde. Some of the latter did not rally to his assistance very readily, and, at the head of some raw levies, he was discouraged by receiving a check from the troops of Hocquincourt. Then he tried to come to terms with the Queen and even went so far as to give her a promise to offer no opposition to the return of the cardinal. The Queen then made a cat's paw of Condé, by seizing this opportunity as an excuse to recall Mazarin ; but, shortly after getting her way on this point, she broke off her negotiations with the prince.

Although there was nominally peace, many of the aristocratic Frondeurs were intriguing and caballing; and, between these and the Court party, others were hesitating or wavering. Some of the late leaders of the Fronde were in favour of making a real and lasting reconciliation, or, as it was then termed, "accommodation," with the Court, and those who desired the contrary were much divided in opinion as to the most judicious course to be followed. It may be sufficient to quote De Retz's observations that " M. de Bouillon, who was in no manner pleased either with the prince or with the Court, did not help to fix the resolutions of the party "—the New Fronde—" because the difficulty of keeping fair with both sides confounded at noon the

views he had had two hours before, either for or
against an accommodation. M. de Turenne, who
was not better pleased with either side than his brother,
was not so decisive in state affairs as in war." As for
Turenne's friend, Madame de Longueville, she "was
sometimes for an accommodation because La Rochefoucauld desired it ; at other times she was for a rupture
because it would keep her from her husband, whom
she never loved ".

Direct contemporary evidence is always worthy of
consideration, and De Retz shall now be called in as a
witness concerning an obscure action of Turenne's.
Upon the credibility of De Retz, who is often quoted
in these pages rather as a gossip than as a witness, no
opinion shall be expressed.

" Immediately after the prince's [Condé's] leaving
Paris and going to St. Maur, Messieurs de Bouillon
and De Turenne waited upon his Highness there,
offering him their service publicly, and in the same
manner with those that seemed the most deeply engaged with him. The prince has told me since, that
the day before he left St. Maur to go to Trie, after
which he returned no more to Court, Mr. de Turenne
was still so positive in promising to serve him, that he
even accepted of a writing signed with his own hand,
whereby the prince ordered La Moussaye, who
governed for him in Stenay, to put that place into Mr.
de Turenne's hands ; and that the first news he [Condé]
heard of him [Turenne] afterwards, was that he was
going to command the King's army. I must desire

you to observe that of all the men whom I have known,
the prince was the least capable of a premeditated im-
posture.   I never durst bring Mr. de Turenne to explain me this to the bottom; but what I could indirectly
draw out of him is, that as soon as the prince was set
at liberty, he had all imaginable reasons to be ill pleased
with his manner of proceeding in respect to him: that
he [Condé] preferred before him, in everything and in
all manner of ways, Mr. de Nemours, who came not
nigh to him in merit, and who besides had not rendered
him near so many services, for which reason he thought
himself free from his first engagements to him.   I must
likewise desire you to observe that I never knew anybody less capable of a base thing than Mr. de Turenne.
Let us therefore once more acknowledge that there are
points in history inconceivable even to those that have
been nearest to the facts."

When Turenne and Bouillon, says De Retz, "had
left the prince's party, they lived very retired in Paris,
and except their particular friends, they were seen
by few persons".   De Retz was one of these and
he tried to gain them over to the interests of the
Duke of Orleans; but Turenne's utter contempt for
Orleans, and the dislike of Orleans to Bouillon,
stood much in the way of such an arrangement.
Meanwhile an emissary named Berthet was sent to
Paris for the express purpose of winning Turenne
and Bouillon to the interests of Mazarin.   Their meeting was to be managed by the Princess Palatine, of
whom De Retz once said he did "not believe that

Queen Elizabeth of England had greater capacity than she ".

The princess invited Turenne, Bouillon and De Retz to "her house betwixt twelve and one at night, where," says De Retz, "she presented Berthet to us, who . . . told us that the Queen, who was resolved to recall the cardinal, was unwilling to execute her resolution without hearing what we had to say to it. Mr. de Bouillon, who swore to me an hour after in the presence of the Princess Palatine that he had not to that day received any proposals from the Court, at least in form, seemed to me embarrassed; but he got off in his usual manner, that is, as a man that knew better than anybody I have ever seen how to speak the most when he said the least. Mr. de Turenne, who was more laconic, and in truth much more frank, turned towards me and said : ' I believe that Mr. Berthet pulls by the sleeve all those he meets in the streets, to ask their opinion about the return of the cardinal, for I do not see any more reason to ask it of my brother and me, than of all those who have passed this day over the Pontneuf'. . . . Nothing was more ridiculous than to see a little insignificant fellow . . . take it upon him to persuade two of the greatest men in the world to commit the greatest piece of folly imaginable, which was to declare for the Court, before they had taken any measures there. They would not therefore hearken to what Berthet said to them at that time, but they entered soon after into sure measures with the Court. Mr. de Turenne had the promise of commanding the armies, and Mr. de

Bouillon had assurances given him of the immense recompense which he has since had in lieu of Sedan."

When the Duke of Orleans, who was one of the leaders of the New Fronde, heard that Turenne and Bouillon were about to leave Paris to serve the King, he gave orders, as Governor of Paris, that they should both be arrested, and he told De Retz what he was doing. Although De Retz was of the Duke of Orleans' party and Turenne had now become a political enemy, De Retz still had a regard for him as a personal friend; and he saved both Turenne and Bouillon from arrest by contriving to delay the execution of the order and by giving them immediate warning.

In 1652 Turenne and Bouillon were loyal to the King and in favour both with the Queen and with Mazarin, who had now returned to the French Court, in defiance of the offer by the French Parliament of 50,000 crowns for his head. The cardinal once more acted as supreme ruler in France; but Louis XIV., although only fourteen years old, had come of age and nominally enjoyed the full powers of a reigning monarch.

The King's army was placed under the command of Turenne, in conjunction with the Marquis of Hocquincourt; for Mazarin would not trust it entirely to Turenne after his recent disloyalty. Its total strength, including a force of 5,000 men brought from Champagne by Mazarin, did not exceed 9,000, the greater proportion of which was cavalry. The soldiers of

the different contingents were distinguished by their
scarves: the King's own troops wore white scarves and
the levies recruited by Mazarin wore green scarves,
while their enemies, the troops of Condé, wore scarves
of a pale brownish colour, known by the name of
Isabel.[1]   The royal army, the Court, and Mazarin
were at Poictiers, nearly 200 miles to the south-west
of Paris, while the army of the Fronde, which numbered
14,000, was stationed between Montargis and the Loire,
under the Duke of Beaufort, and Beaufort's brother-in-
law, the Duke of Nemours.   Condé had gone to the
borders of Spain to negotiate with the Spaniards and
to raise followers in Guienne.

Mazarin wished to remove the Court to Gien, a
town about forty miles to the east of Orleans.   For
this purpose both Court and army went to Tours and
up the Loire, where they were received into every
city, except Orleans, with open gates.

Beaufort formed a plan for crossing the Loire, by
the bridge of Jargeau,[2] a few miles to the east of Orleans, and seizing the person of the King, as well as

[1] Not long before the time of which we are writing, the
Spaniards were besieging Ostend, and the Archduchess Isabel,
wishing to encourage the troops, and thinking that the city would
almost immediately surrender, made a vow not to change her linen
until she entered it.   The siege lasted three years longer and meanwhile her linen, as might indeed be expected, lost its whiteness.
To comfort her, her ladies-in-waiting had their linen dyed to match
hers, and called the colour Isabel.

[2] It was at Jargeau that Joan of Arc's troops took Suffolk
prisoner, shortly after the siege of Orleans.

those of the Queen and the cardinal, as they passed along the road towards Gien. This plot would probably have succeeded had not Turenne, suspicious of this bridge, ridden hurriedly to it, with a couple of hundred horse and, with that small force, stopped four regiments of Beaufort's cavalry as they were in the act of crossing it. Hastily forming a barricade on the south side of the bridge, Turenne held the position against almost overwhelming numbers for about a couple of hours, when his own troops came to his rescue. His defence was the more meritorious because, as he himself says, "the enemy's cannon all the while annoyed us very much". In a letter immediately afterwards Turenne modestly wrote in a postscript: "Something has happened at Gergeau, but 'tis of no great consequence". The Queen, however, said in the presence of the whole Court that Turenne "had saved the kingdom," when that "something happened".

A peculiar condition in the rival armies, at this time, was that on neither side were the generals on good terms with each other. Hocquincourt was jealous of Turenne on the one side, and Beaufort and Nemours were actually quarrelling on the other. Whether Turenne was enabled to foster this quarrel does not appear; but one of the maxims attributed to him is: "If you have to do with a confederate army, endeavour to break down the confederacy by raising discord and jealousy amongst their generals".

It was the month of April, and it was impossible

to find provender for the horses at Gien. The King's army, therefore, leaving the Court at Gien, moved a little to the west, Turenne going to Briare and Hocquincourt to Bléneau, both keeping only their infantry with them, and allowing their cavalry to disperse in search of forage.

One day Turenne went to dine with Hocquincourt, and, having observed the disposition of his men, told him "that he thought them very much exposed, and therefore advised him to contract them". Hocquincourt was annoyed at being offered advice by Turenne, and did not act upon it.

Having returned to his own quarters at Briare, Turenne heard, the next evening, that the rebel army had attacked Hocquincourt's camp and routed it. Without losing a moment, Turenne ordered his infantry to prepare to start at once to the relief of Hocquincourt, and he sent officers to bring on the cavalry, which was foraging in the neighbouring villages. This time he had not allowed any of his horse to wander more than three miles away in search of provender. He marched without a guide, although the night was very dark. Presently he saw flames rising in the distance, in the direction of Hocquincourt's camp. There was no longer any doubt about Hocquincourt's disaster, and Turenne, well aware of the feebleness of both Beaufort and Nemours, quietly remarked that the Prince of Condé must have arrived.

This turned out to be true. Condé, having heard

of the quarrelling between Beaufort and Nemours, had
secretly left Guienne, accompanied only by his son
and Rochefoucauld, and had ridden some two hundred
miles, past hostile fortresses, through hostile cities, and
right across a hostile country.   After extraordinary adventures and, as Napoleon says, "after escaping a thousand dangers," he had reached Beaufort's army, just in
time to take advantage of Hocquincourt's careless disposition of his troops, at Bléneau, where he put him to
flight and sacked his camp.   By this victory, with his
great superiority in numbers, Condé had every hope of
seizing not only the person of the young King, but
also that of his hated enemy, Mazarin.

Perceiving that their commander was advancing
against Condé, Turenne's generals pointed out the
dangers of proceeding against an enemy largely outnumbering him and flushed with victory; and they
urged him to retire upon Gien, for the protection of
the King and the Court.   But, the evening before,
Turenne had noticed an advantageous position, which
he determined to occupy, and, in spite of their remonstrances, he went on silently and deep in thought.
"Never," he afterwards said, "did such a multitude
of dreadful things crowd into the imagination of one
man, as filled mine at that time.   I had not long been
on good terms with the Court ; and had but lately
received command of the army which was to defend
it.   That man who has distinguished himself ever so
little is sure of being envied, and of raising enemies.
Some I had, who declared in all places that I still

11

carried on a secret correspondence with the prince [Condé]. The cardinal did not believe it; but he, perhaps, the very first misfortune which should have befallen me, would have entertained the same suspicion. Besides, I knew Marshal d'Hocquincourt, who would certainly have said that I exposed him, and [that I had] not brought him the least succour. These were very troublesome thoughts, and the worst of all was, the prince was advancing towards me, victorious and with a superior force." [1]

Turenne had good reason for thinking that Hocquincourt would say that he exposed him and brought him no succour if he did not go to his assistance. In spite of all, as will now be seen, that Turenne did to help him, two years later St. Evremond heard him say : " I remember well that Turenne suffered me to be beaten by the Prince of Condé [at Bléneau] when the Court was at Gien ; perhaps I may find an opportunity to be even with him ". [2]

Turenne's army of 4,000 men, and Condé's army of 14,000, passed each other during the night without being aware of it; but, in the morning, they both discovered their propinquity by the sound of each other's drums and bugles. Turenne, however, had reached his desired position. He had in front of him a narrow defile, with a wood on the right, and a lake and a bog on the left. Immediately opposite this defile

[1] *Histoire d'Henri de la Tour d'Auverne*, tom. ii., pp. 204, 205.

[2] *Works of St. Evremond*, vol. i., p. 182.

he concealed a strong battery of guns. Contrary to the advice of his staff, Turenne did not place any infantry in the wood, because he feared that, if he did so, Condé's infantry might attack them and bring on a general engagement, in which, with his inferior numbers, he would certainly have been beaten. Meanwhile, Condé was advancing towards this narrow passage, which lay on his direct road to Gien.

Having drawn up his troops about a musket-shot from the wood, Turenne rode through the defile with ten squadrons and, as soon as Condé could see him, he led his men back again, as if retreating in alarm. Condé was not to be so easily deceived, especially when he observed Turenne's forces stationary on reaching the opposite end of the pass; and he halted and hesitated for some time at his own end of it. In order to induce Condé to advance, Turenne then turned away from the defile with his troops, as if intending to retreat. On seeing this, Condé sent fifteen or twenty squadrons into it. As soon as some of these squadrons had got through it, Turenne wheeled about and attacked them with his whole force, causing them to hurry back into the narrow passage in confusion. At the moment when the defile was thus overcrowded, Turenne unmasked his battery of artillery, which "did dreadful execution on the enemy, who, in their hurry, trod down each other in heaps," as the Duke of York describes it. In the evening Hocquincourt joined Turenne with such forces as he had rallied or saved out of his army.

11 *

Then, says Turenne, in his *Memoirs*, "both armies stood looking at each other till night, and afterwards retired on both sides, the King's army to Briare, and that of the Prince to Chatillon. . . . Some days afterwards, the Prince departed from Chatillon; his army made the best of its way to Montargis, and he himself went to Paris, where he thought his presence was necessary." It was indeed urgently needed there. During his consequent absence from his army, he left it under the command of General Tavannes.

Napoleon praises Turenne for his execution of this "able and successful manœuvre to impose on Condé" —not for undertaking the manœuvre. Napoleon points out that Turenne had no intention of maintaining his position, which is proved by his stationing his army in a situation for easy retreat, and by his having carefully avoided the temptation to place any of his infantry in the wood. It is true that musketeers concealed under its cover could have slaughtered Condé's cavalry as it passed through the defile; but the consequence might have been a general action, in which Turenne, with his inferior numbers, would inevitably have been defeated. "When once an affair has commenced partially," says Napoleon, "it gradually becomes general." Turenne, continues Napoleon, "kept his troops together, sufficiently near the defile to render its passage dangerous to the prince, and to annoy him by a fire of a battery planted so as to play through the whole length of the defile, but sufficiently removed to prevent the compromising of any part of his force. This circumstance may appear trifling, but it is one of those trifles which are the indications of military genius."

Much as Napoleon praises Turenne's tactics in this affair, and while fully admitting his "talent and prudence" in the execution of the "delicate manœuvre," he blames his strategy.   In short, he maintains that the manœuvre ought not to have been undertaken at all.   "As soon as Turenne had mustered his cavalry, he should have retired towards St. Fargeau and not have returned and marched forward until after his junction with Marshal d'Hocquincourt."   The position had been as follows: Condé had been in the north and had advanced towards the south, upon Bléneau.   Bléneau, Briare and St. Fargeau form a triangle, Bléneau being in the north, Briare in the south-west, and St. Fargeau in the south-east, the sides of the triangle varying from ten to fifteen miles in length.

"The rules of war," says Napoleon, "require a division of an army to avoid engaging alone a whole army, which has already obtained victories.   It is risking a total and irretrievable overthrow; the Prince of Condé had above 12,000 men, and Turenne only 4,000."   Again, he says: "The rendezvous for the two armies in quarters was fixed too near the enemy: this was an error; the point of junction for an army, in case of surprise, should always be fixed in the rear, so that the troops may reach it from all the cantonments before the enemy.   On this principle, it should have been fixed between Briare and St. Fargeau."   It will be remembered that Napoleon made a somewhat similar criticism of Turenne's selection of a rendezvous for his cavalry before the battle of Marienthal.[1]

Voltaire, however, says that it is difficult to decide which general deserved most praise, Condé for his victory at Bléneau, or Turenne for robbing him of the fruits of it; but, says he, if Condé had not been checked by Turenne, he would probably have captured the King, Mazarin and the whole Court. De Retz also divides his praises. He says that "they both did what the two best generals in the world would have done!" Napoleon, on the contrary, finds fault with each of them. We have already seen his criticism of Turenne's strategy, and he says that Condé "did not display in this campaign, the daring spirit which distinguished the general of Freiburg and Nördlingen; he ought not to have suffered himself to be overawed at Bléneau by demonstrations; even when united, the two royal armies were inferior to his; he ought to have been convinced, as by demonstration, that there could not be any considerable force before him; he contented himself with an insignificant advantage, and stopped short at preliminaries, without pushing his enterprise to a conclusion. With a little of his habitual daring, he must have obtained the last favours of fortune: he neglected to gather the fruits of his own calculations, and of Marshal d'Hocquincourt's error."

[1] See chapter vii.

CHAPTER XIII.

THE task of a general is infinitely increased when, in addition to the ordinary duties of a campaign, he has to protect a Court, including the person of a King driven out of his own capital, wandering aimlessly and unwelcome among his own dominions, and perpetually shadowed by an enemy consisting of his own subjects. And a yet further and very serious addition is made to these increased difficulties when the general wishes one thing and the Court another. Turenne sometimes found it little, if at all, easier to drive the Court than to drive the enemy where he desired. Eventually, however, by making a long détour to the east, with Turenne's and Hocquincourt's armies between it and the rebel army, the Court reached St. Germains.

Tavannes then established his forces at Étampes, a town about twenty-five miles south of Paris, and Turenne and Hocquincourt made their headquarters at Chartres, about thirty miles to the west of Étampes. Chartres and Étampes lie in the richest corn-growing district of France; and Chartres, which is a very much larger town than Étampes, is one of the principal French corn markets. The rebels fortified Étampes, for it was an important position to them, as it lay on the direct road from Paris to Orleans.

The Duke of Orleans had now joined the Fronde, and it had been suggested to him, some little time before the Court passed Orleans, that he should go to that city and enlist the services of its citizens. The cowardly Duke refused to go there himself, as the disposition of the inhabitants seemed rather doubtful; but he gladly sent his much more courageous daughter. We may be introduced to that young lady by Madame de Motteville, who says: " She had beauty, intelligence, wealth, virtue, and royal birth. . . . Her beauty, however, was not without its defects; and her mind was not always in a condition to please. Her vivacity deprived her actions of the dignity desirable in a personage of her high position, and she was too readily carried away by her emotions."

Pitiable was the position of the authorities in the city of Orleans! A representative of the King had appeared at one of its gates and demanded admittance for some of Turenne's troops which were on their way thither; and while the functionaries were in the act of pondering about a reply, they were informed that an emissary was demanding admittance at a gate on the opposite side of the city. There they found the Duke of Orleans' daughter, clad in armour, with many other Amazons attired like herself, accompanied by the Duke of Rohan, several members of Parliament, and a band of gay young men from Paris. This picturesque force was as imposing as it was brilliant, but it savoured some-

MADEMOISELLE,

what of comic opera, and the rulers of Orleans would
necessarily reflect that, insignificant in comparison as were
the King's representatives at the other gate, so far as
appearances were concerned, they would soon be
followed by much more able-bodied warriors than this
second Maid of Orleans, her pretty companions, and
her troop of boys and politicians. Unable to decide
between loyalty to the lord of their city and province
on the one side, and loyalty to the King of their country
on the other, they determined to be neutral and refused
admittance to the representatives of both.

Later in the day they were quietly congratulating
each other upon their prudence, by which they imagined
that they had insured themselves against all danger of
Mazarin's much-dreaded resentment, when news was
brought to them that Mademoiselle de Montpensier
was in the middle of their city, haranguing a crowd of
her father's subjects and demanding their own immediate presence and loyal homage.

Mademoiselle, by dint of persuasion and bribes, had
induced some boatmen to get her into the town; and
they had succeeded in doing so by rowing her across
the river and breaking down a disused doorway in the
walls, through which they gave her entrance. Concerning the negotiations, demurrings, upbraidings,
waverings and consultations which followed, ending in
the triumph of one bold-faced but half-frightened girl
over a whole pack of both military and civic authorities,
the reader must be referred to the entertaining pages
of Mademoiselle de Montpensier herself. To complete

the comedy, Turenne's troops did not attack Orleans after all, but left that city, its authorities, and its Mademoiselle severely alone.

Turenne strongly advised the King to enter Paris with his army; but, for purely personal reasons, Mazarin would not hear of it, because he knew himself to be so hated by the Parisians that he feared for his own safety. Meanwhile, Mazarin was secretly, and as it turned out ineffectually, trying to negotiate terms with Condé. De Retz, now like Mazarin a cardinal, although nominally an ally of Condé, was endeavouring to get him out of favour with the Duke of Orleans as industriously as the Duke of Orleans' daughter, Mademoiselle de Montpensier, was endeavouring to get him into it. The reason of this was that De Retz wished Orleans to place the government in his own hands instead of in those of Condé, while Mademoiselle was now in love with Condé, whom she had formerly hated, and hoped to marry him whenever his very excellent but very delicate wife should die.

OPERA-
TIONS
BEFORE
ÉTAMPES,
May, 1652.

When Turenne was contriving an attack upon Étampes, Mademoiselle de Montpensier was about to return from Orleans to Paris, and, to do this, she would have to pass not only through the rebel army at Étampes, but also through the region held by the royal army, as Turenne had posted some troops between Étampes and Paris. She therefore sent a trumpeter from Étampes to Turenne, with a request for a pass, which, after some delay, he granted to her. Nor was this all; for he expressed a hope that she would pay him a visit, on her way, and inspect his troops. During the delay just mentioned, Mademoiselle says she amused herself by stopping all the couriers, taking their letters, opening and reading them; "for I had really nothing else to do. Some I found charged with despatches, others with family matters or love-letters, ridiculous enough. . . . When they were of no advantage to my own party, I turned them into a source of merriment."

Turenne happened to hear that Tavannes' men had not been foraging during Mademoiselle's visit, probably as he thought, because there had been in-spections and reviews for her entertainment, and he believed that, as soon as she left Étampes, his enemy would find it necessary to send out foragers on an un-usually large scale to make up for lost time. He also expected that the principal officers would accompany her during the first part of her journey towards Paris. Thinking, therefore, that a large number of Tavannes' soldiers would be absent for foraging purposes, and that many of their officers would be away, as a guard of honour to Mademoiselle, on the morning of her departure, Turenne and Hocquincourt agreed that it would be a favourable moment for an attack. They proposed to make a long night-march by a considerable détour to intercept the foragers, and to enter and take possession of the comparatively defenceless city in their absence.

Unfortunately, when, after a very wearisome but admirably conducted night-march, Turenne and

Hocquincourt arrived at the critical spot exactly at the critical moment, there were no foragers to intercept. On the contrary, Tavannes' troops were all drawn up under arms, on the plain outside the city, for an inspection by Mademoiselle, who was just then driving away from them and from Étampes, on her way to Paris.

Great as was the surprise of Turenne at finding the rebel army drawn up under arms, the surprise of Tavannes at the unexpected appearance of the royal army was even greater, and he hurried his men back into Étampes so vigorously that they fell into some confusion. Of this confusion Turenne and Hocquincourt determined to take advantage, and they attacked the enemy's troops as they were passing through the suburbs.

The rebels made a gallant defence, and the battle was long and obstinate; but eventually the King's troops forced their way into the suburbs, entirely defeating, says Turenne, after a fight of three hours, "nine regiments of infantry, and four or five squadrons of cavalry," taking "2,000 prisoners, and a great number of officers". The King's army, says the Duke of York, lost 500 men. Brilliant as was the action of the royal troops in this affair, Étampes was not taken; in fact the town itself was not even entered; the royal army was withdrawn to Etrechy, a place about three miles off, and the next day it returned to Chartres.

Hocquincourt was now sent to take command of the King's army in Flanders, and Turenne was left in sole command of the army in France. He removed it from Chartres to Paliseau, a town about eighteen miles to the north of Étampes, so as to cut off all communication between the rebel army and Paris. He also sent some cavalry, for the protection of the Court at St. Germains, and he took possession of St. Denis, then fully four miles distant from the northern walls of Paris. Here he left a garrison, and we shall hear again of this fortress before long.[1]

Turenne then moved to the South, to lay siege to

[1] Turenne was buried at St. Denis. It is remarkable that, during the French Revolution, in 1792, the tombs of three celebrated men who had been so much associated in life—Turenne, Richelieu and Mazarin—should have been defaced at the same time. Again, in 1793, says Alison (*History*, vol. iii., chap. xiv.), "a furious multitude, headed by the revolutionary army, precipitated itself out of Paris ; the tombs of Henry IV., of Francis I., and of Louis XII., were ransacked, and their bones scattered in the air. Even the glorious name of Turenne could not protect his grave from spoliation." The bodies of "kings, queens and heroes were thrown into a vast trench and destroyed by quicklime. The body of Du Guesclin was lost in this way. That of Turenne alone escaped, not from any reverence for his memory, but from the fortunate circumstance that, after it had been ordered to be thrown into the common tomb, two of the officers of the Museum of Natural History requested to have it, as being 'a well-*preserved mummy*,' which might be of service to the science of comparative anatomy. It was delivered to them accordingly, and carried to the Jardin des Plantes, where it lay for nine years in a storehouse between the skeletons of a monkey and a camel. In 1802, however, Napoleon heard of the circumstance, and had the body of the illustrious warrior removed to the church of the Invalides, where it now reposes beside his own mortal remains." During the French Revolution his body, so little altered as to be recognisable from his portraits, had been exposed in a glass case for the amusement of the populace.

Étampes, with 6,000 foot and 4,000 horse, against the enemy's 4,000 foot and 3,000 horse. Unfortunately he was lamentably short of the "tools and warlike stores" necessary for a siege, and, as a result, his "line of contravallation" proceeded very slowly. The enemy made frequent sallies to interrupt it, and there was a great deal of fighting and much loss of life on either side. The details of the siege of Étampes are fully described in the *Memoirs of the Duke of York*, which were handed by him to Turenne's nephew, Cardinal de Bouillon, and also in the *Life of James II.*, written from King James's own manuscripts and diaries.

James, Duke of York, had taken service under Turenne, at the age of nineteen, a few weeks before the first attack upon Étampes. Turenne "gave him a reception suitable to his birth ; and endeavoured, by all possible proofs of affection, to soften the remembrance of his misfortunes". A little later in the campaign, Turenne employed the Duke of York to write despatches from the front to his brother, the Duke of Bouillon. And, as a substitute for his own defects of vision, Turenne frequently kept the Duke at his side, "to observe as exactly as he could and inform him what the enemy were doing". Turenne is reported by Burnet[1]—no friend of the Duke of York —to have said of him that he "was the greatest prince and like to be the best general of his time".

In one of the attacks during the siege of Étampes, Turenne's own regiment specially distinguished itself.

---

[1] *History of His Own Times*, vol. i., p. 168.

DUKE OF SCHOMBERG.

His captains, says the Duke of York, took the colours in their hands and marched with them at the head of their men, till they "came up to push of pike," and he adds that Turenne was of opinion that it would have been impossible for the men to have done so much if their colours had not been always before their eyes. "And this," says he, "was what partly determined the regiments afterwards to procure new colours, the old corps, as well as the rest, having till then through a mistaken glory, affected to have their colours so tattered and ragged, that oftentimes there was nothing left but the staff."

Besides the Duke of York, another foreigner, who had volunteered, was serving under Turenne. This was Count Schomberg, who was wounded before Étampes while standing beside the Duke of York. Although then allies, these two men were to meet again on opposite sides, nearly forty years later, at the battle of the Boyne, in which James II. was defeated and Schomberg, though victorious, was killed.

Just as Turenne had half finished undermining a portion of the wall of Étampes, and had a reasonable hope of taking the town in a few days, his operations before it had to be given up altogether. Some little time before the siege of Étampes, the Duke of Lorraine had assured Mazarin that, if allowed to raise troops in Lorraine, he would hasten with them to join them to the army under Turenne. Pleased by this promise, Mazarin had ordered Marshal de la Ferté, the Governor of Lorraine, to give the Duke the privilege of levying troops, and to furnish him with whatever provisions he might require for his march. With 10,000 men the Duke of Lorraine then marched towards Paris, being permitted to forage as he passed through France.

When Lorraine, with his army, was within a few miles of Paris, it was discovered that, instead of going to the assistance of the King's army, as he had promised, he was in reality going to join his forces with the army of the rebels. As a matter of fact, before he had made his promises to Mazarin, he had been already hired by Spain to proceed against the army of the King of France. He afterwards admitted that he had very nearly thrown over the Spaniards, in their turn, as he came near Paris. Mademoiselle de Montpensier rode out to inspect his troops. "The cavalry were very fine," she says; "but the infantry nothing to speak of. There were among them some Irish, who in general have nothing to recommend them but their bag-pipes." Possibly Mademoiselle may have confused the Irish with another Celtic nation.

News was presently brought to Turenne that Lorraine was on his way to attack him. If Turenne had remained at Étampes he would soon have found himself between the armies of Tavannes and Lorraine; therefore he raised the siege of Étampes, and hurried northwards to meet Lorraine. So few horses had he that he was obliged to send to St. Germains to beg for every available remount. The courtiers and the King and the Queen-Mother sent him their private carriage horses; and, even with all these, he had to take some of his guns on first, and then send back the horses which had dragged them to bring on those still remaining behind.

Lorraine, he heard, was at Villeneuve St. Georges, a town near the Seine, rather more than twenty miles north-north-east of Étampes, and nine or ten miles from Paris; and he was very anxious to fight a decisive battle with Lorraine before Tavannes could join forces with him. To this end, Turenne marched as quickly as he could; but a small river, which runs into the Seine, being in his way, when he was almost within sight of Lorraine's camp, he had to make a night-march to get within fighting range of his enemy, a position which he succeeded in attaining at daybreak on the 15th of June.

As Lorraine "expected every moment the arrival of the [rebel] army from Étampes, he flattered himself with the hopes of amusing the Viscount by negotiations";[1] thinking it wiser to refuse battle until the junction of the two armies should make victory a certainty. While he had been still pretending to be on his way to help Turenne, Lorraine had succeeded in getting the yet uncrowned Charles II. of England into his camp, and he now sent word to Turenne that Charles would negotiate terms of peace if his brother, the Duke of York, would come over to his camp for an interview with him. To this Turenne consented and negotiations were opened. Charles felt in a very awkward position. He had just been at the French Court, and although we learn from Madame de Motteville that "the King and he behaved together

[1] Ramsay.

12

like young princes who felt embarrassed by each
other's presence"; he was under the protection
of the King; but he was under pecuniary obliga-
tions to Lorraine, who was also his personal friend.
While the negotiations were in progress, Turenne kept
drawing nearer and nearer and planting his guns in
more and more advantageous positions. It was only
at the last moment that Lorraine, after a good deal of
swagger, consented to Turenne's terms, which were
that Lorraine should at once desist from making a
bridge of boats, which he had begun, across the Seine,
that he and his army should be out of France within
a fortnight, and that he should give his word never
again to help the rebel princes against the King. On
the other hand, says De Retz, Turenne consented to
Lorraine's demands "that what troops belonging to
the princes were in the Prince of Condé's camp, might
safely come into Paris; and that provisions should be
furnished by the King's order to the Duke of Lorraine's
troops during their retreat; . . . Mr. de Turenne saying
that he was persuaded the Duke of Lorraine's army
would save the King the trouble and expense of furnishing them with provisions, because they would take care
to provide for themselves upon the road; and as for
the liberty that was asked for the troops of the princes
to get safely into Paris, Mr. de Turenne granted it with
joy, because he was sure that that would more alarm
than encourage the city." Turenne dictated the route
which Lorraine's army was to take within an hour, and
it lay through a long and narrow pass, in which,

for the moment, Lorraine would be completely at Turenne's mercy.

It was well that Turenne had chosen this route for his adversary, and that he took the precaution of standing to arms as soon as Lorraine had started; for the retiring army had only just got well into the pass, when the rebel army from Étampes came into sight from the opposite direction.   If that army had appeared a couple of hours earlier, Lorraine would doubtless have fought instead of accepting Turenne's terms; and Turenne, with 7,000 men against Lorraine's 6,000 and Tavanne's 5,000 or 6,000, would have been in an exceedingly perilous position.   As soon as Tavannes had learned what had just occurred, he withdrew his army and retired to St. Cloud.

If the royal army had been defeated at this conjuncture the political history of France would have been considerably altered.   Great credit is due to Turenne; but Napoleon slightly qualifies it by saying that "Turenne's march against the Prince of Lorraine was attended by every possible advantage".

The Parisians were furious with Lorraine for submitting to the terms of Turenne, and they were very angry with Charles II. and the Duke of York for their reputed share in the negotiations.   The Queen of England and Charles II. and their household "were kept in the Louvre without daring to go out; for the people said: 'You wish to render us as miserable as yourselves, and are doing as much to ruin France, as you have done, and are doing, to ruin England'".[1]

[1] *Memoirs of Mademoiselle de Montpensier.*

CHAPTER XIV.

SHORTLY after the events recorded in the last chapter the Court was again in a fidget and on the move. First it went to Melun, about twenty-five miles to the south-east of Paris, and, a little later, to Lagny on the Marne, about fifteen miles due east of Paris. Thither also went Turenne with his army and he was joined by La Ferté, who reinforced him with 3,000 men, bringing up the strength of the royal army to between 10,000 and 11,000. The Court presently moved on to St. Denis, and Turenne went there, too, encamping his army about three miles from the town. Meanwhile Condé, who had been ill, joined the army of the Fronde, which had marched towards Paris from Villeneuve St. Georges, and he encamped at St. Cloud.

In Paris the Duke of Orleans, the head of the New Fronde, became in a fever of alarm when he found that the royal army was on the north of the city, and that the rebel army was on the south-west of it. Apart from any question of the shame of betraying his own party, he was afraid to admit the royal army into Paris, because, as head of the Fronde, he dreaded the vengeance of Mazarin. And as that vengeance would be greatly increased if he should make an armed

resistance in the case of an attempt by the royal army
to enter Paris by force, he was equally afraid to admit
the rebel army, which was the army of his own party,
the Fronde.

To make matters worse, the temper of the Parisians
themselves was very undecided, and many of them
were as much frightened as Orleans himself: more
they could not have been!   The civic authorities were,
indeed, in a very awkward predicament; for on the one
hand they had denounced Condé as a traitor, and,
on the other, they had set a price upon the head of
Mazarin.   Under these distressing circumstances the
heroic Duke of Orleans gave orders that neither army
was to be allowed to enter Paris; and, pretending to be
very ill, this leader of men got into bed and refused to
see anybody.

Turenne was now determined to force a battle upon
Condé, and, to understand his movements, we must
consider their relative positions.   Condé was south-
west of Paris, at St. Cloud, which is on the west bank
of the Seine.   From St. Cloud the Seine flows in a
north-easterly direction for about eight miles to St. Denis,
which is on the east of the river.   To get at Condé,
therefore, it was necessary for Turenne to cross the
Seine somewhere, and he chose to do so by making a
bridge of boats at Epinay, about a mile from St. Denis.
Condé, hearing of this, hurried towards Epinay with a
small force, hoping to be in time to prevent Turenne's
army from crossing the bridge; but he was too late, as
Turenne had already got most of his artillery upon an

island in the Seine, so as to guard both banks, and had landed a strong force of musketeers on the west bank of the river. There was no alternative then left for Condé but to retire upon St. Cloud. But St. Cloud was no longer a place of safety for his army, since that of Turenne, double its size, was on the eve of advancing upon it; therefore Condé decided to remove it to the east of Paris and to place it between the Marne and the Seine at their junction, near Charenton, a position which it would be very difficult for Turenne to attack. In fact, Condé proposed to occupy very much the same position as that on which the modern Fort of Charenton now stands.

Accordingly that night he made his forces cross the Seine by two bridges, at St. Cloud, to the eastern or Parisian side of the river. He cherished a lingering hope that his army might be admitted into the city, notwithstanding hints that its admission would be refused; and to put the matter to the test, he marched his forces through the Bois-de-Boulogne, led them up to the gate of La Conférence, and asked, not to be allowed to take up his quarters in the city, but merely for permission to march through it on his way to Charenton.

To his vexation, although scarcely to his surprise, admittance was refused; the reason given for this refusal, says the Duke of York, being that although the Parisians "were indeed against the cardinal, and wished his ruin, yet it was unworthy of the Parisians, as they were good Frenchmen, to suffer an army, partly composed of Spanish troops, and the greatest number of whose officers were either subjects to that King, or in his pay, to enter within the walls. . . . That it would look as if they had already submitted to the Spanish yoke, to see so many red scarves strutting through the streets of Paris." Condé, to some extent prepared for the refusal, proceeded to reach the east of Paris by marching under the north wall, which stood near where the Boulevardes de la Madeleine, des Capucines, des Italiens, de St. Denis and de St. Martin now run ; and then to make his way south-east to the junction of the Marne and the Seine, near Charenton.

Although the Duke of Orleans had refused admittance to the army of his own party, his sympathies were with it, and orders had been given that nobody was to be allowed to pass out of any of the gates of Paris, lest an intimation might be given to the enemy of the movements of Condé. Turenne, however, had friends in Paris who put a messenger into a basket and let him down in it by a rope over the wall. On reaching the ground on the other side, he made off with all speed to carry the information to Turenne that Condé was leading his army round the north wall of the city.

It was early in the morning of the 2nd of July when Turenne received this important intelligence. After a brief conference with Mazarin, he collected his troops in his camp and started at about 4 A.M. in pursuit of Condé, sending orders to General la Ferté to

BATTLE OF THE FAUBOURG ST. ANTOINE, 2nd July, 1652.

hurry after him with the artillery, which had been placed on the island in the Seine, as well as with the infantry which had been posted on the western side of it ; an operation which, be his expedition what it might, would necessarily occupy considerable time.

Condé had passed between Montmartre and the walls of Paris before Turenne came within sight of him.   When Turenne, who had ridden forward with ten or a dozen horsemen, reached La Chapelle, a place about a quarter of a mile inside the modern fortifications on the north of Paris, but more than a mile from the walls at the period which we are studying, he caught a glimpse of the rear of Condé's infantry passing through the Faubourg St. Martin, and rounding what was then the north-eastern corner of the walls of Paris. He observed that Condé had posted some infantry about the windmills and small houses in the suburb to protect his rear ; and, as soon as he could get some cavalry up, he attacked them and routed them.   A strong force of his horse having arrived shortly afterwards, it attacked a rearguard of Condé's, consisting of 200 or 300 horse, close to the Hospital of St. Louis, a little to the south-west of Belleville, and cut them to pieces.   Then it made several charges against the rear of Condé's infantry, took a good many prisoners, and spread disorder in the ranks, much where the Boulevard Voltaire now runs.

Things were going so badly now in Condé's rear that he faced about and ordered his artillery to return and fire upon Turenne's cavalry ; and he recalled his

van, part of which was already at Charenton. Turenne's
cavalry was now near the Faubourg St. Antoine; but
he ordered a halt to await the arrival of his infantry and
artillery.

When his infantry came up, Turenne still thought
it dangerous to advance against Condé's guns until
the arrival of his own, and another difficulty against
which he had to contend was that Condé's musketeers
had taken up their positions behind barricades, which
they found ready-made. "These barriers," wrote
Turenne, "the people of Paris had made, on purpose
to secure themselves against the scouts of M. de
Lorraine's Army, while he was at Villeneuve St.
Georges."

Condé's infantry, therefore, though inferior in
numbers to the troops of Turenne, had superiority in
position. Yet Turenne felt confident that he had only
to await the arrival of his artillery to insure the capture
of his enemy. On the south of Condé's army ran the
river Seine; on its western side stood the walls of Paris,
with the gate of St. Antoine closed against it and the
great towers of the fortress of the Bastille frowning
above it. On the north of it, and commanding its
eastern side also, was the powerful army of Turenne;
for Condé, finding his rear hard pressed, had brought
back his troops from the front and had concentrated
them in the Faubourg St. Antoine. In fact his rear
had now become his front. Turenne, accordingly, had
caught Condé in a trap and was only pausing until his
guns came up to demolish him. As those guns had

been carried across the water in two ferry-boats,[1] and mounted upon the island in the Seine, near St. Denis, he did not expect to see them for some time.

Soon after Turenne had left St. Denis, Mazarin had awakened the King and the Court. Both King and cardinal wished to see the battle, and the rising ground above Charonne offered them a splendid opportunity of doing so. While the Queen went to the chapel of the Carmelite convent at St. Denis and spent the whole day on her knees before the Sacrament, only rising from them to go to the grating when messengers from the King brought news of the battle,[2] Mazarin and Louis XIV., then a boy of fifteen, took up their position on the hill of Charonne, probably somewhere near where the cemetery of Père la Chaise[3] now stands.

The King and cardinal reached this eminence when Turenne had driven the enemy into the Faubourg St. Antoine with his cavalry and had halted to await the remainder of his forces. His inactivity puzzled the cardinal, who sent a message to him asking why he did not attack. Turenne replied that he was waiting for the remainder of his forces. When Mazarin presently saw the infantry arrive and Turenne still stationary, he sent another message asking what he was waiting for now. Turenne replied that he was

[1] *Memoirs of James II.*, vol. i., p. 98.

[2] *Memoirs of Madame de Motteville* (1902), vol. iii., p. 75.

[3] Père la Chaise, from whom the cemetery takes its name, was then living, and he became confessor to Louis XIV.

waiting for his artillery, and also for his implements
for breaking or pulling down the barricades and garden
walls behind which the enemy was sheltered. Mazarin
sent again to advise him to waste no more time, but
to attack with his infantry and cavalry. Turenne
replied by begging him to have a little more patience;
but again the cardinal sent a message to Turenne,
and this time it took the form of an order to attack at
once. Turenne also received a message from his
brother, the Duke of Bouillon, who was with the
Court, to which he had only recently been reconciled,
warning Turenne that, if he put off his attack any
longer, it would be thought that he did so out of friendship for Condé. Indeed, as the Duke of York wrote,
Turenne himself was fully aware that he "was not yet
so well established in the opinion of the Court, nor his
integrity so thoroughly known that he durst hazard it
by refusing to act against their orders, though they
were contrary to his own judgment".

Much against his will, therefore, Turenne gave
orders for an immediate attack upon the barricades.
The suburbs of St. Antoine consisted of three principal
streets leading to the gate of the city, with narrow
streets crossing them, forming "a kind of duck's foot,"
as one historian of the battle described them. Having
extended his troops in a curve as far as the river, so
as to guard every outlet, Turenne ordered three simultaneous attacks. One of these attacks was made upon
a barricade in a narrow street, which ran into the
market-place of the faubourg. It was gallantly carried

by the infantry, in spite of musketry fire and peltings
with stones from the windows of the houses on either
side.   Unfortunately, the Marquis of St. Maigrin, who
was in support of the infantry with the King's Horse-
Guards, instead of waiting until the infantry had dislodged the enemy from the houses on each side of the
narrow street, pushed through the ranks of the infantry
with his cavalry to pursue Condé's men as they fled
from the barricades.   Just as they nearly reached the
market-place, they were met by five and twenty officers,
headed by Condé himself, who charged them in the
narrow street, while a heavy fire was poured down
upon them from its windows on both sides.   The
Marquis of St. Maigrin, the Marquis of Nantouillet,
and many of the troopers were killed on the spot, and
the Marquis of Mancini, a boy of seventeen and a
nephew of Mazarin, received a wound from which he
afterwards died.   The King's Horse-Guards then
retired in something very like a rout, scattering the
infantry of their own side before them in their panic.

Turenne's own regiment valiantly ousted the enemy
from several gardens and houses ; but when it heard
of the flight of the Horse-Guards and the infantry
accompanying them, it refused to proceed farther.
A regiment of cavalry was behind it, and, suddenly,
such a heavy fire was opened from loop-holes in a
wall on the flank of these horsemen that all their
captains, except one, were killed, as well as many of
the men.   The rest, says the Duke of York, "absolutely ran"; but they were rallied by their few

remaining officers, and showed great bravery during the rest of the action. "This particular deserves the rather to be remarked," says he, "because 'tis very seldom known, when soldiers have been once frightened so as to run, that they have ever performed any good action the same day."

Meanwhile, in the third attack, the lieutenant-colonels of two of Turenne's battalions were killed as they were marching to the attack. A furious fusillade was poured upon the troops from a loop-holed wall. Although suffering tremendous losses, the King's infantry pushed on right up to this wall "till they had placed themselves under it betwixt the holes which the enemy had made in it. Being lodged there, a new manner of fight began, there being only the wall between the two parties for not being able, on either side, to do any great execution with their muskets, they heaved massy stones against each other over the wall, shot their pistols through the holes, and thrust their swords through the crannies; one party endeavouring to maintain possession, and the others to make them quit it."[1]

It has already been seen that Condé with a small party of officers had turned back a whole regiment of the King's Horse-Guards in a narrow street; and, as the battle progressed, the officers, on both sides, took more and more part in the hand-to-hand fighting. "There were then more officers than soldiers in the

[1] The Duke of York, in Clarke's *James II.*

fray, the great Turenne and the great Condé, within pistol-shot of each other, fighting themselves, hand to hand, and showing an admirable contrast between martial fury and intrepid coolness. 'Did you see the Prince of Condé?' was afterwards asked of Turenne. 'I did not see one Prince of Condé,' replied he, 'I saw more than a dozen!' So rapidly did this hero appear to rush from danger to danger, from exploit to exploit. It is related that M. le Prince, who wore a breastplate, and was more active than anybody else, was so stifled with his armour that he was obliged to have himself disarmed and unbooted, and to throw himself quite naked upon the grass in a field, where he rolled like a tired horse.   Then he dressed and armed and returned into the conflict."[1]

Ramsay says that both Turenne and Condé were covered with blood, though not with their own ; that Condé was in a fury, but that Turenne, if physically hot, was mentally cool.   It must have been galling to him to reflect that much of this bloodshed might have been spared to his own men, if he had been allowed to await the arrival of his artillery.

When La Ferté at last came up with the artillery, Turenne gave orders that a general attack should be made as soon as the guns had delivered a heavy fire. Magnificent as had been the defence of Condé against largely superior numbers—at least 11,000 against 5,000

[1] St. Aulaire's *History of the Fronde*, vol. iii., p. 191, quoted in Lord Mahon's *Life of Condé*, p. 230.

—Turenne now felt that he had him completely at his mercy. The combined attack of artillery, musketry and cavalry that followed soon told its tale.

Presently Condé's troops began to retire and even to disappear with unaccountable speed. For a moment Turenne was puzzled; and then, to his astonishment and his vexation, he saw that the great gates of St. Antoine had been thrown wide open and that his enemy was escaping from him into the city of Paris. Instantly he ordered his cavalry to charge his retreating foes in the rear, while the gateway was crowded with the entering troops, and without doubt it would have inflicted terrible slaughter; but just then the guns on the great tower of the Bastille began to boom, and Turenne's horsemen were exposed to a murderous artillery fire.

Among the most interesting of the delightful pages of Mademoiselle de Montpensier are those giving an account of her proceedings on this eventful day. They describe her vain attempts to persuade her cowardly father, the Duke of Orleans, to be a man for once, and to act quickly and decisively on that critical morning; they tell us how she found him shamming illness, but, in reality, frightened almost to death, with a carriage in waiting at a backdoor to carry him post-haste to Orleans, in case of need, and how she alternately coaxed and scolded him until he gave her his authority to go in person to the Hôtel de Ville, and there to demand full powers in his name; they inform us of the hesitation and the vacillation, but the final consent of the municipal authorities, and, with many graphic details, they give us a vivid picture of Mademoiselle hurrying—and only just in time—with the powers thus conferred upon her to the gate of St. Antoine, which she ordered to be thrown widely open, and of her rush into the tower of the Bastille, where she made its governor give orders that its guns should be fired upon the troops of Turenne.[1]

Thus was Turenne foiled, at the last moment, in his attempt to capture Condé and his army ; but while we may sympathise with our hero in being robbed of the fruits of his victory, it is difficult to avoid sympathy with Condé in his escape, when we reflect upon the inferiority of his numbers and the splendour of his defence.

[1] Mademoiselle de Montpensier gives us the story of her meeting with Condé at the Porte St. Antoine : " He was in a deplorable state : his face covered with dust, his hair dishevelled, his neck and shirt stained with blood. Although not wounded, his cuirass bore the marks of blows ; and he carried his naked sword in his hand, for he had lost the scabbard. He gave it to my equerry, and said : ' Ah, Mademoiselle, I am in despair : I have lost all my friends '. He was much cast down ; for he wept bitterly, as he exclaimed : ' You must excuse the grief in which you see me '. It had been said that he cared for nobody ; but I had always found him attached to his friends, and kind to those he loved." As a matter of fact, several of his friends whom he then believed to be dead, or mortally wounded, recovered.

CHAPTER XV.

IT might be expected that rest and repose would have been the well-earned reward of Condé, his officers and his troops, when, wearied and blood-stained, they staggered through the gates into Paris; but they neither sought it, nor obtained it. Space cannot be spared to describe the disorders or the riots, the massacres or the political complications which followed during the first few days after the entry of Condé and his troops into that city.

The riots were succeeded by a duel between the brothers-in-law, the Duke of Beaufort and the Duke of Nemours. It may be remembered that those two very inefficient generals had been in command of the army of the Fronde which opposed the army under Turenne and Hocquincourt on the Loire, when the latter generals were on bad terms and the former were actually quarrelling.

Although, at the battle of St. Antoine, Beaufort and Nemours had sunk their differences sufficiently to agree to defend a barricade together, as soon as Nemours had partially recovered from some wounds which he received on that occasion, he challenged Beaufort. When they met to fight, on the ground behind the Hôtel Vendôme, Beaufort exclaimed: "Ah!

my brother, what a disgrace this is to us! Let us forget the past and be friends!" To which Nemours replied: "You rascal! I will either kill you now, or you shall kill me!" And then he aimed his pistol at Beaufort and pulled the trigger; but it missed fire, whereupon he rushed, sword in hand, at Beaufort, who was obliged to fire in self-defence, when three of his bullets struck Nemours in the head and killed him. Two of the seconds in this duel were also killed, and one was dreadfully wounded.[1]

After the battle of St. Antoine the Court returned to St. Denis and remained there. A few weeks later news was received that a Spanish army—with the perfidious Duke of Lorraine, who had joined it, making in all 20,000 men—had entered France in the extreme North, and was marching through Picardy towards Paris. Mazarin was much alarmed, as the Court might very soon be between this large force and the much smaller army of Condé then in Paris. He

---

[1] After the duel Condé, Mademoiselle de Montpensier and several others went to condole with the widow of Nemours. She was in bed, says Mademoiselle de Montpensier, "senseless—the curtains open, and everybody around her. . . . Amidst all this desolation, Madame de Béthune said something, I know not what, in so lamentable a tone that it set off Madame de Guise laughing, who was yet the most serious person in the world, so that the Prince (of Condé) and even myself, who heard it, burst out into a violent fit, of which we were quite ashamed." They then went to condole with Nemours' brother. "We were again almost tempted to laugh; for he, too, was in bed, with all the curtains drawn, and spoke to us very lugubriously through them" (*Memoirs*, vol. i., p. 299).

therefore proposed to remove the Court either to Rouen or to Dijon; but, on inquiry, he learned that neither of those cities would consent to receive it.

Mazarin then talked of taking the Court to Lyons; but Turenne begged him not to remove it so far from Paris, pointing out that if the royal army had to go so far South to protect the Court, all the fortresses in Picardy would fall to the enemy. He also urged that the moral effect of such a retreat would be most disastrous among the Parisians, who, he had reasons for believing, were already growing heartily sick of Condé and his Spanish, or semi-Spanish, army. He besought the Queen and the cardinal on no account to appear to be retreating, much less flying, but simply to take the drive of fifteen miles to Pontoise, where he would have a strong force ready and would undertake to protect the Court. This advice was fortunately followed.

The army of Turenne lay between the Court and Paris; and the rival armies were anxiously watching each other. Even when ready to fly at each other's throats, they could be courteous. While Mademoiselle was visiting the rebel army at Charenton, it was agreed between Condé and Turenne that hostilities should be suspended. In a letter to Condé, she says Turenne and De la Ferté "presented me with many fine compliments, and declared that I was to command, and to consider myself mistress of their army as well as of our own".

Shortly afterwards Turenne advanced to oppose

13 *

the Spanish army with a force of less than half its number. This bold step succeeded. The Archduke contented himself with a victory over the Duke of Elbœuf and 600 men, and retired into Flanders, leaving Lorraine, with his army of 10,000 men, to winter in Champagne. Turenne then retired towards Paris and encamped his army four miles to the north-east of St. Denis.

Bad news then reached Turenne in a report of the serious illness of his brother, to whom he was devotedly attached, and, a few days later, that illness terminated fatally. Death came to the Duke of Bouillon at a moment when he was in high favour at Court and when his opinion was much consulted and carried great weight with the Queen and even with the cardinal. Had he lived longer, he might have become one of the Queen's principal counsellors; it was even thought by some that he might have become a rival to Mazarin himself. He was a man of great determination of character, even to severity. When he was in command of the troops of the Fronde at Bordeaux, he was informed that the royal army had taken a small neighbouring fort, and that, by Mazarin's orders, the commandant of the fort had been hanged as a rebel. Without a moment's hesitation, Bouillon sent for a captain of the Novailles regiment, who had been taken prisoner some time previously. He was found playing a game of cards with some ladies, and he went to Bouillon without the slightest suspicion of any impending evil. Bouillon ordered him to be

instantly hanged and that his body should be fastened
on the wall of the city as a reprisal. Even in those
days many of his friends considered his conduct cruel
in this case.

Shortly after the death of Bouillon, negotiations
took place between the Court and the princes. The
latter hinted that if Mazarin could be banished all
would be well. In the hope of thus pacifying the
people of Paris, Mazarin left the Court, ostensibly for
ever, and retired to Bouillon, on the Belgian frontier.
The King then opened a Parliament at Pontoise; so
there was now one Parliament at Pontoise and another
in Paris. Underhand negotiations were being attempted
in all directions. Each side was watching for an opportunity of attacking the other; yet everybody was tired
of fighting. The leading politicians were all prepared
to throw over their allies and their friends, if they
could gain anything by so doing.

Now that the Spanish army was withdrawn to
Flanders, Turenne supposed that Lorraine would not
renew hostile operations until the spring. He was
therefore surprised on receiving information that that
uncertain Duke was marching towards Paris. At
once Turenne started to meet him and, on the 4th of
September, he had reasons for believing that Lorraine
was advancing to join his forces with those of Condé,
which Turenne learned were either leaving, or had already left, Paris. Suspecting that a juncture would
be attempted at Villeneuve St. Georges—a place with
which we are already familiar—he marched thither

in order to prevent it, and arrived just at the time when the quarter-masters of Condé and of Lorraine were beginning to mark out the lines for the encampment of their approaching armies.

Although Turenne thus put a stop to the junction of his two enemies at the particular spot which they had selected, those generals successfully acccomplished their purpose at a place about a mile and a half to the west of it, near the small castle of Ablon.

In some ways Turenne's position was a strong one. He had a wood on his right, the town and the river Seine on his left, and the river Yerre at his rear, while in his front stood five redoubts, which had been made by Lorraine on the memorable occasion when Turenne had forced him into a futile promise never again to make war against the King of France. All that Turenne accordingly had to do, to fortify his position, was to continue the lines between these five redoubts.

Notwithstanding these advantages, Turenne was now in peril. As he had left a strong force to protect the Court at Pontoise, the army he now had with him was scarcely more than half the strength of the combined armies of Lorraine and Condé; having made a forced march, in the hope of preventing the juncture of Condé with Lorraine, he had brought very few stores with him; and he was greatly disappointed at finding scarcely any provisions in Villeneuve St. Georges either for man or for beast. On the very night of their arrival some of the troopers were reduced to feeding their horses on vine leaves. Nor was their unhappy condition unknown to Condé, who, although so much stronger in numbers, determined, instead of attacking Turenne, to keep him fast in what the Duke of York calls his "narrow nooke" and thus starve him out.

Starved out he undoubtedly would have been, had he not had the good fortune to find four or five large boats, by the use of which and every gate to be found in the town, together with the timber of some of the houses which he had pulled down to supply it, he contrived to make a bridge across the Seine.

Fortunately, some of his cavalry which had been at Montrond came to Corbeil, about seven miles higher up the river. These Turenne ordered to remain there and to protect his men when they went out on foraging expeditions. Condé's army had at first lain between Villeneuve and Corbeil. Had it remained in that position Turenne says his own army would have been starved out of its camp in four days. As it was, his foraging expeditions, during the six weeks he remained at Villeneuve, were conducted under very great difficulties, and the Duke of York even goes to the length of saying: "It may with truth be said that the French Monarchy was reduced to that extremity, that its preservation depended on each of these convoys, the loss of but one being capable of inducing that of the whole army".

Napoleon finds fault with both Turenne and Condé for their conduct at this juncture. "Turenne's stay at the camp of Villeneuve St. Georges during six weeks, in presence of two armies superior in strength," says he, "was very hazardous. What motive could have induced him to incur so much danger? His camp was not too strong to be forced, and such an occurrence would have been his ruin, and that of the Court party. His situation appeared so critical that it retarded the submission of Paris."

Of Condé he says: "After his junction with the Duke of Lorraine, as he had such a superiority in strength, it is not easy to understand why he was satisfied with entrenching[1] himself on the heights of Limeil—a place within cannon-shot of Turenne's outposts—instead of attacking the King's army: he might have had as much artillery as he pleased, being so near Paris; and nothing but a decisive victory could, under the circumstances, retrieve his affairs and maintain his party in the capital. *Condé, on that day, was not sufficiently daring.*"

Towards the end of September Turenne prepared to leave his camp. The reason he himself gives for doing so is this: "At last, the roads grew so bad by the continual rains, that the horses could not go so far for their forage as before: so that we were obliged to think of breaking up". But the Duke of York adds another reason. He says that the Parisians were "discontented that the princes kept up the war at their gates"; for Condé's army, after having been, as

---

[1] The Duke of York says that Condé made these entrenchments very deep.

we saw, for some time in Paris, now kept foraging
between Villeneuve and Paris, as also did Lorraine's.
The Parisians, heartily tired of all this, were in treaty
with the Court. "And now," says the Duke of York,
"a negotiation being on a good footing, the Court
sent to know of the two Generals"—Turenne and La
Ferté—"whether they believed it practicable to dis-
engage the army, from the post it was in without
running any hazard, and to find means to join the
King, in order to favour the treaty which was on the
anvil."

On the 4th of October, as soon as it was dark, that
is to say at about half-past six or seven o'clock,
Turenne took his army across the Yerre, the small river
which lay in his rear, by fourteen bridges, which he had
made ostensibly for foraging purposes, and marched
in exactly the opposite direction from Paris, to Corbeil,
where he had given orders to his cavalry, there
stationed, to make some entrenchments. The bridges
were broken when the last men had crossed them, to
prevent pursuit by the enemy. The night-march was
conducted with great silence and secrecy; and it was
not until the next morning that the enemy discovered
the escape of the army of Turenne.

After resting a day at Corbeil, Turenne marched
slowly to Meaux, about twenty-five miles to the east
of Paris, always keeping in order for an attack, which
he constantly expected, and would probably have received, had not Condé been unwell and obliged to
return to Paris. When Condé heard of Turenne's

escape, says Mademoiselle, "he was in a perfect
fury," and he exclaimed : "We ought to put bridles on
Tavannes and Vallon ; they are nothing but asses ".
From Meaux Turenne moved his troops to Senlis, a
place somewhat less than thirty miles from Paris in a
northerly direction.

Condé now made a false move. Out of temper
with the vacillating Parisians, who kept complaining of
the drain made upon their resources by the foraging
parties of the armies of Condé and Lorraine in their
neighbourhood, and finding some difficulty in procuring further provisions, he withdrew his forces to
join them with those of Spain, at Laon, some seventy
miles to the north-east of Paris. Although this gave
him a very powerful military position numerically, it
left Paris at the mercy of the King's troops and lost
him the allegiance of its inhabitants.

Turenne was not slow in taking advantage of this
opportunity. Leaving his army under the command of
La Ferté, he hurried to the Court at Pontoise and
urged the King and the Queen to enter Paris immediately. The counsellors of the Court opposed this
advice ; but Turenne insisted "that they ought to take
advantage of the Prince of Condé's absence, and not
give the Parisians time to" recover from their present
ill-humour with "the Frondeurs ; that as (Turenne's)
officers daily left the army for want of money, the
King would soon be left without troops ; that the
Court would not be in a condition, the next campaign,
to make head against the enemy, whose forces would

then be augmented ; that the Parisians would be less inclined to receive the King, and that other cities would follow the example of the capital". Against all this the Queen's counsellors objected that the Duke of Orleans, and, what was much more to the point, his clever and courageous daughter, would order the Parisian soldiers to seize the King, the Queen and the Court, if they entered Paris without the support of a very formidable military force. Their fears on this point were not shared by Turenne, who felt sure that, if the King went into Paris, the Duke of Orleans would very soon run out of it. Nor was he much mistaken in holding this opinion.

The King and the Queen yielded to the entreaties of Turenne, and, having made up his mind to go to Paris, Louis XIV. wrote to the Duke of Orleans to inform him of his decision. Upon receiving this letter, the Duke sent for Cardinal de Retz, to whom he said that he had "almost a mind to shut the gates against the King". De Retz says that he told him he had no reason to be alarmed, at which he "uttered five or six oaths one after another," and told De Retz to come again in the evening. When De Retz did so, he found him talking to the Duchess and in a fine fury. He was speaking "as if he had been armed cap-à-pie, and ready to cover the plains of St. Denis and Grenelle with blood and slaughter". The Duchess was trying to pacify him, but in vain. "I will make war to-morrow," replied the Duke, in the tone of a warrior. "Not a doubt of it, Sir," said De Retz. And, as the

Duke continued to state his warlike intentions, De Retz continued to assent to them, much to the disappointment of the former, who wanted to be able to say that he had wished to fight, but had reluctantly yielded to the entreaties of De Retz that he should sheathe his sword. The Duke left them for a few minutes, when the Duchess, "half laughing and half crying," said to De Retz: "Methinks that I see Harlequin telling Scaramouch: What fine things I would have said, if thou hadst not had wit enough to contradict me". When the Duke came back, he said that, although all the world knew that he could prevent the King's return to Paris with ease, if he so pleased, he thought that for the sake of the peace of the State he should permit it. The Duchess felt so ashamed of this sudden collapse that she said: "This way of reasoning, Sir, might become the Cardinal de Retz, but not a son of France". At this he became as angry "as if she had proposed to throw him headlong into the river". "Retire, then, Sir, immediately," added she. "And where the devil shall I retire?" said he.

When the Court was passing through the Bois-de-Boulogne, on its way to Paris, a report was brought to the Queen that the people were rising in rebellion and that it would be most perilous for the King to enter the city. The Queen got out of her coach and, summoning Prince Thomas, and the Marshals de Turenne, de Villeroi and du Plessis, "held a council in the open field". With the exception of Turenne, her council was unanimous in advising that the Court should go back and not enter Paris.[1] But the Queen, who was naturally courageous, "followed without once hesitating the advice of Turenne and, accordingly, the King at the head of his guards entered the city, through St. Honoré's Gate, was received everywhere with acclamations and was followed to the Louvre by a crowd of people, who were for ever crying: Long Live The King". As might have been expected, the Duke of Orleans bolted!

On the evening of her arrival in Paris, the Queen held a Court at the Louvre. Turenne, who attended it, found himself standing next to De Retz, who had come to do homage at the Court, although he had belonged to the party opposed to it and had acted as right-hand man to the Duke of Orleans. As we have seen, De Retz had once saved Turenne from arrest by a timely warning, and now Turenne endeavoured to do the same good office to De Retz. "Do you think yourself safe here?" said he. De Retz squeezed his hand and loudly replied in the affirmative; but only because he had observed that "a great Mazarinian" had overheard the question; for he confesses that this assertion of his safety was "only bragging". Some of the courtiers flattered the Queen upon the acclamations of the populace as she had driven through the streets of Paris; whereupon Turenne whispered in the ear of De Retz: "They did the like lately for the Duke of Lorraine".

[1] So says Ramsay. But the *Mémoires du Maréchal du Plessis* (Guyot, 1850, p. 435) state that all were agreed that the Court ought to proceed into Paris without hesitation

The King was liberal in the matter of amnesties. "The Prince of Condé was the only one who refused to accept of the pardon: he chose to go over to the Spaniards and lose all his estates."[1]   But although he became the ally of Spain, and formed what is sometimes termed the Spanish Fronde and sometimes the Provincial Fronde, the Parisian Fronde was now at an end.

Having seen the King securely established in Paris, and having obtained considerable reinforcements, with the expectation of more to be brought to him by Mazarin from Sedan, Turenne, at the end of October, advanced against Lorraine and Condé.   He made the long march of more than one hundred and twenty miles to the relief of Bar-le-Duc, which was besieged by the enemy. Half-way thither he had to pass through Épernay, where, says the Duke of York, he was "obliged to stop a whole day, because the soldiers, in coming thither, found so great a quantity of new win (*sic*), after the Vintage in a Country plentifully stor'd with that liquour, that of all the foot there came not enough up to the quarter, to make the ordinary guard for the Duke and Mr. de Turenne; so that they stirr'd not till the 4th" (of November).

Fortunately for Turenne, Count Fuensaldagne, who was in command of the Spanish army, had marched away with it, being in a hurry to go into winter quarters; for the Spaniards did everything by rule. If it was the usual time for going into winter quarters, into

[1] Ramsay.

winter quarters they went, whatever might be the circumstances of a campaign. Their machine-like movements, their punctilious military etiquette, and their red-tapism proved maddening to Condé.

Bar-le-Duc would have been relieved with far greater ease had it not been for what the Duke of York calls "the rashness and indiscretion of Monsr. de Roussillon . . . that addle-headed Governour" of the town. In this siege Lorraine lost his best general, who, after supping with Condé, and getting very drunk, tied a white napkin round his head to make himself the more conspicuous and, out of sheer drunken bravado, rushed out, exposed himself to the fire of the enemy, and was shot, before Condé, who ran after him, could catch him.

Nor was it only on the side of the enemy that an officer lost his life, at Bar-le-Duc, through drink. During the same siege Turenne ordered General du Tott to conduct the assault upon a part of the town which had been taken by the enemy. Du Tott had "drunk more than ever Commander ought to do," says the Duke of York, who adds that he never saw any other officer drunk in the French army. Foolishly rushing forward far before his men, opening a door in an exposed position, and standing vacantly in the doorway, the poor, tipsy Du Tott "was shot dead". But what else can one expect when people *will* fight in a champagne[1] district?

[1] The Bar wine is not, strictly speaking, classed as a champagne, but it is of that character. Champagne, exactly as we drink it, was not made until later than the days of Turenne.

Cardinal Mazarin, who was on his way to return to Court, now that the King's power was firmly established, brought valuable reinforcements to Turenne at Bar-le-Duc, and he was present at its relief.

Being in need of provisions, Turenne quartered his men in St. Michel, a town under the governorship of La Ferté, without asking leave of that general. He had asked for provisions to be brought out of it; but, as difficulties were made and time was pressing, he had no alternative but to enter the town and take them. So angry was La Ferté, when he heard of this, that he hurried thither from a place thirty miles distant and summoned Turenne to leave the town, a summons which Turenne obeyed. "But Mr. de la Ferté," says the Duke of York, "was so much enraged by seeing that some of the men had been bolder than became them in their quarters, taking more than meat and drink, that as they were marching out, he himself, attended by his guards, fell upon such of them as stragled or were loytering behind, hacking and hewing them as if they had been Enemys." Turenne may have been wrong, in the first instance; but most certainly La Ferté was wrong in the last. This incident made ill blood between the two generals, and it was long before they were thoroughly reconciled.

Mazarin would not listen to Turenne's representations that his men were worn out, that, owing to the severity of the frost, thirty or forty soldiers died in a day, and that it was cruel to keep the troops any longer out of winter quarters. At the siege of Vervins, which followed, when Condé's soldiers, on its walls, loudly cursed Mazarin, the King's soldiers shouted "Amen" in reply, so incensed were they at being still kept in the field by the cardinal. After the fall of Vervins, Mazarin, in the month of February, consented to a termination of the campaign.

According to Napoleon, Turenne's strategy, recorded in this chapter, was open to criticism; so also, perhaps, may have been his conduct at St. Michel; but the events of the later months of 1652, so far as Turenne was concerned, are chiefly interesting because of the excellent advice already mentioned, which, on at least two very critical occasions, he gave to the Court, advice which probably saved the Crown of France for Louis XIV.

CHAPTER XVI.

A MOST important event now occurred in Turenne's private life. Soon after his return to Paris, early in the year 1653, when he was at the age of forty-two, he married a great lady, a great heiress and—a point upon which he laid much importance—a great Protestant. Charlotte de Caumont was the only daughter and the sole heiress of Armand de Nompar de Caumont, Duke de la Force and a Marshal of France. Of this lady Ramsay says: "Her birth and fortune distinguished her less than her virtues and superior understanding ; noble, elevated sentiments, with those parts of knowledge that are the least common among the sex, were in her accompanied with sweetness and modesty, an inexpressible delicacy and sweetness of manners : to say all in a word, *she was worthy of the Viscomte de Turenne*". It will be observed that Ramsay says nothing about her looks; and, when excessive stress is laid upon a lady's virtues, without any mention of her beauty, it may be generally assumed to have been somewhat deficient.

In his notes to *Bayle* (vol. iv., p. 331) Des Maizeaux says: "It is not unusual to see persons of quality very virtuous, and very zealous for religion, and at the same time so jealous of their rank, and so fond of receiving a great deal of honour, that they are always upon their punctilios on that account. Madame Turenne is an example of it. Her virtue and piety are not more memorable than her exact precautions to preserve the privileges of highness, and the precedence she pretended to above the duchesses."

Whatever may have been the charms of the Viscomtesse de Turenne, her husband had to tear himself away from them in about three months, that is to say in June, 1653, as his services were required in the wars. Although Paris was now quiet and loyal, Guienne was in a state of insurrection in the South, while, in the North-east, the enemy was within a hundred miles of Paris, at Rethel, and it also occupied Rocroi, Dunkirk, Gravelines and Mardyck. Another very serious matter was the disproportion between the rival forces. Turenne and La Ferté between them had only 7,000 infantry and 5,000 cavalry, with which to defend a large space of country and to garrison several fortresses, whereas the Spanish army, with those of Condé and Lorraine, in the north-east of France and Flanders, numbered 30,000. These are the statistics given by Ramsay; but Napoleon, although giving the same numbers to the enemy as does Ramsay, puts the King of France's troops at 6,000 infantry and 10,000 cavalry.

Information reached Turenne that one of the enemy's army corps was on the Sambre in the North, and that another was more than 120 miles distant from it, in the East. He at once decided that this was an

14 *

opportunity that might never occur again of regaining
Rethel (which lay between them); he therefore hurried
thither and retook it in a few days—it capitulated on
the 8th of July, 1653—while the Spaniards were trying
to make up their minds which army corps to send to
its relief.

Turenne then marched towards the North and soon
found himself within reach of the enemy, whose force,
at that particular point, consisted of 16,000 infantry,
11,000 cavalry and between thirty and forty guns.
The King and the cardinal now came out to Turenne
in order to hold a Council of War. At this council
one proposition was to make use of half the army for
garrisoning the frontier fortresses, and to use the other
half for dogging the enemy on his march, carrying off
his convoys and threatening his communications. Another proposition was to keep the army intact, to defend the passage of the river Oise by taking up a
strong position behind it, and to centralise any reserves,
which might be obtained from the Provinces, before
Paris. The Oise, it will be remembered, flows in a
south-westerly direction, from near the Flemish frontier,
until it joins the Seine, about a dozen miles to the north-
west of Paris.

To both of these plans of campaign Turenne raised
objections. The King's army was too small to divide,
he said; on the other hand, to defend the passage of a
river like the Oise would be impossible. Turenne proposed to march with the whole army within a certain
distance of the enemy, to weary him by threatening

movements, but to avoid a general action, and thus to wear away the weeks and months between June and the time for going into winter quarters.

If, says Turenne, he had decimated his small army by garrisoning the fortresses, the enemy would have been relatively strong enough in numbers to have marched to Paris; and, if he had kept behind the Oise, for the purpose of preventing a passage of that river, supposing the enemy had attacked one of the fortresses or cities on the farther side of it, it would have taken him some time, perhaps several days, to cross the river and to go to its relief; whereas, by crossing the river at once and keeping within a few miles of the enemy, if that enemy were to besiege a place, Turenne could go to the assistance of its garrison in a few hours.

In carrying out his proposition, to which the King and cardinal had agreed, Turenne had extraordinary luck. If Condé had been commander-in-chief of both of the allied armies Turenne would probably have met with disaster; but, fortunately for Turenne, the Archduke kept the exclusive command of his own army and would brook no interference. Again, the objects of the Archduke and of Condé, although those two generals were allies, were totally different. Condé's object was to reach Paris, to revive the Fronde in that city, to encourage the revolt in Bordeaux, and to raise an insurrection in Central France. The Archduke on the contrary, cared not a jot or a tittle for either Paris or the Fronde, or Bordeaux, or Central France. His sole object was to enlarge the frontier of Flanders, for which purpose he desired to take a few of the French fortresses; but he had no intention of advancing to Paris or to Central France, or of fighting a general action, unless indeed an opportunity should occur of defeating the French army, with little or no risk or trouble.

Under these peculiar circumstances Napoleon admits that Turenne's line of conduct was likely to succeed; but, says he, "it would have been very dangerous in any other conjuncture. To march by the side of an enemy twice your own strength, is always a difficult operation: there are few positions strong enough to protect an army so inferior in numbers. Nor does it appear that he took the precaution to pitch his camp every evening in a chosen position: on the contrary, he frequently encamped in very bad positions, where his army was in imminent danger."

Whether Turenne was aware of the diversity of the objects of Condé, on the one hand, and of the Archduke, on the other, may be doubtful; but he certainly was well aware of the difficulties and drawbacks likely to be met with by a French general when in alliance with a Spanish army; for he had experienced them himself when fighting with the Spaniards for the release of the princes. It was this knowledge, with his own intelligent inferences therefrom, which justified him in a proceeding which would have been otherwise exceedingly dangerous.

"Achilles," says Napoleon, at the end of the same chapter, "was the son of a goddess and a mortal. This is emblematical of the genius of war. The divine part is all that is derived from the moral considerations of the character, the talents, and the interests of your adversary : as well as of the spirit of your own troops, whether they feel strong and victorious, or whether they fancy themselves feeble and beaten.   The mortal or earthly part of arms, are entrenchments, positions, orders of battle, and all that appertains to the combination of physical means and methods."

Now Turenne exhibited his genius in "the divine part of war" by his "moral considerations of the characters" of Condé and the Archduke.   That they would not and could not work harmoniously together, he felt assured.   As to their " talents," those of the one were so ill-balanced, in relation to those of the other, that the equilibrium of their strategy was certain to be upset, and their "interests" were quite conflicting enough to neutralise each other.

Ramsay gives more unqualified praise to Turenne's management of this campaign than does Napoleon. He compares him to Fabius Maximus, in always encamping on eminences or places otherwise difficult of access.   "Whenever the enemy halted, he stopped likewise, and when the enemy marched, he followed them, keeping along the side of them at a considerable distance, and posting himself so that he could not be forced to fight against his will."   And Ramsay compares Condé with Hannibal in trying every stratagem to force a general action on Turenne.   "Sometimes he drew near the French and beat up their quarters : at other times, he removed to a great distance, that he might induce them to decamp and surprise them in some march, where he might have an advantage over them."

In a work written for the general reader by a writer ignorant of military matters, it is unnecessary to follow all Turenne's marches and countermarches during this campaign in detail. But some little must be said about them. Much of his success in shadowing a superior enemy, without approaching him too closely, necessarily depended to a great extent upon successful scouting, a military art which must have developed considerably during the twenty-one years which had passed since two rival armies—that of King Charles I. and that of the Parliament—wandered about Warwickshire, for several days, before they could find each other. Every morning, says the Duke of York, Turenne "went out of his quarters . . . by sunrise, slenderly attended," to make observations and to receive intelligence from his outposts.

While avoiding contact with his enemy, Turenne embarrassed him by stopping his convoys. When the enemy besieged Roye, a place of no great importance, Turenne resisted the temptation to risk a general engagement by attempting to relieve it; and allowed the allies to amuse themselves by taking it. When they had done so, he says, "they began to be very much at a loss what to do next : they did not dare to advance into a country where they had no places, while an enemy lay within three hours' march of them ".

Near Peronne, a town on the river Somme, about half-way between Amiens and St. Quentin,[1] Turenne had a very narrow escape. The enemy had made a forced march and Turenne was surprised on his flank, in a very bad position. This position, which was held by the troops under La Ferté, was commanded by a hill up the farther side of which the enemy was advancing. On discovering their dilemma, both La Ferté and his men were panic-stricken and retreated in a confusion which began rapidly to spread among the other troops. In this difficulty, says Napoleon, any ordinary general would have withdrawn his troops to Peronne,[2] a mile and a half off, crossed the Somme there, and protected himself behind the river; a course which would have disheartened his troops, encouraged his enemy, and only postponed a general engagement; for, unless he remained where he was to guard the bridge at Peronne, the enemy would have crossed it and pursued him. "Turenne," continues Napoleon, "risked everything and marched to meet the enemy." He had just time, and only just, to ascend the hill from which the danger lay. Had the enemy reached it first, he would inevitably have sustained a crushing defeat. With some of his troops in a condition of

[1] It was at the battle of St. Quentin, in 1871, that the French army of the North, raised for the relief of Paris, under Faidherbe, was defeated by the German army under Von Goben.

[2] Peronne seems fated to be the scene of battles. It was taken by Charles the Bold in 1465, and it was before its walls that the Emperor Charles V. met with defeat in 1536. It was captured by Wellington in 1815, and by the Germans in 1871.

panic it was an exceedingly difficult, even a speculative, proceeding, but it was accomplished, barely accomplished, it is true; but still accomplished! Instantly Turenne gave orders to make five redans, which the men, having now regained their confidence, worked at with a will, as well as in self-defence.

But the enemy had double Turenne's numbers, and Condé determined to attack him at once. Even with his improved position, Turenne says, "'tis more than probable that we should have fought with ill success that day". The Spanish General, however, absolutely refused to attack. It was nearly three o'clock; three o'clock in the afternoon was not the proper hour for beginning a battle; his men had had a long march; the end of a long march was not the regular time for fighting, and Spanish generals never did anything except at the regular time. It was the time for resting, and a rest they would take. After a good night's rest, they would very soon demolish the French, who could not possibly escape them in the meantime.

When the morning came, however, the Spaniards found that Turenne, who did *not* take a rest, had spent the night in entrenching himself and had made his position so strong that an attack would have been most hazardous. During the next few days there were some skirmishes and then the enemy moved off to invest Guise, a town about sixteen miles to the east. Turenne heard in time of this intention, and as Guise, unlike Roye, was a place which it would have

strengthened the enemy's position to possess, Turenne
sent 2,500 men into it.   Happily, on the way thither
the allies, who would otherwise have reached it before
Turenne, were delayed, owing to some trouble being
raised by Lorraine; and, when they came to Guise,
which they had calculated upon taking by surprise
but found already garrisoned, they did not invest it.
After a fortnight's rest they made a march of more
than forty miles to Rocroi, besieged it, and took it in
something under a month.

Turenne did not go to the relief of Rocroi, because,
owing to the large woods surrounding it, the army
which reached it first had an enormous advantage;
but he endeavoured to counterbalance the loss of
Rocroi by laying siege to Mouzon,[1] a very important
fortress on the Meuse, half-way between Sedan and
Stenay, which was in the hands of the enemy.   Mouzon
capitulated after a siege of seventeen days.   Here, says
the Duke of York, Turenne had no engineer and was
obliged to contrive and superintend all the siege works
himself.   Nothing further of any great importance
took place in this campaign, after which both armies
went into winter quarters.

While that campaign was in course, the people of

[1] Like so many of the important places in Turenne's campaigns, Mouzon has much later military interests.   It was at
Mouzon that MacMahon crossed the Meuse with his army, in his
attempt to march to the relief of Bazaine, in 1870; and, in the
same year, only six miles from Mouzon, the Saxons surprised and
captured 3,000 French soldiers, placed there to defend the passage
of the Meuse.

Bordeaux had submitted to the King. This was a terrible disappointment and discouragement to Condé. He was still further disheartened by the loss to his interests of his brother, the Prince of Conti, who availed himself of the King's amnesty and pardon, and became a royalist.[1] At about the same time a much more surprising secession from the rebels to the Court was that of Madame de Longueville, who gave up politics, as well as other things which it was quite as desirable that she should forgo, returned to her husband, and eventually devoted herself entirely to religion.

Meanwhile, all was not going smoothly among the allies. Charles, Duke of Lorraine, began to demand either the restoration of some of his ancient territory in Lorraine, or some of the places which might be captured by the allies in France. So importunate and troublesome did he become[2] that the Spaniards, to put an end to the nuisance, quietly arrested him, and sent him off as a prisoner to Spain, where he was

[1] In the first war of the Fronde, when Mazarin invested Paris, Condé was on the side of the Court, while his brother, Conti, who was on the side of the Fronde, was made commander of the rebel army within the city. Conti was very ugly, and Montglat says that Condé, on seeing a pet monkey chained up in the young King's room, made a low bow before it and said : " I salute the generalissimo of the Parisians ".

[2] Before this campaign Lorraine declared that he would not embark upon it unless a certain very pretty *bourgeoise* of Brussels came and asked him to do so. The whole council was obliged to go in procession to the girl and to her parents, to induce her to present herself before Lorraine and beg him to go to the war for her sake (Lord Mahon's *Life of Condé*, p. 248).

detained until the Peace of the Pyrenees. They placed his troops under the command of Duke Francis of Lorraine, his brother, with whom he had quarrelled.

This campaign of Turenne's was another instance of successful strategy with little fighting. Commanding an army less than half as numerous as that of his enemy, he prevented the threatened advance on Paris; he succeeded in driving the invading forces farther towards the frontier than they had been before the campaign began; he recovered Rethel, and he fully made up for the loss of Rocroi by taking Mouzon. In the game of war Turenne often resembled a chess-player who checkmates his adversary without either losing or taking more than a piece or two.

CHAPTER XVII.

IT was fortunate that the Kings of France used to be crowned at Rheims; for although the coronation of Louis XIV. and its attendant ceremonies, military displays, and entertainments considerably delayed the opening of the campaign of 1654, the journeys of the officers and troops who took part in them had brought them a long way on their route for the war.

The submission of Guienne had liberated a number of the King's troops, and the army of Turenne was now somewhat stronger than it had been in the campaign of the previous year; yet even now that of the enemy far outnumbered it. As we have seen, the military operations of 1653 had ended by the taking of Mouzon; and the new campaign began with the siege of Stenay, an important fortress which had long served as an asylum for the Fronde, about fifteen miles to the south of Mouzon. It will be remembered that Turenne himself had stayed some time there in the company of that archconspiratress Madame de Longueville, when he was about to fight against the King's troops for the relief of the princes.

Expecting that the siege of Stenay would be particularly galling to Condé, as it was his own property,

Turenne anticipated a strenuous effort for its relief, and he had everything in readiness to give Condé a warm reception as soon as he should appear before it with the allied armies.   But that warm reception was never given, for the simple reason that Condé and the allied armies never did appear before Stenay.   While Turenne was daily expecting them, they were 120 miles away, besieging Arras.

Arras, whose railway station is familiar to travellers from Paris to Lille, which is about fifteen miles to the north of it, was a very important fortress; if it fell, all the acquisitions of the French in Artois would be in the greatest danger.   The fortress itself was a very strong one; but unfortunately, at the time when Condé and the Archduke sat down before it, its garrison happened to be very weak; and the forces brought up to lay siege to it, on the 3rd of July, 1654, amounted, says Turenne, to 25,000, while he states that the total forces which he could collect at Peronne, before proceeding to the relief of Arras, did not exceed 14,000 or 15,000.

In leaving Stenay to its fate, and by making forced marches to Arras, Condé, for once, had outwitted Turenne, who never suspected him of any such design. On the other hand, with no forces coming to its relief, Stenay was doomed, and, feeling certain of its capture, Turenne left the siege to be conducted by Hocquincourt, one of his generals; but he was unwilling to begin operations against the besieging army at Arras, until he could be reinforced by his troops which would be liberated when Stenay should fall.   Therefore he

made his headquarters at Peronne, some thirty miles
to the south-east of Arras, and employed himself in
making observations and despatching scouts for information.

Condé and the Archduke had very wisely marched
their armies to Arras with extraordinary expedition,
so as to invest the place before Turenne could throw a
strong garrison into it, and so far all was well for them ;
but, in making so rapid a march, it was impossible to
carry with them either the provisions or the ammunition necessary for the siege.   Turenne's first opportunity, therefore, was to try to intercept their convoys.

. The allies dared not carry gunpowder in carts
while Turenne's cavalry were patrolling the country ;
so they had it carried in bags of fifty-pounds weight,
each bag being fastened behind the saddle of a trooper.
One night, says the Duke of York, a drunken soldier
fired a pistol at his lieutenant, thereby igniting one of
these bags of gunpowder "behind the Lieutenant's
horse, which taking fire, blew it up, and so, from one
successively to the other who was next, it spread through
the whole regiment ".   This regiment consisted of "six
score going from Douay to the enemy's camp, all of
them, officers as well as soldiers having behind them a
bag of powder, besides about four score horses laden
with hand grenades, which were led by countrymen on
foot ".   All of them, says the Duke, were "blown up. . . .
Indeed it was a very dismall object to behold a great
number of poor men, who were brought into camp with
their faces disfigured and their bodies burnt by powder,

so that few recovered, their companions having been all killed outright."

Although not intending an attack until his reinforcements should arrive from Stenay, Turenne marched to the village of Mouchi le Preux, which stood on a hill, overlooking the plain of Arras, about four miles to the east of the walls of the city, and about two from the nearest camp of the enemy. From this position he was able to send out scouting parties every night to endeavour to intercept the enemy's convoys on their way from Cambrai and Douay; but on such a flat country it was impossible to prevent all of them from getting through to the enemy's camp.

Turenne's inability to attack, on account of his numerical weakness, enabled the enemy not only to complete his lines round Arras for the siege of that city, but also to dig elaborate trenches for defence against the army of Turenne, which was about to attempt its relief. The allied armies, therefore, lay between an inner and an outer circle of entrenchments.

Ramsay thus describes the entrenchments made by the Spaniards between their own army and the relieving army. The "lines of circumvallation were 12 foot broad and 10 deep, with an advance ditch, 9 foot in breadth and 6 in depth," and they "had built redoubts and little forts at certain distances, planted artillery in all parts, and raised *Epaulments* to cover themselves from the cannon. In the space between the circumvallation and its advance ditch, they had dug 12 rows of holes or little wells 4 foot deep, and a foot

15

and a half over, disposed chequer-wise, and in the
intervals, they had fixed palisades a foot and a half
high to stop and hamper the horses." As, in addition
to all this, the Spaniards had to make their entrenchments on their own side for the siege of Arras, they
must have done a prodigious amount of digging.
These entrenchments, says Napoleon, enabled the
Archduke to continue the siege for thirty-eight days.
Without these entrenchments "he would not have been
able to carry on the siege twenty-four hours".

Hocquincourt's army arrived from Stenay on the
17th of August, and this reinforcement, together with
the garrison inside Arras, placed the King's troops
almost on a numerical equality with that of the enemy,
which had lost a good many men in the open trenches
during the month which had passed since the trenches
had been completed and the actual siege had begun.
But Napoleon, in speaking of this very siege, says that
engineers require a besieging army to be seven times
the number of the garrison; when, therefore, a relieving army comes to the assistance of the garrison, the
besieging army ought to be equal to the relieving
army, plus seven times the garrison itself. At that
rate, if the garrison of Arras was 5,000 and the relieving army 20,000, the besieging army should have been
$7 \times 5 = 35,000 + 20,000 = 55,000$. As the besieging
army was much below that strength, its only hope of
safety lay in making, in addition to the contravallations
for the siege, circumvallations, *i.e.* very formidable entrenchments, against the relieving army. These terms

are only used here to explain their meanings on the accompanying plan of the siege.

Modern weapons, to some extent, must have upset the above calculations, as in the siege of Paris 236,000 Prussians were sufficient to shut up and reduce by famine a garrison of 300,000 French soldiers.[1] At Kimberley, 5,000 Boers besieged a garrison of 4,730. At Ladysmith an army of 22,000 besieged a garrison of 13,000, while an army of observation of 8,000 defeated a force of 18,000 on its way to the relief of Ladysmith. At Port Arthur the besieging army with the army of observation cannot have greatly exceeded in numbers the army which attempted to relieve it, combined with its garrison.

A good deal of skirmishing went on before Arras between the King's troops and those of the allies, who were sent out to bring in convoys; and, after the arrival of Hocquincourt, he and Turenne took St. Pol, a village to the west of Arras, and also the Abbey of St. Eloy, which stood about three miles to the north-west of it. Both places had been garrisoned, but made a weak defence.

The positions of the armies were then as follows: On the south-east Turenne on the left, and La Ferté on the right, were encamped side by side, their left resting on the river Cogeul and their right on the river Scarpe. In their centre was the hill of Mouchi le Preux, upon the front of which they placed their guns, while from either side of the hill entrenchments were

---

[1] *Ency. Brit.* (9th ed.), vol. ix., p. 467 c.

carried to the rivers. Altogether, it was a very strong position! On the opposite side of Arras, to the northwest, Hocquincourt was encamped on a steep hill called Cæsar's Camp, his left resting on the river Scarpe, while a tributary of the Scarpe flowed round his right and under his front, joining the Scarpe below the corner of his left front.

Within the enemy's entrenchments, Condé lay in the south, the Archduke in the east, Fuensaldagne in the north, and Fernando de Solis in the west.

When Turenne, with his troops, having helped Hocquincourt in taking St. Pol and St. Eloy, was returning to his own camp at Mouchi le Preux, he took the opportunity of riding along the enemy's western, northern and eastern lines—carefully avoiding the southern lines for a reason which will presently appear. This reconnoitre, he says, "gave us great lights, both how to make the attack, and as to the road we were to take to the making it. . . . None but a few skirmishers came out of the lines, which M. de Castelnau went and took a close view of, and the cavalry marched all the time within the reach of a three-pounder cannon-shot." Turenne noticed that the lines in front of Dom Fernando Solis's were "very naked," and then he rode past the quarters of Fuensaldagne and the Archduke, the whole ride occupying about a couple of hours, in the course of which he made very careful observations. "The cannon of the Spaniards," says Ramsay, "killed several of his soldiers." According to the Duke of York, "there was never a squadron but lost

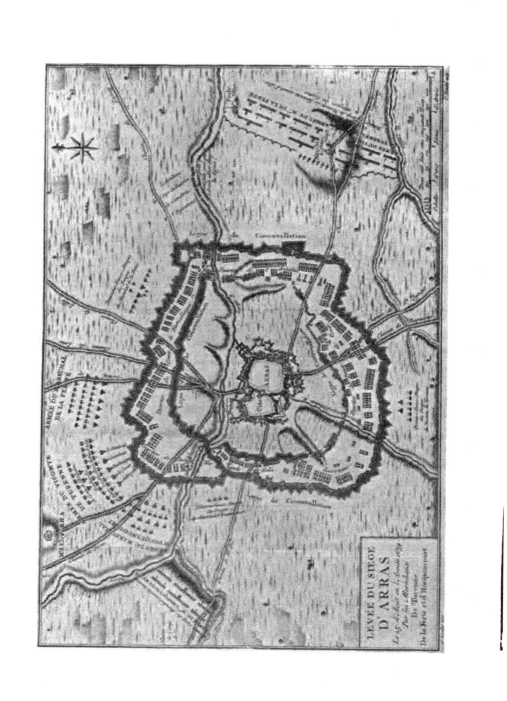

LEVÉE DU SIÉGE
D'ARRAS

two or three men, without reckoning horses ". Some
old and experienced officers murmured at Turenne's
thus exposing his men without apparent necessity;
but, continues the Duke of York, some time afterwards "these gentlemen were sensible of their error,
after that we had forced [the enemy's] lines, since it
was at that very time that he chose, as he was exposing himself, as well as others, the place where to attack
them : and, if he had not approached with all the
troops he had with him, the enemies' advanced guards
would not have retired as they did, and he could not
have taken notice of everything with so much exact-
ness ".

As he was riding near the enemy's lines, some of
his staff took the liberty of expostulating with him
about his own personal danger, and of saying that the
enemy could come out of his lines, at any point, attack
Turenne and defeat him.   Turenne replied that no
doubt this was true, and that it would be exceedingly
dangerous to ride so close to the lines in front of the
camp of Condé, which, as has been remarked, he carefully avoided; but, from his own experience of the
Spanish army, he felt certain that, before stirring a
foot, Fernando de Solis would send to consult
Fuensaldagne, the generalissimo, that Fuensaldagne
would then send to consult the Archduke, that the
Archduke would then send to Condé, and would
summon a Council of War to decide whether, on the
whole, it would be better to send out a force to attack
Turenne, as he rode past the lines, or whether it would

be wiser to refrain from doing so. Long afterwards, Condé told the Duke of York that exactly what Turenne anticipated had happened, and that by the time it had been decided to send out troops to attack Turenne, he was safe back again behind his own entrenchments.

Having discovered the weakest places in the enemy's lines, Turenne was anxious to attack, and his anxiety on this point was increased by a message which he received from the governor within the city of Arras, to the effect that he had very little ammunition remaining and that, unless the siege were raised very shortly, he would be obliged to capitulate.

It is difficult to ascertain fully the position of Turenne towards the other French generals and to make out whether he was at that time commander-in-chief, in the modern sense of the word. When he proposed the attack, at a Council of War, all the generals opposed it, with the exception of the Count of Broglie and the Duke of York; but La Ferté and Hocquincourt raised stronger objections than any of the others. Turenne at last seems to have got his way, not by command, but by sheer force of argument, backed up by an order from the Court urging a speedy attack.

Great preparations were made for the attempt; fascines for filling in ditches, hurdles, and other implements for enabling soldiers to make a passage over entrenchments were procured in abundance. Turenne spent much time in explaining to his officers the mea-

COMTE DE GRAMMONT.

sures which they were to employ. The Duke of York
says that "public prayers" were said "at the head of
each battalion and squadron, for several days before,
and as many as could confessed and received the
Blessed Sacrament," and he expressed his confidence
that "no army ever showed more marks of true devotion than ours at that time".

A couple of days before the attack was to be attempted, Turenne and a good many of his officers
were riding about examining the lines of the enemy
opposite to, but at a respectful distance from, the
quarters of Condé, when they were attacked by some
of Condé's cavalry, and a squadron of their own cavalry
which was with them was panic-stricken and fled. Con-
sequently Turenne and his officers were obliged to
pocket their pride and run away as fast as their horses
could carry them, with their foes in full pursuit, greatly
to the vexation of Turenne.

In the midst of all this grave anxiety there was
a somewhat disconcerting arrival at the camp of
Turenne in the person of that lively courtier, the
Comte de Grammont, who had ridden thither for
the fun of seeing a battle. This gifted amateur
amused himself by going alternately from one rival
camp to another, having friends in both, to whom
he related the latest gossip and scandals of the Court
which he had just left. He had the impudence to
tell Turenne that unless he were victorious Mazarin
would hold him personally responsible for undertaking
an enterprise of which the cardinal strongly disap-

proved, and to tell Condé that, if he were taken prisoner, Mazarin intended to have him beheaded. Having been informed by Turenne that he proposed to attack the lines of the enemy on the following morning, Grammont rode across to Condé and made him a present of this important secret. From what followed it may be assumed that such was Condé's opinion of Grammont that he did not believe it. In an epitaph on Grammont, written long before his death, by St. Evremond, are the rather lumbering lines :—

> We may once more see a Turenne ;
>   Condé himself may have a double ;
> But to make Grammont o'er again,
>   Would cost dame nature too much trouble.

It was by night that Turenne determined to make his grand attack. The reason he gave for this, says the Duke of York, was that "in the night time, no one of the enemy's quarters durst come to assist another ; that each fearing for itself because of false attacks"—for the making of false attacks in three separate places was part of his plan—"no one would venture to quit its ground, or at most would only aid its next neighbour till break of day, before which we should have made a passage through their lines". Of the making of this attack by night, Napoleon says: "Nocturnal marches and operations are so uncertain, that although they sometimes succeed, they more frequently fail".

The attack was to be made on the point farthest

from the camps of Turenne and La Ferté, at the
north-west corner of the enemy's lines, behind which
lay the quarters of Fernando de Solis; but three small
bodies of troops were despatched to make feigned
attacks, the first on the south of the lines, opposite the
quarters of Condé, the second on the north-east,
opposite the quarters of Fuensaldagne, and the third
on the west, opposite the more southern portion of
the quarters of De Solis.

Soon after dark Turenne and La Ferté started RELIEF OF
with their troops. They crossed the river Scarpe by ARRAS, 24th
August, 1654.
four bridges, which had been previously constructed
over it, and marched first to the north, straight away
from Arras, and afterwards to the west. As every
soldier was wanted for the fighting lines, the baggage
and transport in the camps were left unprotected, and
orders were given that they were not to be removed
till it was broad daylight, when they were to be brought
on as might best be managed.

A night had been chosen on which the moon would
be shining during the first half of the march, when the
French troops would not be visible from the positions
of the allies; but on which it would be dark during the
second part of the march, when they would be advancing towards, and in full view of, the enemy's lines.
The first part of the march was made in great silence
and in excellent order. The night was fine and still,
and there was bright moonlight until the troops came
to the appointed and only halting-place. Soon after
that had been reached the moon went down, intense

darkness set in, and a fresh breeze sprang up. Just
before the moonlight failed the troops had been drawn
up in order of battle. Turenne was in the centre, La
Ferté was on his left, and Hocquincourt, whose troops,
although they had no distance to come, had not yet
arrived, was to be on his right. The infantry were
drawn up in two lines, and each battalion had four or
five squadrons of horse behind it carrying fascines and
hurdles, wherewith to cover the holes made by the
enemy for the purpose of stopping cavalry and imped-
ing infantry.

The time arrived for the attack; but not so the
forces of Hocquincourt, who was, however, on the ground
himself. He begged Turenne to wait for his troops;
but Turenne said that was impossible, and, riding in
front of the whole army, he led it to the attack in person.
It advanced in the dark to within half-cannon-shot of
the enemy's lines without being discovered.

Suddenly the darkness was illuminated by a blaze
of light along the whole line of the advancing army.
"Our foot," says the Duke of York, "at once lighted
their matches. They made a glorious show, which
appeared the more by reason of the wind, which kindled
them and made them blaze through the darkness of the
night."

Almost immediately three of the enemy's guns fired
at Turenne's army, and lights gradually appeared all
along the Spanish lines. Turenne's officers then
advanced boldly; but not so the men. The Duke of
York declares that he "never knew them to go on so

unwillingly as then ".   Yet, owing to the "vigour of the
officers who led them " and to the pressure of "the horse
by keeping so close to their rear," they "stopped not
till they came to the Line itself, where the resistance
they found was not so great as they expected ; for in a
very little time all our five battalions made themselves
masters of that part of it which they attacked.   Then
the horses brought up the fascines and covered hurdles,
and after doing so retired a little to the rear.   The
engineers then set to work to make a safe road-way
through the entrenchments, by which the cavalry might
enter the lines."   To encourage his men, the Duke of
York was injudicious enough to order his kettledrum
to be sounded, which drew upon his men the fire of the
enemy.   "The kettledrum was soon silenced, he (*sic*)
being the first man killed" in his squadron.

La Ferté was less successful than Turenne, "having
not put his men so soon in order, as Mr. de Turenne
had," for although they advanced right into the ditch,
they were beaten off and came running away to
shelter themselves amongst the horse which the Duke
commanded.   They were in terrible disorder.   The
officers were loudly complaining that their men had
refused to follow them into the enemy's trenches, and
the men were crying out that they had only fled in
following their own flying officers.   Worse still, the
disordered mob not only made confusion among the
cavalry, but, through carrying their lighted matches,
drew the fire of the enemy upon it.

We learn from Turenne that it took his sappers,

or such of his soldiers as he employed in engineering work, "a good half-hour in filling up the ditches". When this had been done over a space sufficiently wide for horses to pass over the entrenchments, Turenne's cavalry dismounted and led their horses over the roadway into the enemy's lines.

A scene of great confusion followed. The Spaniards were in confusion from fright; the French were in confusion from the eagerness of each man to be before his neighbour—not in defeating the enemy, but in looting the enemy's camp; and the confusion of both was worse confounded by the darkness, by the uncertain flickering of matches and torches, and by the dazzling glare of some burning huts, which had been set on fire by the French soon after they entered the Spanish lines. Squadrons of cavalry belonging to the rival armies passed through each other, in the darkness, without recognising that they were foes. In the weird lights and shadows caused by the burning huts and the torches, others imagined foes where none existed. Here and there, on either side, a detachment would gain a temporary success or be driven away into the darkness. Frequently troops found themselves close to unexpected entrenchments; for those made by the Spaniards as a defence against the relieving army, and those made for the siege of Arras, were at distances from each other varying from less than a quarter of a mile to three-quarters of a mile; and the river Scarpe, which crossed both, formed another embarrassing barrier.

When, with the early morning, it became light enough to distinguish objects clearly, and the Spaniards could see that the space between their defensive and offensive entrenchments was filled with French troops, they were more terror-stricken than ever. Condé, who had ridden up with some cavalry, was asked by the Archduke what he would advise to be done, and when he observed the panic of the Spaniards he recommended the Archduke to retire; but he himself attacked and put to flight some of La Ferté's squadrons. Turenne witnessed this attack, and, when he saw that the flying Frenchmen were not being chased imprudently by their pursuers, he felt pretty certain that the attack must be under the command of Condé. Condé, on his part, when leading his cavalry in pursuit of La Ferté's runaways, perceived some guns admirably posted on an eminence in front of him, and, thinking that the commander of so well chosen a position could be none other than Turenne himself, he gave orders to halt. Yet, so great was the confusion among the French troops, in consequence of their leaving the ranks for purposes of pillage, that Turenne says he would have been forced to withdraw his army for protection into the town of Arras, if Condé had been able to bring up infantry with him as well as cavalry. As it was, with such forces as Turenne could persuade to deny themselves the pleasures of plunder, and with the help of the cavalry, which now made a sortie from Arras, he was able to put to rout the totally demoralised Spaniards.

Condé rallied his scattered troops, quitted his entrenchments and retired in good order to Cambrai; the Archduke and the Count Fuensaldagne fled in a terrible hurry with only a squadron or two, to Douay, and the other generals of the Spanish army galloped away as best they could, with fragments of their forces. They lost 3,000 men in killed, wounded and prisoners, and they had to leave behind them 63 guns, 2,000 waggons, 9,000 horses, " all the equipage of the officers, and the baggage of the whole army ". Turenne, who received a contusion from a musket-bullet, did not lose more than about 400 men.

The French Court came to Arras after its relief, and then went to Paris, followed by La Ferté and Hocquincourt. Turenne marched eastwards, some fifty miles, to Quesnoy, a fortress near the Flemish frontier, which he took in two days. In September he marched southwards, to Cambrésis, and demolished some castles on the frontier. Then he sent his troops into winter quarters, and went to Paris, where, Ramsay tells us, "his presence was like to be necessary".

CHAPTER XVIII.

THE purpose for which the presence of Turenne appeared likely to be necessary was to quell a riot in the streets of Paris, for there seemed to be some danger of a revival of the Paris Fronde. One symptom of this was a friction between the King and the Parliament about a new coinage.

De Retz, who had been arrested and imprisoned at Nantes, having heard of this, had managed to escape from prison, and was riding off towards Paris, to "show himself to the people in the public market, and make new barricades," when he observed a soldier galloping in pursuit. In getting his pistol ready he frightened his horse, who swerved and threw him. Although his collar-bone was broken by the fall, the dignified cardinal managed to crawl away on foot and to hide in a haystack. Going thence under cover of the dark to the house of a friend, he got a change of clothes, and then he embarked in a fishing-boat which landed him on the coast of Spain. There he had great difficulty in accounting for himself and experienced some disagreeable adventures; but eventually he reached Rome. Thanks to his absence from France, the threatened rising of the Fronde fell through. There

was still, however, much discontent. Louis XIV. went
to the Parliament, seated himself on his throne, and
"without any preamble forbad the Parliament to concern itself in public affairs and then, rising hastily, went
out, being determined not to hear any remonstrance.
Notwithstanding this prohibition, the Parliament continued to assemble, and the minds of the members
grew every day more and more soured."[1]

The popular hatred of Mazarin became fiercer than
ever, while the cardinal, on his part, became more
despotic than ever. Cardinal de Retz, although in
Rome, was intriguing through his agents in Paris; and
another intriguer, through the medium of his Parisian
friends and admirers, was the Prince of Condé. At
this critical juncture Turenne, by the request of Mazarin, acted as a peacemaker between the King and the
Parliament, and, thanks to his good offices, all disputed matters were sufficiently smoothed over in the
early summer for the campaign to begin in June.

We have now to consider a campaign in which,
says Napoleon, "Turenne constantly observed the two
maxims: 1st. *Never attack a position in front, when
you can obtain it by turning it.* 2nd. *Avoid doing
what the enemy wishes; and that simply because he
does wish it. Shun the field of battle which he has
reconnoitred and studied; and more particularly that
in which he has fortified and entrenched himself.*"

Turenne began by besieging and taking Landreçies, without which, as it was some miles nearer the

[1] Ramsay.

interior of France, it would have been impossible to hold
Quesnoy.   The operations which followed were conducted for some time within the triangle made by
Landrecies, Bouchain and Valenciennes, each side of
the triangle being only a little over or under twenty
miles in length.

Not far from Valenciennes Condé was nearly, and
ought to have been, taken prisoner.   The Spanish
army was retiring from a position it had occupied,
and the Spanish generals had undertaken to protect
Condé's rear; but the Spanish troops entrusted with that
duty, on seeing a strong body of French approaching, scampered off, to take care of themselves, without
troubling their heads about, or warning, Condé, who was
then left with a very small force.   The French troops
in question were twelve squadrons and two or three
battalions, under General Castelnau, to whom Turenne
had given orders to press on and deliver a sudden and
very energetic flank attack.   But when Castelnau was
approaching Condé's little force, says the Duke of
York, he "suffered himself to be amused by some of
the Prince of Condé's officers, who being in the rear of
their troops and seeing him advance at the head of his,
desired to speak with him upon honour : to which having
consented, because they were his old acquaintance, he
ordered his troops to halt a little, and, while they were
complimenting one another, the Prince of Condé
hastened his troops forwards, and Castelnau was duped ;
a fellow who was left behind, on the top of a small hill,
having given the officers the signal, they took leave of

16

the Lieutenant General and galloped after their troops. This unseasonable piece of civility gave the enemy time to cross the Schelt before we could come up with them."

One fault is apt to lead to another, and so it was with Castelnau. In order to screen his stupid error from Turenne he told him a lie. He represented that he had put the enemy to a headlong flight and that Condé's last squadron had been so sorely pressed that it had been obliged to swim the river to effect its escape. Believing this story, Turenne repeated it in a despatch to Mazarin, a despatch which unfortunately was intercepted by the enemy, and fell into the hands of Condé, who was furious. He sent a most insulting letter to Turenne, accusing him of lying, and bitter ill-feeling continued between these two great generals from that date till the Peace of the Pyrenees, four years later. Before this quarrel, even when antagonistic in warfare, their personal relations had been most friendly. During their campaigns against each other, it is said, they kept up a correspondence ; if Turenne beat Condé in a battle, he very fully and very courteously explained the means by which he had succeeded ; and, when Condé gained a success, he wrote to Turenne asking him whether he approved of his tactics.[1]

The sieges of the fortresses of Condé and St. Guislain were successfully accomplished by Turenne, and in November he received orders to go to the Court at Compiègne, on a matter of great importance. The matter in question was as follows :—

[1] *Louis XIV. in Court and Camp*, p. 84.   By Col. A. C. P. Haggard.

Hocquincourt had fully expected to be made commander-in-chief, and he was very angry with Mazarin for having given that office to Turenne. To keep Hocquincourt quiet and, as he thought, out of harm's way, Mazarin had made him Governor of Ham and Peronne. At the time when Hocquincourt was nursing his wrath against Mazarin for putting him on the shelf, one of the great ladies of the Provincial Fronde happened to come in his way, and promptly made him fall in love with her. Perceiving the temper he was in, she communicated with Condé, who made him an offer of the post of Lieutenant-General of Flanders with 100,000 crowns down in cash, if he would deliver up Ham and Peronne into the hands of the Spanish army.

Mazarin heard of this offer, sent for Turenne, and suggested to this general that the King's army should march at once to Peronne for its protection. Turenne objected that as the Spanish army was at Cambrai, and Condé's army only half a dozen miles from Peronne, a movement of the King's army in the direction of the latter town would be anticipated by the enemy; and that if Peronne and Ham should be lost, there would probably be a general insurrection throughout France. He suggested, instead, that negotiations should be opened with Hocquincourt. The cardinal said that for the King to stoop to bargaining with one of his own rebellious subjects would be intolerable, with which Turenne quite agreed; but, at the same time, this practical and cool-headed general gave it as his opinion that, of the two, it would be a

16 *

lesser evil than to lose Ham and Peronne and to risk a dangerous insurrection.

Finally, Mazarin took the advice of Turenne. The negotiations lasted a fortnight, during which Hocquincourt gave alternate audiences to the envoys of the King and the envoys of Spain, "not concealing from either party what the other offered him, as if he had been free to make what choice he pleased". After much haggling, the impudent Hocquincourt struck a bargain with the representatives of the King. He was to receive 200,000 crowns down, and to lose his governorship, but it was to be given to his son. Thus the disgraceful affair ended; Turenne, adds Ramsay, "saved his country by this method, and disposed Mazarin to finish without violence an affair which, had he employed force, might have had fatal consequences". The troops then went into winter quarters and Turenne to Paris. Thither also went another general, Duke Francis of Lorraine, who shared the vacillating spirit of his family—vacillating, at least, where they thought it to their interest to vacillate—and made an excuse of the continued detention, by the Spaniards, of his brother (whom he hated and was only too glad should be detained), for deserting the Spaniards and allying himself to the King of France, whose fortunes he thought seemed just then to be in the ascendant.

But a more important potentate than Francis of Lorraine had noted the improvement in the prospects of France and determined to make an alliance with her. Towards the end of the year 1655, Cromwell,

who had long wavered as to whether he should take
the side of France or that of Spain, came to the conclusion that France was going to win, and, in accordance
with that conclusion, he made a treaty with Mazarin.
Charles II. had already left France for Brussels,
where he signed a treaty with the King of Spain and
sent peremptory orders to his brother, the Duke of
York, to leave the service of France and join him there.

Mazarin was, at the same time, anxious for a treaty
with Spain, his object being to negotiate a marriage
between Louis XIV. and the Infanta, presumptive
heiress to the Crown of Spain.   Philip IV., however,
refused to listen to such a proposal.   On the contrary,
he prepared to carry on the war in the following year
with increased vigour.   Dissatisfied with the conduct
of the previous campaigns, he recalled Fuensaldagne
and persuaded the Emperor to find other employment
for the Archduke.   Then he substituted, for these
generals, Marshal Caracena, an experienced veteran,
but a true Spaniard in his phlegmatic deliberation,
and Don John of Austria, his own bastard son by
an actress in Madrid, a young man full of energy, but
almost without education, and as yet without experience.

The negotiations which Mazarin had attempted
with Spain delayed the opening of the campaign of
1656.   It was not until June that Turenne laid siege
to Valenciennes, then a strong fortress on the river
Scheldt.   It is now in France, a few miles from the
frontier of Belgium.   The surrounding country is very

flat, and, in the seventeenth century, the sluggish river formed morasses both above and below it. Its garrison consisted of 2,000 foot and 200 horse; but 10,000 of its inhabitants[1] were capable of bearing arms. The river ran through the town, and Turenne took up his quarters on the east side, with Lorraine to the south of him, on some slightly rising ground. La Ferté took up his position on an incline to the west of the town, on the opposite side of the river. Valenciennes was, at that time, one of the principal towns of the Low Countries and it served as a magazine for the military stores of Spain.

It was known to Turenne that the Spanish army of 20,000 men was on its march to the relief of the fortress; so the first thing he did was to make entrenchments, not against the fortress itself, but for his own defence against the army of relief; and in six days this "circumvallation" was completed, with a double ditch defended by palisades. He had arrived before Valenciennes sooner than La Ferté, who had been ill, and he had planted a double row of palisades along La Ferté's lines for his protection; "but La Ferté, on his arrival," says Napoleon, "out of a mere spirit of contradiction, had them pulled up".

The Spaniards flooded the country round the fortress by drawing up all the sluices. Turenne employed several regiments of foot and nearly all his horse in carrying fascines to strengthen a dyke against

[1] Valenciennes, the town celebrated for the lace bearing that name, has now more than double that number of inhabitants.

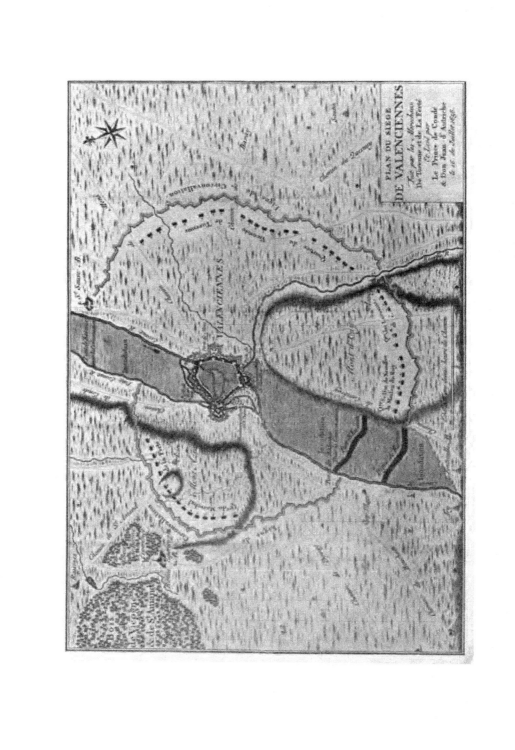

PLAN DU SIEGE
DE VALENCIENNES

the water. This required enormous labour ; the men were working in water up to their waists ; but their efforts were successful, so much so, in fact, that they were enabled to divert some of the water in such a manner as to flood one quarter of the city.

When the Spanish relieving force arrived, it spent the first week in entrenching itself. The French infantry, which was about 12,000 strong, was necessarily much scattered in guarding entrenchments of seven or eight miles in circumference; and, with a relieving army of 12,000 men close at hand, Turenne felt the necessity of watchfulness, especially when, after eight days, the enemy's entrenchments were evidently completed, and the withdrawal of the transports denoted readiness for immediate action. The day that this happened Turenne fully expected an attack either that afternoon or during the coming night. Accordingly he sent to La Ferté warning him to be "upon the watch and to place guards everywhere : but the Marshal looked upon the Viscount's advice as an affront and slighted it ".[1]

When darkness came on, although no attack had RELIEF OF yet been made, Turenne ordered his regiments to re- VALENCI- ENNES main under arms, and the event was just what Turenne BY THE SPANI- had anticipated. Early in the night his lines were at- ARDS, 16th July, 1656. tacked. He made a vigorous resistance and the enemy was quickly repulsed. In fact the weakness of the attack led Turenne to suspect it to be a mere feint. Presently news was brought to Turenne that heavy

[1] Ramsay.

musketry fire had been heard to the left, more than a couple of miles off, on La Ferté's side of the river.   It was now clear to Turenne that the enemy's attack in force must have been made upon the lines of La Ferté. Immediately he despatched two regiments to cross the bridge of boats on the left and to hasten to the relief of that general; and he ordered four more regiments to follow them as soon as possible.   By the time he had given his own generals their orders and galloped round to La Ferté's quarters, he found that the two regiments he had sent on had been defeated, that the four which followed them had then halted, that the Spaniards had begun by entering La Ferté's lines at a point which had been practically unguarded, and that in his quarters there was now a regular rout.   Turenne did his best to save the situation, but it was too late.   The battle had not lasted more than a quarter of an hour. La Ferté himself had been taken prisoner, with more than 400 of his officers and nearly 4,000 of his men, and before long the sounds of cheering, which could be heard in the distance, proclaimed that the town of Valenciennes had been relieved.

Nothing was left to be done by Turenne but to order a general retreat and, if possible, to save the guns. Many of his men were three miles away and he lost half of them : some of his " tents and baggage " had also to be left behind.   At first all was confusion, "but in a short time he got into such good order that the enemy durst not pursue him ".[1]   Well might Turenne

[1] Ramsay.

say : "A fine retreat is looked upon by many experienced officers as the masterpiece of a good general, for which nothing should be neglected that can render it safe and honourable".

His staff to a man recommended him to retire rapidly into Picardy ; but, contrary to the advice of all his generals and in spite of their urgent remonstrances, when he had marched about a dozen miles, he halted and turned round to face the enemy, near Quesnoy.   He knew that if he made a full retreat the Court would be thrown into a panic, that the discontented throughout France would join in the insurrection of Condé, and that, in all probability, the Parisian Fronde would be revived.   Therefore, although he had now no entrenching tools—they had been left before Valenciennes in his flight and it would have been useless to waste labour with weak substitutes—he awaited in open camp the approach of his formidable foe.

When the enemy came in sight Turenne's men began hurriedly to prepare the transport for flight, whereupon Turenne rode up to them, fired a pistol at the nearest man thus engaged, and forbade the rest to leave their posts on pain of death.

So puzzled were the Spaniards, when they observed Turenne's army awaiting their arrival with tents standing, that they did not know what to do.   Fearing some trap, they waited a couple of days and then moved off to besiege the fortress of Condé.   Perceiving their intention, Turenne sent 1,000 of his cavalry, each trooper carrying a sack of corn behind him, to victual the place. But he knew that he was not strong enough to save either Condé or Quesnoy, the fate of both was sealed, and he retired to a strong position between Lens and Arras.

Soon afterwards a little incident occurred which exhibited the character of Turenne. When a convoy was being taken to Arras under the charge of the Count of Grandpré, that young officer stayed behind, having an assignation with a lady. During his absence from his post the convoy was attacked by the Spaniards and was only saved from capture by the courage of a major. When Turenne was privately informed of Grandpré's ill-conduct, he said in presence of his officers: "The Count of Grandpré will be very angry with me for having given him a private commission, which kept him at Arras at a time when he would have had an opportunity of showing his bravery". On Grandpré's return, he heard what Turenne had said, although fully aware of his delinquency. Going into Turenne's tent, he threw himself on his knees and begged for forgiveness. Turenne "spoke to him with a paternal severity," and with such good effect that the young Count became "one of the ablest captains of his age".

Unable to interfere with the proceedings of the Spaniards, Turenne besieged La Chapelle. Condé came to its relief; but his troops were so wearied out by a long march through rain and mud that they rested two days before attacking, and this delay just enabled Turenne to take the fortress. He afterwards relieved

St. Guislain and was thus enabled to end this disastrous campaign with a couple of slight successes.

For the defeat at Valenciennes, Turenne receives a scolding from Napoleon. "The army commanded by Turenne," says he, "was superior both in number and quality to the Spanish army; how came he to allow it to approach his quarters at Valenciennes, and not to march out of his lines to give it battle? His lines were far from equal to those at Arras; and Marshal de la Ferté's position was evidently unsupported, separated from the rest of the army by a river and an inundation of 1,000 toises"—an obsolete word meaning six feet—"this circumstance alone ought to have determined him to engage."

But after condemning Turenne for being defeated at Valenciennes, he gives him unstinted praise for awaiting the enemy in his position near Quesnoy, against the advice of every member of his staff. This, says Napoleon, "was because he had more talent than they: men think only of avoiding a present danger, without troubling themselves about the influence which their conduct may have on subsequent events. With common minds the impression of a defeat wears out but slowly and gradually."

As an example of courtesies between enemies, it may be mentioned here that when, after this campaign, Condé was seriously ill at Brussels, the Queen-Dowager of France sent a Parisian physician, in whom she knew that Condé placed great confidence, to attend him.

CHAPTER XIX.

WITH all his holy horror of Popery and Kingcraft,
Oliver Cromwell was quite prepared to ally himself
with the most autocratic of kings and to make use of
the most intolerant of Papists when it suited his purpose so to do. After much wrestling with the Lord,
he had come to the conclusion, towards the end of 1656,
that it would be to his interest to be on a firmer footing
of friendship with France than that already obtained,
and early in 1657, after considerable bargaining, an
offensive and defensive alliance was concluded that was
to last for twelve months. Sir John Reynolds was sent
to Calais with 6,000 splendid English infantry, one half
to be in the pay of the Protector and the other half to
be in that of the King of France. The combined
forces of England and France were to endeavour to
seize Dunkirk, which, when taken, was to be made
over to England as a return for her services in the war.
If either Gravelines or Mardyck were taken first, that
fortress was to be held as a hostage by England until
she received Dunkirk. It will be necessary now to
bear in mind that Calais, Gravelines, Mardyck, and
Dunkirk are all on the north-east coast of what is
now France, Gravelines being about a dozen miles to

the east of Calais, Mardyck about five miles to the
east of Gravelines, and Dunkirk some six or seven
miles to the east of Mardyck.

Turenne started on his campaign in May to lay
siege to Cambrai. The very evening after he had
arrived before it he learned that Condé had marched
from Valenciennes, which was only fifteen miles to the
north-east, and would shortly arrive to the relief of
the fortress. Turenne, says Ramsay, " being persuaded
that the Prince would fetch a compass to avoid the
French camp, he went and posted himself in a place
where, according to all the rules of war, Condé must
pass. By good fortune for the Prince (Condé) his
guide misled him, and brought him by the high road."
The consequence was that Condé met with but a weak
opposition and was able to enter and to relieve the
fortress ; therefore Turenne "thought proper to raise
the siege ". On hearing of this Turenne's enemies in
Paris spread a report that he had treacherously allowed
the Spanish troops to relieve Cambrai, out of friendship
for Condé, for they hoped by this calumny to induce
Mazarin to recall him. In this they happily failed.

"During this time," Ramsay tells us, "the Prince
of Condé and Don John of Austria made several
marches and counter-marches to amuse the Viscount,
divert him from his purpose, and fall suddenly upon
Calais."

The Duke of York who, it must be borne in mind,
was now fighting for the Spaniards against the French ;
instead of, as before, for the French against the

Spaniards, describes the long march, the object of which, he says, in the very words of Ramsay, was "to fall suddenly on Calais". The Prince de Ligny was to approach a part of the town without the walls, adjoining the quay, at low water. Had he been once master of that position, the place could not "have held out above twelve hours, the garrison being weak, as well as the town on that side of it. But he coming half an hour too late, the water was then so high that it was impossible for him to pass." So the only result of the attempt was to give "the town a hot alarm," and to demonstrate to the governor "the weakness of that part," which he immediately strengthened. "And thus we failed of our design, having made so great a march for so little purpose."

After the capitulation of Montmédy, which had been besieged and captured by La Ferté, Turenne marched to besiege St. Venant—a place little known now, but then an important frontier fortress on the river Lys. The Duke of York shall describe an incident that occurred during this siege. "We arrived at Calonne on the Lys within a league of St. Venant which M. de Turenne was besieging, and the lines whereof were already so far advanced that this consideration and the disproportion of forces by no means allowed of any endeavours to relieve the place. We only studied how to cut off the enemy's provisions and prevent the passing of a convoy of four or five hundred waggons which were to go the next day from Béthune to their army. . . . We were ready to break up camp at dawn of day." It was represented to Don John "that the least delay would give the convoy an opportunity to enter the lines; but whatever could be said to quicken him, the army stirred not till noon". When it at last arrived at the place where the convoy would inevitably pass, Don John and Caracena "would needs, according to their custom, take an afternoon nap". They had not long been asleep, when the Duke of York saw Turenne's convoy coming "in all haste". The Duke went to the Prince of Ligny, the general of the horse, and urged him to attack. The Prince "answered he saw the thing as well as he, that it was the easiest thing in the world to carry off the convoy, but that he durst not attack it without orders from Don John or the Marquess of Caracena". Still less "durst he" disturb the siestas of those worthy generals. The Duke "conjured him not to lose so fine an opportunity by being over-scrupulous; but his reply was that [the Duke] knew not how far the Spanish severity went; that by falling on without orders, it might cost him his head". As a consequence of allowing the convoy to pass, not a waggon of it was lost to Turenne. St. Venant capitulated on the 29th of August, after a magnificent attack on its supposed impregnable counter-scarp by Cromwell's pikemen from Hampshire and Huntingdon. During this siege Turenne was so short of money, with which to pay the English troops that he was reduced to breaking up his own plate and distributing morsels of the silver among the men.

The Spaniards might have prevented the fall of

St. Venant had they not withdrawn with the object of taking Ardres, which had then a garrison of only 300, while Turenne was occupied at St. Venant. And Ramsay tells us that, if they had attacked Ardres "the same night they arrived before it, they would have carried it, but they lost twenty-four hours in making an useless circumvallation". While the Prince of Condé was "suffering these delays with the utmost impatience," the Spanish generals made matters worse, by determining to hold a Council of War, at which still more precious time was lost "in superfluous reasoning . . . about an enterprise which required not the least reflection".

At last a decision was arrived at; but, at the same time as the decision, arrived Turenne, who had hurried to the relief of Ardres as soon as St. Venant had fallen. Then the Spaniards made off for the coast and Turenne followed them until they were under the protection of the guns of Dunkirk.

It was too late in the season to begin a siege of that fortress, so Turenne attacked Mardyck, took it in a few days, and handed it over to the English troops, according to the agreement. The young King and the cardinal joined the French army during the siege of Mardyck. Madame de Motteville says that, on this occasion, Louis XIV. "lived like a private person, dining with Cardinal Mazarin or the Viscomte de Turenne: he had no officers, and neither servants nor money". After taking Mardyck, Turenne tried to take Gravelines;[1]

---

[1] It was off Gravelines that the Spanish Armada had been defeated, some seventy years earlier.

but, as an old writer describes that fortress, "It is very strong, by reason that they can drown it round in four hours, so as no land shall be within a mile of it". And so it happened on this occasion. They drew up their sluices and any approach to it became impossible.

Thus ended a tedious and indecisive, although by no means unsatisfactory, campaign, during which Cromwell grew very impatient and perpetually pestered his French allies with remonstrances, as well as with suggestions which it was impossible to carry out. Yet this campaign was a necessary prelude to its very important successor.

The year 1658 did not open auspiciously for the French. The pardoned rebel, Hocquincourt, now openly allied himself with Condé, and persuaded the Mayor of Hedin to deliver that town to the Spaniards. Meanwhile Cromwell was haughtily calling upon the French Government to fulfil its treaty by besieging Dunkirk.

The French army was early in the field. The siege of Dunkirk is so much the most important incident of this year that we will not linger over the military operations which preceded it. Although plenty of rumours had reached the Spaniards, at Brussels, to the effect that the French were going to besiege Dunkirk, they were convinced, says the Duke of York, who was with them, that Turenne's real objective was Cambrai, and that he purposely spread reports about an intended attack upon Dunkirk for the purpose of in-

17

ducing the Spaniards to withdraw their forces from
Cambrai to Dunkirk, and thus leave Cambrai very
weakly protected.

The country round Dunkirk is a wilderness of
sandhills, raised by the fierce northerly gales. These
white sandhills go by the name of Dunes. On the
south side of this sandy plain were canals and morasses.
When Turenne was approaching Dunkirk, all the low-
lying land about the town was under water. From
flooded fields, again, he had suffered much on his
march thither. It had been an unusually long winter
and the roads were in a fearful state. He had been
advised that it would be impossible to take cannon
with him; but he persisted in doing so and he succeeded in the attempt. It was a most miserable march!
Much time and labour had been spent in filling up
ditches and making bridges, and sometimes the soldiers
were wading through deep water, holding their muskets
above their heads.

Cromwell sent a fleet to blockade the harbour of
Dunkirk, as well as 5,000 or 6,000 infantry with some
guns to be added to the army of Turenne. The
English regiments, now that Reynolds was dead, were
under the command of Lockhart, the English Ambas-
sador at Paris, who was suffering agonies from a most
painful complaint, and, at the great battle about to be
described, he drove about in a carriage.[1] Not long

[1] The Emperor, Louis Napoleon, was suffering from the same
malady at the battle of Sedan, where he also watched the fighting
from a carriage.

afterwards he was drowned when crossing the Channel to pay a visit to Cromwell.

"The first days of the siege," says Turenne, "we suffered very great hardships from want of food for the men and of forage for the horses," and he adds that the English, "who behaved very well, brought very few conveniences to the siege". The King, the cardinal, and the Queen came to Mardyck to be witnesses of this important siege; but they were greatly in the way, and happily they were persuaded to return to Calais. Much more welcome were some barques, bringing provisions for men and horses, palisades and siege tools.

During the early days of the siege the enemy's cavalry made frequent sallies, under the protection of their guns; but they were invariably driven back and Turenne was able to proceed with his entrenchments. He was anxious to complete those works, because Don John was expected daily, if not hourly, with a relieving army; and for several nights Turenne never went to bed.

On the eighth or ninth day, some of the enemy's cavalry were seen approaching, but were driven back by Turenne's troops; and he learned later that in this slight affray "a musket-ball," as the Duke of York writes, struck that arch-traitor, Hocquincourt, "in the belly and killed him on the spot". Of this Napoleon remarks: "A just punishment for his crime!"

The next morning, the 13th of June, the whole army of relief was observed advancing along the coast from

17 *

the east. The sea was on its right and the canal from
Furnes to Dunkirk on its left. A line of infantry
marched before the cavalry. "The artillery was not
yet arrived," says the Duke of York, who was in the
march, "nor the tools for breaking ground; scarce
was there powder sufficient for their infantry; thus
unprovided of whatever was most necessary for a
battle, we encamped at less than twice the distance
of a cannon-shot from the enemy." Napoleon says:
"The Spaniards were so certain that their mere appearance would relieve the place, that they presented
themselves without artillery and without tools to entrench themselves with; their park [of artillery] had
been accidentally delayed on the road".

That evening Turenne says he "sent orders to
all the quarters to rendezvous at his order, two hours
before day"—*i.e.*, at 1.45 A.M., as the sun rises at 3.45
on the 14th of June—being "presently sensible that
there was nothing to be done but to fight" the enemy
the next day.

The Spanish generals were in no such hurry. As
he says himself, the Duke of York, being at supper
with the Marquis of Caracena, "expressed his dislike
of their encamping without lines or the least thing to
cover them, and his fixed belief that if the French did
not attack them that night, they would infallibly give
them battle next morning". Caracena replied: "That
is what I desire". "I am well acquainted with M. de
Turenne," said the Duke of York, "and I venture to
promise that your desire shall be gratified."

At about 5 A.M. the next morning the Duke of York and Condé, hearing that the French were on the move, mounted their horses and rode to the outposts, where they saw artillery and cavalry marching towards them.   They galloped back to tell Caracena, who, annoyed at being disturbed so early—it was one of the hours for being in bed; so in bed, of course, he was lying—pettishly replied that no doubt the French were only going to attack the outposts.   Provoked at Caracena's indolence, Condé said: "Artillery are not generally used in capturing outposts"; and turning to the young Duke of Gloucester, he said sharply: "Have you ever seen a battle won?"   Receiving a reply in the negative he said: "Then in half an hour you will see one lost!"   Further reports confirmed the approach of the French, and delay for another moment became impossible even to the Spanish general.

The rival armies were numerically pretty even, each numbering about 14,000, but the French had 8,000 infantry to 6,000 cavalry, while the Spaniards had 6,000 infantry to 8,000 cavalry; and, as Napoleon observes, the ground was "ill adapted to horse"; therefore, in his larger proportion of infantry, Turenne had a decided advantage.   Another, and a great, advantage on the side of Turenne was that he not only had his own artillery on the field, but also the support of the guns from the English ships, which kept annoying the right flank of the Spaniards, whereas the Spanish artillery had not yet arrived and the enemy

had not a single gun with which to defend himself.
Moreover, the Spaniards had not been expecting an
attack that morning, therefore they must almost inevitably have formed themselves into battle array with
undue hurry, and undue hurry generally entails confusion.

The Battle of the Dunes, as it was afterwards
called, was fought on the sands between the sea on the
north, and the Furnes and Dunkirk canal on the south.
Turenne drew up his army in three lines. He placed
the English troops on his left, next to the sea, and the
French on the right, resting on the canal. His guns
were in front of either flank. In the opposing army
Don John was on the right and Condé was on the left.
Where there was cavalry, and cavalry largely prepon-
derated, there was a line of infantry in front of it.

Turenne had five guns at each wing of his army,
and they were fired four or five times before the rival
infantry and cavalry came into contact. Two battalions
of English pikemen, on Turenne's left, began the
attack, and began it too soon, by running forward,
getting out of line with the front rank of the French
army, and advancing against a Spanish battalion which
was posted upon the highest of the sandhills. Colonel
Fenwick, who was in command, halted at the foot of
the sandhill to give his pikemen time to take breath
before charging up the hill. Meanwhile his musketeers
opened fire upon the Spaniards, who returned it with
vigour, Colonel Fenwick falling to one of their bullets.
His second in command, Major Hinton, then led the

attack. The Englishmen scrambled up the soft, yielding surface of the mound, says the Duke of York, who was watching them from the Spanish ranks, and they "stopped not till they came to push of pike; where notwithstanding the great resistance which was made by the Spaniards, and the advantage they had on the higher ground, as well as that of being well in breath, when their enemies were almost spent with climbing, the English gained the hill and drove them from off it". He might have added that these English soldiers had been marching all night; for such was the fact.

When the English came down the hill, on the Spanish side, the Duke of York charged them with his cavalry; but the sandhills afforded very unsuitable ground for horses to gallop over, and the pikemen made such a stolid resistance that, says the Duke, "I was beaten off, and all who were at the head of my own troop were either killed or wounded, of which number I had been, had not the goodness of my armour preserved me".

If, says he, "they whose business it was to have taken advantage of it" had sent some cavalry to the flank and rear of the English infantry, which had out-marched the French, those Englishmen "might have paid dear for their rash bravery"; but "the opportunity was let slip" by the Spanish officers. The Duke met the Marquis of Caracena, who asked him why he had not charged the enemy. "I have already done so," replied the Duke, "and I have been worsted for my pains."

The English were now advancing out of sight behind some sandhills, and the Duke of York, who had rallied some cavalry, ordered a Spanish officer to attack them in front with some infantry, while he attacked them in their flank with his small body of cavalry. Although the Spanish infantry only appeared in front of the English without attacking them, the distraction prevented the Englishmen from noticing that the Duke of York, with his horse, was charging upon their flank. " I charged that battalion so home," says he, "that I broke them, doing great execution upon them to the edge of the sandhill next the sea." It seems that the ranks, which he "broke," were those not of pikemen, but of musketeers; for he continues: "not so much as one single man of them asked quarter or threw down his arms; but every man defended himself to the last: so that we ran as great danger by the butt end of their muskets, as by the volley they had given us".

Condé, on the Spanish left, was meanwhile making a valiant effort with his cavalry; but the Spanish centre soon fell into hopeless confusion before the vigorous onslaught of Turenne's troops. Condé's cavalry, alarmed at seeing the rout of the Spanish troops on their right, were still further discouraged at seeing Condé himself hurled to the ground; and they turned and joined in the flight before Condé, who, as it happened, was unhurt, had had time to mount another horse in place of the one which had been shot under him.

As to the Spanish infantry, which the Duke of York had ordered to charge the English front, while he attacked its flank, "discovering from the top of the sandhill, where they were, that our whole army was in rout, they scattered, and every man endeavoured to get off, which few of them were so lucky as to perform". It was indeed something like a rout ! Turenne says that "there were between three and four thousand of the enemy made prisoners, and a thousand killed and wounded" ; but the French loss was comparatively slight.

On the evening after this great victory, Turenne wrote the following laconic description of it to his wife : " The enemy came to us and God be praised they have been defeated : I was pretty busy all day, which has fatigued me : I wish you good night : I am going to bed ".

A letter of a very different nature about this battle is said to have been suggested to him. It is asserted that he was offered some of the highest dignities as a bribe, if he would consent to write a letter attributing to Mazarin the credit of having conceived the entire plan of operations which led to the victory. Turenne replied that his signature should never cover a fraud.[1]

Napoleon's criticisms of this affair are interesting. "Don John," he says, "deserved his defeat for advancing within sight of Turenne, without artillery or tools to entrench himself with. It was not with such

[1] *Lives of Cardinals Richelieu and Mazarin* (1854), p. 104.

culpable negligence that Turenne presented himself before the lines of Arras" (as we saw in Chapter XVII.). "He," that is to say Turenne, before Arras, "might have occupied the position of Mouchy by ten o'clock in the morning; but he took care not to do so: he remained all day behind a rivulet, and, in the evening took up his position: he therefore had the whole night in which to entrench himself."

But, while describing the Battle of the Dunes as "Turenne's most brilliant action," he says that his victory " was to be expected". He had a superiority of three to two in infantry, over "ground ill adapted to horse, which rendered the superiority of the Spaniards in cavalry useless to them. Turenne had artillery, and his enemy had none." And "the English ships, at anchor in the roads, cannonaded the right flank of the Spaniards ". Turenne's "order of battle was parallel, he had no manœuvre to execute, nor anything out of the ordinary course to perform ". When he resolved to attack he was unaware that the enemy's artillery had not yet arrived; but he was right in attacking before the enemy had had "time to entrench themselves". Yet he has a fault to find with Turenne.

After the Battle of the Dunes Turenne continued the siege of Dunkirk, which fell in ten days. Now Napoleon says : "After the taking of Dunkirk, and so brilliant a victory as that of the Downs, . . . Turenne might have done more than he did. He ought to have struck a grand blow and taken Brussels, which would have rendered the French arms far more illustrious, and accelerated the conclusion of peace. An event of such importance would have produced the fall of all the smaller places. Turenne infringed the rule which says : 'Avail yourself of the favour of Fortune, while she is in the humour : beware that she does not change, through resentment of your neglect : she is a woman '."

Great credit had been given to the English troops in the description of this victory in these pages ; but it is only fair to say that there were several English, Scotch and Irish regiments in the vanquished army— Lord Ormonde's, Lord Bristol's, the Duke of York's, Lord Middleton's and King Charles's royal regiment of Guards, afterwards called the 1st Guards, and now known as the Grenadier Guards.

If the taking of Dunkirk did honour to the French army, the delivery of Dunkirk to England was a humiliation to French pride. Turenne endeavoured to make up for its loss by capturing for France, Furnes, Dixmunde, Gravelines (after a siege of twenty-six days), Ypres, [1] and Oudenarde, an unfortified city on the Scheldt, within thirty-five miles of Brussels. It was then generally expected that he would advance to Brussels, but Turenne himself explains his reasons for not doing so. "Having only some field-pieces, and but two or three days' provisions, he could not enter upon a siege." He chose the alternative of proceeding

---

[1] At the siege of Ypres the English delivered such a brilliant assault that, when it was over, Turenne embraced their leader and called him one of the bravest captains of the period.

against the maritime towns, and conquered the whole country between the Lys and the Scheldt, two rivers which are twenty-five miles apart on the present Belgium frontier, but join at Ghent. Leaving garrisons in the important fortresses, Turenne went to Paris in December, about six months after the Battle of the Dunes. This campaign had been long and wearying; but its effects, if not immediate, were eventually decisive; for, as there were no fortresses beyond those already captured by Turenne, the King of Spain was afraid lest, in another campaign, the French troops should capture all his territory in the Low Countries.

Before the end of the year 1658 an event had happened which had a considerable influence upon European politics. Within three months of the Battle of the Dunes Cromwell lay dead. Little less influential upon the affairs of Western Europe was the recovery from the jaws of death of a neighbouring potentate. For ten days in July the young King of France had lain in a most critical condition; and, when his health and strength were completely restored, the Queen-Mother told Mazarin that she felt it to be a matter of conscience to show her thankfulness by putting a stop to the effusion of Christian blood and making peace with her brother, the King of Spain.

CHAPTER XX.

'Tis less to conquer, than to make wars cease,
And, without fighting, awe the world to peace.—HALIFAX.

IT appeared, at the end of the last chapter, that
Turenne's victories had made the King of Spain desire
peace with France, and Mazarin, again, on his part,
had his own reasons for desiring peace with Spain.
He still cherished his project of a marriage between
the young King of France and Maria Theresa, the
Infanta of Spain, and he thought that Spain's present
embarrassments offered a peculiarly favourable opportunity of accomplishing it.

To France the year 1659 was one not of warfare
but of diplomacy. After negotiations, which lasted
during many months, the Peace of the Pyrenees—so
called because the conferences between the representatives of France and Spain were held near that
boundary between the two kingdoms—was concluded
in November, after a war which had lasted twenty-four
years. By this agreement France retained many of the
places she had conquered, such as Philippsburg, Montmédy, Arras, Lens, Gravelines, Landreçies, and all the
fortresses in Artois, as well as some on the frontiers of
Spain.

At about the same time a marriage contract was made between Louis XIV. and the Infanta, Maria Theresa, with the agreement that she was to renounce her rights to the Crown of Spain. Condé was forgiven and his honours and estates were to be restored to him; but he was to be Governor of Burgundy instead of Guienne. The Duke of Lorraine was to retain his duchy, but his capital was no longer to be fortified; and, in order to put him out of the temptation of placing his military services and those of his troops at the disposal of the highest bidder, he was to have no troops at all for the future. As will be seen later, however, he contrived to raise some.

The choice of a spot among the Pyrenees for negotiating the peace, and the marriage with the Infanta, brought both diplomatists and the Court from Paris to those mountains. In these days of admiration for mountain scenery, it is interesting to observe how differently it was regarded in the seventeenth century. Madame de Motteville writes of the "frightful mountains" which she saw on this occasion. "I was amazed," she says, "to find that the agreeable and the horrible made an admirable blending of the different beauties of nature. From space to space among these high and monstrous mountains are very beautiful valleys". Of Lourdes, a place now celebrated for such different reasons, she says: "It appears to have been placed on the French side to defend the entrance and the exit against the Spaniards, in case they had the audacity to attempt to enter France on that side".

After the peace had been finally settled, Turenne spent much time in seeing to the defence of the fortresses. He had also the difficult task thrown upon him of the reduction of the army, which he carried out with every possible consideration for his officers and his men. He also arranged for the reception of the troops of Condé into the army of the King.

In the spring of 1660 Louis XIV. was married to Maria Theresa. At the dinner which followed, the King of Spain asked the Queen-Dowager of France if Turenne was present; and, when she had pointed him out, the King said in a low voice: "That man has given me many bad nights".[1]

Louis XIV. was anxious to make Turenne Constable of France, the highest dignity in the gift of the Crown, and he deputed Mazarin to inform him that it would be offered to him, but that it was a post which could only be held by a Catholic. On hearing of this condition, Turenne, gratefully and respectfully, but very firmly, declined it. The King then made him " Marshal General of his Majesty's Camps and Armies " and Governor of Limousin.

" It appears by several letters to the King of Great Britain and the Duke of York," that Turenne "was in close correspondence," after the death of Oliver Cromwell, "with the Royalists in England, and that he contributed more than any other stranger to the

---

[1] On the other hand, De Retz declares that he never slept so soundly as he did in misfortune; and, curiously enough, St. Evremond makes a similar statement about their contemporary, Mademoiselle de Beverweert.

happy restoration of Charles II."[1]   Probably his personal friendship with the Duke of York may have influenced Turenne in this direction.   He not only corresponded with General Monk, but sent a special envoy to England to confer with him.   Having obtained the consent of Louis XIV. he proposed, "at his own expense to assist the King of England in ascending the throne of his ancestors: he requested the Duke of York to come to Amiens and offered him his regiment of foot, consisting of 1,200 effective men, together with the Scots gendarmes, ammunition and arms for 4,000 or 5,000 men; provisions to subsist them two months; ships to transport them into England; passports to embark at Boulogne the troops the Duke had in Flanders, and lastly all his credit for borrowing the necessary sums.   The Duke of York having joyfully accepted these offers, Turenne sent him a letter for the King's Lieutenant at Boulogne, who promised to furnish all the vessels belonging to the ports of his government even to his fishing smacks." And the Duke of York, in his own *Memoirs*, says that, besides all this, Turenne insisted upon his accepting a personal present of 300 pistoles, or about £240 sterling.   The Restoration of King Charles II., however, was effected without any necessity for foreign intervention or assistance.

Peace had not long been made between France and Spain, before Turenne, who "was ever fond of procuring succour for distressed Princes," advised

[1] Ramsay,

Louis XIV. to assist Alfonso, King of Portugal, in
his war with the King of Spain. Richelieu had
always supported and encouraged Portugal, in order
that it might reduce the power of Spain by proving a
constant thorn in her side, just as he had supported
and encouraged Scotland, for the purpose of serving
as a thorn in the side of England ; and Mazarin, in his
wars with Spain, had practically supported Portugal
by giving the armies of Spain more than enough to
occupy their attention in Flanders, as well as on the
northern frontier of Spain itself. But, now that peace
had been made between Spain and France, Spain was
able to concentrate its army for the destruction of
Portugal. Louis XIV., without nominally breaking
his treaty of peace with Spain, agreed to send money
and a general to the assistance of Portugal against her
powerful neighbour. Turenne proposed the Count of
Schomberg as a general for this purpose, for being a
German by birth, although he had served in the
French army, his appointment was likely to give less
offence to Spain than that of a Frenchman. Schomberg, although already a distinguished general, was
somewhat out of favour at Court, not on account of
any demerits of his own, but because his wife and the
Queen-Dowager had quarrelled about a chemise.

Meanwhile, Charles II. of England arranged a
marriage between himself and the Infanta of Portugal ;
and another match was made between Henrietta, the
sister of Charles II., and Philip, the new Duke of
Orleans ; for Gaston was dead. Charles II. had no

18

money to give as a dowry to his sister; but Louis was clever enough to offer to buy Dunkirk from Charles, thus providing him with funds for his sister's dowry and a large balance in hand. To this bargain Charles agreed. In the course of his life Louis XIV. showed many kindnesses to the Stuarts; but he never lost sight of his own interests in so doing; and he once observed that he felt the natural antipathy towards the English, which was said always to have existed between England and France.

The period during which these events took place was essentially a period of intrigues, and while they were yet in progress the arch-intriguer of Europe showed unmistakable symptoms of being about to intrigue no more. As a result, intrigues were doubled! Never, says Voltaire, was there more intriguing in any Court than during the fatal illness of Cardinal Mazarin. Every beautiful lady at the Court flattered herself that she would become a sort of governess to a prince of only twenty-two, who had already nearly sunk so low as to offer his crown to his mistress; all the young courtiers expected that the reign of Louis XIV. would now become a reign of favourites; each Minister of the Crown hoped to take the place of Mazarin; and nobody believed that a King, brought up without any knowledge or cares of business, would either care or dare to take upon his own shoulders the burden of the Government of his country.[1] They were all mistaken!

Cardinal Mazarin died in 1661. "He showed no

[1] *Siècle de Louis XIV.* (ed. 1835), vol., i., p. 112.

LOUIS XIV.

fear of death," said Montglat, "but an incomprehensible attachment to money to his last breath."[1]   "Whenever," says Madame de Motteville, who hated him, "he had moments of reprieve, he was often seen to be busy weighing the pistoles which he won at cards, in order to stake the lightest of them on the morrow." But there is rebutting evidence.   It is said that he exclaimed : " I feel my end approaching ; I pray God to be merciful to me," and that he asked forgiveness of all whom he might have offended.   His last words are reported to have been, "My hope is in Jesus Christ". If this be true, his end was very different from the deathbed scene of Richelieu, who, when the viaticum was brought to him, has the reputation of having said : " Behold the judge, who will soon pronounce my sentence.   I supplicate him to condemn me, if during my ministry I have had any other object than the good of my country, the service of my sovereign, the glory of God, and the advancement of religion."   The confidence of the dying Richelieu, said the Bishop of Lisieux, who was present, "filled me with terror".[2] Louis XIV., who had already begun to grow tired of being governed by Mazarin, from the time of his death took the reins of government entirely into his own hands.   This he did at the advice of Mazarin himself, who, when he felt that he was dying, warned the King against the great dangers of ever raising a minister

---

[1] *Memoirs of Madame de Motteville*, vol. iii., p. 226.
[2] *Lives of Cardinals Richelieu and Mazarin* (1854), pp. 52 and 113.

again to the height of power which he, Mazarin, had enjoyed.

The King occasionally employed Turenne on diplomatic errands, for which he may have been less fitted than for war. One of these, if not directly dictated by the King, yet at his instigation, was to persuade Mademoiselle de Montpensier to consent to a marriage with the young King of Portugal. We have her own account of it. After telling her that he had always loved her as a daughter and expressing a hope that she would yield to his advice in the most important affairs in life, Turenne informed her that he was anxious to make her Queen of Portugal. Her reply was discouraging: "Get away with you! I will have nothing to do with your Queen of Portugal."

Turenne then said that young ladies of her rank ought to have no will independent of that of the King; and that although the King himself had not directly ordered Turenne to speak to her on the subject, he knew that the King desired the match. The King of Portugal was the kind of youth who could be easily moulded by a wife of strong character like Mademoiselle, who could amuse herself with his great wealth and control him as she pleased.

When he came to describe the proposed bridegroom, he was in an almost ridiculous difficulty; but he did what he could under the circumstances. The King of Portugal, said he, "was tolerably good-looking, fair, and would have been well-made, but that he was born with a paralysis of one side, which made it a little weaker

than the other, yet this was not observable when he
was dressed; he merely drew one leg a little after him.
He could only use one of his arms; but he was beginning to get on his horse without help." His inclinations were neither good nor bad; but, as he was of a
submissive temperament, he would be quite safe in the
hands of so virtuous a mistress as Mademoiselle.

"No," replied she.   "I prefer to be Mademoiselle in France, with 500,000 livres a year, to do
honour to the Court, and to be held in as high consideration for character as for rank."

Turenne then reminded his cousin—for she was a
relation of his—that, high as was her position, she was
still a subject of the King, who was not scrupulous with
those who opposed his wishes, nor hesitated to annoy
them in a thousand ways.

"If the King were to say this to me," answered
Mademoiselle, "I should know how to answer him.
But you are not the King!"

Perceiving that her royal highness was in a passion,
Turenne dropped the subject; but he returned to it a
few days later, and to as little purpose.

The death of Philip IV. of Spain took place in
1665, and, in the same year, England declared war
against Holland.   France intended to join the Dutch
against the English; but the war turned out to be
entirely naval, and the French fleet was unable to join
that of the Dutch before the latter had met with a
defeat from the English, under the Duke of York, off
Lowestoft.

Although Turenne had spent much of his married life on campaigns, he was devoted to his wife, and her death in 1666 caused him great grief. He had indeed been able to be with her more during the last few years of her life than at any other period since his marriage. Some of his letters to her, which are in print, are full of affection; but they are not devoid of candid advice: "Call to mind a little my lessons," he says in one of them. "Avoid dejection of mind: it is the most dangerous of all diseases. . . . I am more hard upon those I love than upon others; but though I take upon me to reprimand, I am not the less sensible of my own faults." On another occasion he seems to have thought that his wife was too severe in her treatment of some girl. "You . . . who exclaim so much how hard it is to win upon a young woman, do you take the proper methods? Let me tell you that roughness and severity beget aversion in young people. . . . Before I turn over, I shall own that what I have just said seems expressed with a little too much dryness: I ask your pardon."

Sometimes the reprimand appears to have come from exactly the opposite quarter; for, in one letter, Turenne writes: "I was some time before I could understand what you meant by a stroke you aim at me; I don't deserve it, and in such affection as ours, little twittings are always out of season. . . . I know very well, that loving me as you do, you will be extremely concerned to find me having so quick a feeling for your reproaches. . . . I impart my thoughts to you ingenu-

ously and they displease you: to confess the truth, I
don't look upon the trouble you are in with the same
eye as if I had found you candid enough to acknowledge certain truths, which seem to me as clear as
day." Towards the end of his letter he becomes more
submissive to the matronly correction. "Notwithstanding anything I have said, I shall not slight your
remonstrances; and I beg you to believe that I am not
insensible how much you love me; it affects me very
much. . . . I was going once to tear up this letter, but
the conclusion will assure you anew of my entire affection."

Almost at the same time as the Viscountess of
Turenne, died also the Queen-Dowager, Anne of
Austria, after a long, tedious and exceedingly painful
illness, which she bore with very remarkable fortitude,
patience and resignation.

On the death of Philip IV. of Spain, the weakly
boy, Charles II., Philip's son by his second marriage,
became King. Although the Queen of France, as Infanta of Spain, had renounced any future right to the
crown of her native country, Louis XIV. claimed that
the Spanish possessions in the Low Countries fell to
her, on the death of her father, by the right of devolu-
tion, according to the laws of the Low Countries, which
ordained that they should go to the issue, whether male
or female, of the first marriage, before that of the
second; and the Queen of France, Maria Theresa, was
the only remaining child of Philip's first marriage.
According to Ramsay, Turenne was the first person

to call the attention of Louis to this right, or, at any
rate, asserted right, of his Queen.

Louis tried to come to some compromise about the
matter with the Queen-Regent of Spain; but, when
she had refused to recognise that the Queen of France
had the shadow of a right to the Low Countries, Louis
made up his mind to take by force what he had failed
to obtain by diplomacy, and he said in confidence to
Turenne: "I will march in person at the head of my
army, but I will learn the art of war under you". Louis,
who was now twenty-nine, was as good as his word.
Having sent Turenne to the war with 25,000 infantry
and 10,000 cavalry, he left St. Germains, on the 16th
of May, 1667, taking with him, as a fellow-pupil, his
recently appointed Minister-of-War, the Marquis of
Louvois. Turenne and Louvois between them, but at
Turenne's initiative, had arranged a new system of
furnishing an army on campaign with supplies, which
the weakness of the Government had hitherto rendered
impossible.

The Low Countries were utterly unprepared for
war. Turenne had already taken Armentières and
Binche, before the arrival of Louis; after that arrival,
Douay, Oudenarde and several other places were taken
without a blow. When they came to Lille it was a
different matter. The governor was an officer of great
experience; it was well fortified, well provisioned, and,
although its garrison of regular troops only numbered
4,200, it contained 20,000 men capable of carrying arms.
The Marquis of Louvois tried to persuade the King

not to attack it; but Turenne was inflexible; and it was well that he was so, for the siege was a great success and the fortress capitulated in seventeen days. The siege works were conducted by Vauban, then a young engineer. His system was quite new to the besieged, who were taken by surprise, confused and bewildered. The King accompanied Turenne when he visited the trenches during the siege, and took an eager, intelligent and active interest in their progress.

The Count of Marsin and the Prince of Lignes, not knowing that Lille had fallen, advanced with 8,000 men to its relief. When they learned that it had capitulated, they retired, but the army of Turenne fell upon their rear, routed them, and took 1,500 prisoners. As the King was present at this engagement it counted as his victory.

The Dutch became alarmed at the successes of their ally; for they by no means desired to have France as a next neighbour, and they began secretly to give assistance to their old enemies the Spaniards. England was as uneasy as was Holland at the advances of the French, and Sir William Temple was sent across the Channel to form a triple alliance between Holland, England and Sweden, for the purpose of obliging France and Spain to make peace. The first three months of the year 1668 were spent in negotiations, military demonstrations, and threatened coalitions. On the 15th of April peace was made at Aix-la-Chapelle. France gave up Franche-Comté, but kept her conquests in the Low Countries, known afterwards as French Flanders; and this treaty had been immediately pre-

ceded by one between Lisbon and Madrid, by which
Spain acknowledged the independence of Portugal.

Four years of peace were to follow; but not of
idleness for France in military matters. Louis XIV.
surrounded his seaports with forts, levelled unnecessary
inland fortresses, and greatly strengthened such as
were of importance. This was a very busy period for
Vauban. People who did not understand his system
were astounded at seeing high walls and towering
battlements disappear, and give place to earthworks,
almost level with the ground. Louis directed that the
fortifications of the important places on the frontier of
French Flanders should be carried forward before any
others, as he was bitterly annoyed with the Dutch for
having made the triple alliance which enforced the
peace, just as he was getting Spain into his power,
also for .representing themselves, on a medal, as the
preservers of the peace of Europe; and he determined
to punish, if not to annihilate, Holland. Though
strong at sea she was weak on land, and Louis had
every hope of success; but he was not going to strike
until certain of victory. Meanwhile, he was doing
something besides improving fortresses. He was endeavouring to prove superior to the United Provinces
by sea as well as by land. His navy occupied much
of his thoughts and increased very rapidly. Altogether,
under the veil of a profound peace, he was eagerly and
energetically preparing for war.

CHAPTER XXI.

MOST of the extant records of the experiences of
Turenne relate to his public career; but, in all bio-
graphical sketches, the private life of their subjects
should not be allowed to pass altogether unnoticed.

We have now to consider a personal matter in the
life of Turenne, which has nothing to do with warfare.
The staunchness of his Calvinism has already been
noticed. It has also been observed that he refused two
splendid marriages rather than take a wife of a religion
different from his own; and, in the last chapter, we
observed that, when the King offered to revive for his
acceptance the office of Constable of France, the
highest in the power of the Crown to grant, but one
which had to be held by a Catholic, Turenne respectfully declined it, on the ground that he could not
change his religion, for even the highest honours of the
world.

But so long ago as two years before that offer was
made to him, he had begun to take a more charitable
view of the Catholic religion. Writing to his wife, from
Ypres, when on a campaign already described, he said,
in 1658: "We had a communion here last Sunday.
M. Brevin made an excellent sermon; one ought to
grow better for such discourses; that is the great point:

but it is very hard to become good; and when I examine myself thoroughly, I find methinks but little amendment. In discoursing on these words: *Go out of Babylon*, he let me understand that he should not have made such post-haste as our Reformers. He has a great deal of knowledge and no bitterness of spirit: he agreed with me that the people of the two religions are not on either side fairly and honestly instructed in the tenets of the other, and that each party represents the religion of the other in such a manner only as may beget an aversion to it; just as in a town where there are two cabals, you never meet with sincerity or candour on either side."

Turenne had probably been considerably influenced by Beaulieu, a Calvinist who held a Professorship of Divinity, founded by Turenne, at Sedan. This Calvinist, says Bayle (*Dic.*, vol. i., p. 705), made "it appear that many disputes, which are thought to be real, are only disputes about words. It is scarce credible how much this method prejudiced a great many ignorant persons against him. They imagined that he endeavoured to bring back the Reformed to the Communion of the Church of Rome." It must be remembered that Bayle wrote from a very anti-catholic standpoint. On the same page Des Maizeaux says, in his Notes, that Turenne was "very fond of re-uniting both religions," or rather of wishing to unite them. In conversation, also, he advanced the view of M. Brevin that "he should not have made such post-haste as our Reformers".

St. Evremond says, in his *Eulogium on M. de Turenne:* "He ever loved to talk of religion, particularly with M. d'Aubigni, and used to say that the doctrine of the Reformed was the soundest, yet they ought not to have made a separation, but to have insensibly distilled their principles into the Catholics". "When a man confesses that he is in the wrong to separate from a Church," answered M. d'Aubigni, "he is in a fair way of returning to it; and if I survive Madame de Turenne, I shall see you in ours." M. de Turenne smiled, says St. Evremond, "but that smile did not sufficiently discover whether he meant to laugh at M. d'Aubigni's prediction or to approve of it".

But was Aubigni fair in hinting that Turenne was afraid of his wife? In 1660 Turenne wrote to her from Amiens: "Let us but lay aside prejudice, and we shall often find in those long declamations that are made against Catholics, a spirit of strife and wrangling, and that some people are so intent upon reforming, that they quite forget charity". In the same letter he says: "I had sent a Gentleman, who speaks English very well, to Monck,[1] to learn his intentions upon his arrival at London. . . . This Gentleman examined the state of religion in England. . . . One sees by this and by the multitude of sects in England"—what would he have said, if he could have known what their number would be now?—"that through a too presumptuous spirit of independency, though there may be good sense and perhaps devotion among them, they have so

[1] The famous English general.

much disfigured religion, that each private man is for setting up a new sect of his particular fashion, and that whoever reads the word of God, and will explain it after his own fancy, goes greater lengths in folly than is easily imagined."

Four months later, in the same year, he wrote to her : " I read this morning a book, which I found at M. Duplessis's, Secretary of State. It is a collection, in French, made at the Port Royal, of what the Fathers of the first centuries have said concerning the Eucharist. The passages are there entire, with the context before and after them, and nothing of the author's own. If the quotations are not fairly made, it is easy to show it ; but I assure you that these passages do not square with what we say.   I believe it is what I write to you from time to time on this head, which draws upon me those reproaches you make me : but nothing can lessen my affection for you."   From this it would appear that Turenne was not afraid of speaking his mind very freely to his wife on the subject of religion ; so M. d'Aubigni need not have insinuated that Turenne wanted to become a Catholic, but was afraid of doing so during his wife's lifetime.   On the contrary, Madame de Turenne herself seems to have been anxious to learn more about the Catholic Church ; for Ramsay says: "This year (1665) died the Viscountess de Turenne, whose virtues cannot be enough admired. Though she had several conferences with the Doctors of the Catholic Church, yet she continued under the prejudices of her education as long as she lived."

Ramsay hints at Turenne's anxiety that, if he made any movement towards the Catholic Church, his wife should go with him, and it may be that, when she seemed to be outpaced, he sometimes paused in his inquiries to give her time to overtake him. But so far indeed was he from merely waiting for his wife's death to become a Catholic, that it was not until two years after her death that he took that step.

"The calm which Europe enjoyed after the peace of Aix-la-Chapelle, allowed the Viscount a great deal of leisure: he employed it wholly in the study of religion, which he had long reproached himself for not having thoroughly examined. From the time of the Peace of the Pyrenees, he had begun to have doubts about Calvinism. The accounts he had frequently from the English, during his intercourse with them, of the multitude of sects that overspread Great Britain, had struck him exceedingly."[1]

When he had become disposed to inquire into the claims of the Catholic Church, he consulted the celebrated preacher, Bossuet, afterwards Bishop of Meaux, with whom he had many conversations. Du Buisson, in his *Vie de Turenne*, published in 1695, says that one of the Fathers of the French Oratory had more to do than any one else with Turenne's preparation for reception into the Church, and that it was conducted as secretly as possible, because Turenne had a great dislike to any fuss being made about himself.

Ramsay says of Turenne that "so long as he

[1] Ramsay.

was not convinced, no human views, no motives of ambition, no temporal interest could prevail with him to change his religion; but, as soon as he saw the truth, he yielded to it, sacrificing his reputation to the unjust suspicions of those who accused him of acting from political views, unworthy of a great soul". If he had become a Catholic some time earlier, no doubt it would have materially assisted his career; but at, and from, the date at which he did so, it in no way influenced his worldly prospects. Of course that entertaining and cynical old sceptic, Voltaire, attributes his change of religion to political motives, on much the same principle that led Bismarck to say when a certain diplomatist was prevented by serious illness from keeping an appointment, "I should very much like to know what his object is in being ill at this particular time". Yet even Voltaire says of Turenne: "It is also possible that his conversion was sincere".[1] A great admission from such a writer!

When, at the age of fifty-seven, he had completely made up his mind to become a Catholic, Turenne decided to make his abjuration before the Archbishop of Paris; but, fearing that, if the day and hour were to be known, the cathedral would be crowded, he did not make his appointment with the archbishop until the evening before it took place.

It will be remembered that Turenne's brother, the Duke of Bouillon, became a Catholic long before his death, and one of the Duke's sons had been made a

[1] *Siècle de Louis XIV.*, vol. i., pp. 186, 187.

cardinal by the time of Turenne's conversion. Possibly conversations with his nephew may have supplemented those with Bossuet and the fathers of the oratory in convincing Turenne of the claims of the Church.

Besides Turenne, several characters figuring in our story, characters formerly anything but saintlike, became what is called in their own language *dévotés*— Cardinal de Retz, Prince de Conti, "the beauty of whose repentance," says Madame de Motteville, "far surpassed the hideousness of his faults," that very political Magdalen, Madame de Longueville, who devoted her later years entirely to religion, and, to some extent, the Great Condé, of whom Bossuet said that, in his last illness, he had "the Psalms always on his lips, and faith always in his heart ".

St. Evremond said of Turenne that, both as a Calvinist and as a Catholic, he "aimed at what was right and good. While a Huguenot, he had no schemes contrary to the interests of the Catholics; when converted, he had no zeal prejudicial to the safety of the Huguenots." Of his excellence, Madame de Sévigné wrote, in a letter to M. de Grignan: "No one believes that sin and evil could have any place in his heart: his conversion was so sincere . . . everybody speaks of the innocence of his manners, the purity of his intentions, his humility far removed from all kind of affectation, his love of virtue for itself, without respect to the approbation of men, and his generous and Christian charity".

There can be little doubt that, in the seventeenth

19

century, some Frenchmen left the Huguenots to become Catholics for the purpose of advancing their prospects of obtaining office or other privileges from the King or the Government. The Bishop of Nismes contrasted Turenne with such as these: "How sincere was his conversion, Gentlemen, and how different from that of those who, forsaking heresy from interested views, change their opinions without changing their manners, who enter into the bosom of the Church only to wound her the deeper by a scandalous life, and from being declared enemies, become rebellious children. Though his mind had escaped the depravation commonly occasioned by the passions, yet he was still the more careful to regulate it; he thought that the innocence of his life ought to be conformable to the purity of his faith: he knew truth, he loved it, he followed it." Shortly after becoming a Catholic, he made a vow never again to commit a certain sin of which hitherto he had not been guiltless. Sometime afterwards, some one who was cognisant of his vow asked him if he had kept it. Turenne replied: "I have never broken my word to man: could you think that I would break it to God?"

After his change of religion he lived a very quiet life in Paris, only associating with a small circle of chosen friends, and he rarely went to Court, except to pay his respects to the King. To his intimate friends his frugal table was always open. "He loved to be gay at meals: he then liked pleasantry, being himself facetious but still with prudence and politeness: few

MARSHAL TURENNE.

people knew more stories or could tell them better."[1]
Several anecdotes are told about his imperturbable good-
temper and his stolid coolness under provocation, during
this period of tranquil life.   In a block in the streets
of Paris a young gentleman, who did not know
Turenne by sight, struck his coachman.   Some one
loudly asked him what he meant by treating a servant
of Marshal Turenne in such a manner.   He immediately went to the door of the carriage to apologise:
"You seem thoroughly to understand the correction
of servants, Sir," said Turenne, smiling.   "Allow me
to send mine to you when they are in need of it."

He often walked alone to hear mass and then took
a turn on the ramparts.   Once he passed two trades-
men, playing at bowls, and, without knowing who he
was, they asked him to decide a disputed game.   He
measured with his cane and gave his opinion, when
the loser began to abuse him in the most violent
terms.   Turenne quietly measured the distances a
second time; and, while he was doing so, some officers
came up and saluted him.   When the man who had
abused him ascertained who he was, he fell on his
knees and begged his pardon.   All Turenne said was:
"My friend, you need not have been afraid that I
should cheat you".

In a theatre, he was sitting alone, on the front seat,
when several strangers from the country swaggered in
and rather rudely asked him to make way for them.
This he refused to do, whereupon one of them had the

[1] Ramsay, ii., p. 357.

19 *

impudence to take up Turenne's hat and gloves, and throw them on to the stage. Turenne said nothing; but he asked a well-known young nobleman, who was standing near, to fetch them for him. Seeing that Turenne must be some one of importance, the strangers asked who he was, and were hastily retiring in great confusion, when Turenne called them back and told them that, if they would only sit close together, there was plenty of room for all of them.

Driving home late one night, his carriage was stopped by highwaymen. The robbers took everything of value that they could find on him, including a ring, which he highly prized quite apart from its intrinsic worth. He promised the men that, if he might keep the ring, he would give them 100 Louis-d'ors, a sum far beyond its value, the next day. They returned the ring to him, and, on the following afternoon, one of them was bold enough to go to his house and, although it so happened that a number of people were visiting him, the man whispered his claim to Turenne, who ordered 100 Louis-d'ors to be paid to him, and, when the robber had had ample time to get clear away, he told the story of his adventure to his friends, saying: "A promise ought to be kept inviolably, and an honest man should never break his word, even when it has been given to knaves".

Of this period of Turenne's life—the quietest period —the Abbot Flechier said: "When he returned from those glorious campaigns that will make his name immortal, he shunned the acclamations of the people,

blushed at his victories, came to hear himself applauded
as one comes to make an apology, and was almost
afraid to approach the King, because he was obliged,
out of respect to him, to suffer patiently the praises
with which his Majesty never failed to honour him.
It was then that, in the sweet repose of a private
condition, this Prince divested himself of all the glory
which he had acquired during the war, and confined
himself to the conversation of a few chosen friends,
exercised himself without noise in civil virtues, and
being sincere in word, plain and simple in action,
faithful in friendship, and great even in the smallest
things, he concealed himself; but his reputation discovered him; he went without a train and without
equipage; but everybody in thought sot him upon a
triumphal car.   People when they saw him, counted
the number of enemies he had conquered, not of
servants that followed him. . . . There is a nobleness
in that simplicity.   The less he was proud, the more
he commanded respect."   With all his humility and
love of retirement, Turenne, as will presently be seen,
was not long to be allowed to enjoy "the sweet repose
of a private condition".

Besides Turenne, another great warrior was proving, as a contemporary writer describes him, "as grand
in his humility and gentleness as he had been in his
victories".   It seemed as if Condé could not do enough
to show his loyalty.   After the King and the Duke of
Orleans, he was the greatest prince in France; but he
now took delight in servile, if highly honourable, duties.

The King, the two queens and the Duchess of Orleans used often to take a collation on their splendid gilded boat, shaped like a galley, on the canal. On such occasions Condé, in his office of grand-master, used to wait upon them and serve them with so much respect that it was difficult to remember that he had lately been a rebel. As to that earliest of all the Frondeurs, Beaufort, he was ever following the King and unwearying in his efforts to please him.

The years which followed the Peace of the Pyrenees provided a period of prosperity to France, buildings and public works made great progress, the arts flourished, and, as has already been observed, while the kingdom was embellished, its fortifications were strengthened ; its army was increased, and its navy enlarged. But meanwhile a neighbouring country had risen in proportion to its size even more rapidly than France. The States-General were now at the very summit of their glory and their greatness.

Louis XIV. had not forgotten that their minute country had practically obliged him to make peace with Spain against his will, nor had he forgiven it for so doing. The Dutch, on the other hand, were still boasting of having been the peacemakers of Europe, and of having compelled the most powerful kingdoms in the world to lay down their arms. They were yet prouder of being the rulers of the seas, and of having sailed up the river Thames and burned the English battle-ships. Their trade was enormous, and their colonies dwarfed those of France. But large

as were their colonies, important as was their commerce, and powerful as was their navy, their army
was insignificant, and Louis hoped to annihilate it.
To do this it was necessary to break up the triple
alliance.

In 1670 his first step in this direction was to make
a secret treaty with England, and for this purpose he
employed Turenne.   Owing to the services which he
had rendered to the House of Stuart, both before and
after the death of Cromwell, Turenne enjoyed the
intimacy of King Charles's sister, the young Duchess
of Orleans.   In making her his friend, the veteran and
staid Turenne now found himself associated much against
his will with the gayest and most frivolous party in the
Court, a party, moreover, strongly disliked both by the
Queen and the Queen-Mother.   Madame, as she was
called, being the wife of the King's brother, remembered, says Madame de Motteville, "with a certain
noble vexation, that the King had formerly disdained
her when she might have expected him to marry her ;
and the pleasure bestowed by vengeance made her
welcome joyfully the contrary sentiments which appeared to be rising in the King's soul towards her.
. . . The daily pleasures, the repasts, the excursions
into the woods lasting till two or three o'clock in the
morning, began to be practised in a manner that had
more than a gallant air, and as if the best of pleasure
would presently corrupt a virtue which had been, with
good reason, all the more admired, because it was
a rare possession at the King's age.   But the sight

alarmed the Queen, who was distressed to find the King so occupied with other objects."

Whatever may have been the King's personal feeling towards Henrietta, Duchess of Orleans, he was anxious to make her useful for political purposes, and he made Turenne visit her every day, and instructed him to spare no pains in enlisting her services as an intermediary with her brother, the King of England. As everybody knows, she eventually did so and the secret treaty was accomplished; but, in the course of the process, there occurred a rather unfortunate incident, or rather an incident which might have proved unfortunate.

The favourite lady-in-waiting of the Duchess of Orleans was a young Marchioness who was even more remarkable for her intelligence than for her beauty, which was very great. Great also was her influence over the Duchess, and Turenne determined to obtain the use of that influence for the political purpose with which he had been entrusted by the King. Accordingly he began to show her a fatherly friendship.

But even increasing years—Turenne was in his sixtieth year—are not an infallible defence against the charms of a pretty woman. It so happened that, in this particular instance, the pretty woman made full use of those charms, and Turenne fell in love with her without being in the least aware of it. One result of this was that he believed he could place the most implicit confidence in her fidelity and secrecy. In the course of his diplomatic endeavours to obtain her influence over the Duchess of Orleans, he incautiously confided to her a secret known only to himself, to the King and to Louvois. The pretty Marchioness could not resist the pleasure of telling it to Lorraine; Lorraine told it to the Duke of Orleans, and the Duke of Orleans informed his brother, the King, that he knew all about it, and complained at not having been taken into confidence on the subject by the King himself. As the King had confided his secret to nobody except Louvois and Turenne, and felt absolutely certain of the trustworthiness of the latter, he sent for Turenne and told him that Louvois had betrayed his trust. Now Turenne disliked Louvois, but he at once declared him to be innocent of all blame in the matter, and confessed his own weakness in having entrusted a State secret to a woman. His candour delighted the King, whose confidence in him was increased, instead of diminishing by this untoward incident.

Turenne would have nothing more to do with the beautiful Marchioness. He studiously kept out of her way, and to the end of his life he felt ashamed of an adventure in which there was nothing immoral, but by which he might have lost the favour of the King. It is said that some time afterwards Lorraine wished to talk about it to Turenne, and that Turenne said: "Then let us begin by putting out the candles".

After Henrietta, Duchess of Orleans, had crossed over to Dover and there obtained a promise from Charles II. to break off the triple alliance, she returned in triumph to Paris and then went to St. Cloud, taking with her Turenne, the Duke of Rochefoucauld, and other friends. In a few days she died very suddenly, and no one in France was more grieved at her death than Turenne.

The year 1671 was spent in negotiations. Sweden, like England, was divorced from the triple alliance with Holland; the neutrality of all the German States and all the Electors, as well as that of the Emperor, was secured, with the exception of the Grand Elector of Brandenburg; but Spain sent 6,000 men to the assistance of the United Provinces. "Thus was the face of Europe entirely changed : France and England, who had contributed to the raising and aggrandising the Republic, were now endeavouring to ruin her : Spain, on the contrary, who had been for an age attempting to destroy the Dutch as revolted subjects, was now their chief support."[1] It will have been by this time observed that, in the seventeenth century, there were very few allies who had not been formerly enemies, or enemies who had not been at one time allies.

The Dutch suffered under the disadvantage of being divided into two factions. One of them desired a Republic, and at the head of this faction were John de Witt and his brother Cornelius, who desired the friendship of France, being well aware that Louis XIV. was better able to defend them against the King of England and the Elector of Brandenburg than either Spain or the Empire, both of whom were hostile, at heart, to the Dutch. The other faction wished for

[1] Ramsay.

the re-establishment of the Stadtholdership, in the person of the young Prince William of Orange, afterwards so well known as King William III. of England. Unlike the republican faction, it dreaded the power and ambition of Louis XIV., and hoped that the young prince might be able to curb them.

Both factions, however, combined to repel the invader. If the two De Witts were well-disposed towards France, they were obliged for the moment to oppose her when she approached, as an enemy, to invade their fatherland. They and William of Orange, with other Dutchmen, formed the staff to arrange the plan of the approaching campaign; in which the Prince of Orange, although only twenty-two, was to be commander-in-chief.

The King of France intended to divide his forces. Both Turenne and Condé were to have leading commands, thus once more fighting under the same flag, although not side by side, or even near each other. Commands were also to be assigned to the Marshals d'Humières, Bellefonds and Créqui, and, as they were likely to be within reach of Turenne, the King, to prevent any dispute on account of rank or precedence, in the case of their forces joining, ordered that, if this happened, Turenne was to be in command of either, or all, of those three marshals. On hearing of this, all three at once refused to serve under Turenne, an act of insubordination which the King punished with banishment. In six months he permitted them to return to France; but never to his service.

That considerable jealousy of a general so successful as Turenne is likely to have existed is sufficiently obvious; but on what grounds any questions could arise concerning obedience to a commander-in-chief appointed by the King is not so clear. That some such questions were mooted, and that they led to remonstrances to the King, is shown by the following memorial of four marshals :—

"Some of the Marshals of France having consulted us in order to know our sentiments with regard to the obedience we ought to pay to the absolute command we have received from the King to take the word from the Viscount de Turenne, Marshal of France, we say and declare, that after the most humble remonstrances which have been made to his Majesty, he persisting in his will, the Marshals ought to submit to that order, there being no reason that can or ought to hinder us from obeying his Majesty's absolute commands. This is our opinion, and as we say and declare, so we most willingly sign it. Grammont, Plessis Praslin, Villeroy, D'Albert."

CHAPTER XXII.

On several occasions we have seen Turenne commanding an army very inferior in numbers to that of his enemy. We shall now find the relative positions completely and largely reversed.

In the campaign against Holland in 1672 the numerical advantage of France was enormous. Louis XIV. had an army of 100,000 men, to which the Elector of Cologne and the Bishop of Münster added 30,000. To oppose the advance of this great army, the Prince of Orange had an active army of 25,000, the Spaniards had 6,000, and there was a garrison of 12,000 at Maestricht. The Grand Elector of Brandenburg, while nominally supporting Holland, did nothing during the first months of the war to help her, although he had a large army at, or near, Berlin. At most the defending force was much less than half the size of the invading force.

Vauban was to engineer the sieges; Louvois, the Minister of War, was to accompany the King on the campaign; 30,000 men were placed under Condé, and the very large army that remained was put under the command of Turenne.

Besides the improvements in the art of fortifications

since the earlier campaigns of Turenne, there were now several important developments in warfare. There was a great increase in the proportion of infantry to cavalry. Even in the campaign of 1667 half the army had consisted of cavalry. Now three-quarters of the troops were infantry, among which there were far more musketeers and fewer pikemen. Instead of the old invariably solid bodies of pikemen—when Turenne joined his first regiment the pikemen were ten ranks deep—with a few musketeers on either side of them and running behind them to reload. Napoleon says, even of the campaign of 1667, that the infantry were drawn up in four ranks, only the fourth being armed with pikes. But in the campaign of 1672, although pikes were still retained,[1] the celebrated disciplinarian, Martinet, had been allowed to equip some regiments with bayonets, which fitted into the nozzles of the muskets. There was also an increase in artillery; there were field guns, and siege guns and mortars. Portable bridges were carried in separate parts, as it was expected that a good deal of the campaign would take place near the rivers Rhine, Meuse and Yssel. Perhaps most important of all, the transport service was reorganised, if not revolutionised; and, in the matter of stores, Louvois had secretly outbidden the enemy for large quantities of provisions, which the Dutch were trying to purchase in the Low Countries for their own use.

Against the skill of two such experienced generals as Turenne and Condé, the Dutch army was to be

---

[1] Pikes were used even in Turenne's last battle.

commanded by a youth of twenty-two, in the Prince of Orange, whose troops were very inferior in quality to those of the French. His soldiers were burghers who had rarely left their homes for military training, and most of his officers were sons of burgomasters or their relatives, without any knowledge of even the rudiments of warfare.

Condé wished to begin the campaign by taking the important fortress of Maestricht,[1] a city on the Meuse, about eighteen miles to the north of Liège, and fifteen to the west of Aix-la-Chapelle. But Turenne persuaded the King to leave it behind with 5,000 men to keep its garrison in check, as he considered that to take so strong a fortress garrisoned by 12,000 men would require a very long siege. But he rendered Maestricht more or less useless in the campaign, by taking Maeseyck, a small town about twenty miles to the north of it, which he ordered to be very strongly fortified and left with a garrison of between 4,000 and 5,000 French soldiers, by this means cutting off the communications between the fortress of Maestricht and Holland.

Turenne then induced the King, after going some distance down the Meuse, to leave that river, to march about five and twenty miles north-east to the Rhine, and take the fortresses on its banks belonging to the Elector of Brandenburg. All of these—Rhineberg,

----

[1] This fortress has been the scene of sieges in 1579, 1632, 1673, 1748 and 1830. It is still one of the strongest fortresses of Europe. A great part of the land around it can at any time be put under water, by opening the sluices.

Burich, Wesel, Rees, and a large number of minor
fortified towns—either opened their gates to the French
troops or surrendered in a few days, and Ramsay
observes that the Dutch "were not much troubled at
the taking of towns which did not belong to them and
were only under their protection".

The French troops, however, were now in Holland,
and had next to consider the army of the Prince of
Orange drawn up behind the river Yssel, a branch of
the Rhine which, instead of running like the main river
to the west until it joins the Meuse at its mouth, flows
due north into the Zuyder Zee.

The French army crossed the Rhine near where
the Yssel branches from it. The summer was exceptionally dry, and the river was abnormally low. Before
a bridge could be thrown across it some of Condé's
cavalry forded it, except for a short space through
which they had to swim. A slight opposition was
made on the opposite side by a small body of
Dutch troops, and the French lost about twenty
men. But the Dutch defence was hopeless against
such numbers, and Condé, who had crossed the river
in a boat with his son, the Duke of Enghien, and
his nephew, the young Duke of Longueville, called
out to the Dutch infantry, who were retiring, that, if
they would lay down their arms, they should have
quarter. Apparently Enghien and Longueville did
not hear this order, for, as Ramsay puts it, "warmed
by the former night's wine," they "advanced imprudently to the enemy," and Longueville, firing a pistol,

shouted: "No quarter". This drew upon them the
fire of the enemy; Longueville was killed on the spot,
and Condé's wrist was broken by a pistol bullet, this
being the only wound that he ever received in his many
campaigns. Notwithstanding his injury, he struggled
on at the head of his troops, till the enemy was
scattered; but his wound was so severe that he was
obliged to resign his command for a considerable time.

The King now put Condé's army under Turenne,
in addition to the troops already serving under him.
His opponent, the Prince of Orange, left garrisons at
some of the fortresses and retired from the Yssel, with
only 12,000 men, into the Province of Utrecht. Over-
yssel and Gelderland were soon overrun by the French
army, and Utrecht gave way a little later. Naarden,
a town on the Zuyder Zee, little more than a dozen
miles from Amsterdam, was taken. This would have
been a most important capture, if advantage had been
taken of it. Nearly all the fortified places surrendered
without any attempt to defend themselves. Napoleon
says of this: "The army took sixty fortified places in
a short time; but there is no glory in conquest where
there is no danger: these places were only garrisoned
by ill-armed militia". The single place where anything like a stand was made was Nimwegen. This
is the first fortress which we read of as having been
subjected to a bombardment by Turenne, and, according to Ramsay, "the bombs had not all the effect
which the Viscount had hoped for," an experience
which has been repeated in the case of many much

20

later generals and bombardments, even with shells
immeasurably superior to the bombs then in use. And,
although the mortars were probably placed very near
the town, "the distance was so great that the greatest
part of the bombs could not cross the river". In spite
of the difficulty experienced by the bombs in crossing
the river, Nimwegen capitulated early in July.

Napoleon criticises Turenne for his conduct of this
part of the campaign. Instead of besieging Nimwegen,
Napoleon says that he ought to have advanced upon
Amsterdam. "When masters of Utrecht and Naarden,
the French might have possessed themselves of
Amsterdam, which would have ended the war. They
knew not how to profit by occurrences. Louvois
thought proper to send back 20,000 prisoners"—these
must have been chiefly the garrisons of the surrendered
fortresses—"who were immediately armed again and
increased the army of the Prince of Orange. He had
the army dispersed in fifty fortresses, by which means
it was so much weakened that it could perform nothing.
They should have demolished forty-five of these places,
carried all the artillery belonging to them into France,
and preserved four or five to facilitate the communications of the army. Turenne enjoyed the principal
share of the King's confidence and it is to him that
these errors ought to be ascribed. It does not appear
that he opposed their commission publicly and with
energy. He might have entered Amsterdam, on the
very day that his troops entered Naarden."

Long before Napoleon, Voltaire held this opinion.

He says (*Siècle de Louis XIV.*, vol. i., p. 160):
"Naarden, in the immediate neighbourhood, had
already been taken.   Four cavalry soldiers, marauding,
went to the gates of Muiden, a place within a league of
Amsterdam, where the flood-gates are by which the
country can be inundated." (In reality it is half way
between Naarden and Amsterdam.) "The magistrates
of Muiden, distracted by terror, were going to give up
their keys to these four soldiers; but, when they saw
that no troops were advancing from Naarden, they took
back their keys and shut their gates.   The least energy
would have placed Amsterdam in the hands of the
King." Perhaps St. Evremond may have been right
when he wrote of Turenne: "He does not so well take
those unforeseen opportunities which produce an absolute victory, and this is the reason why his advantages
are not complete ".

The Dutch now betook themselves to their last and
peculiar resource to defend their capital.   They opened
their sluices, pierced their dams, broke their bridges,
and laid all their country under water.   Holland,
Brabant and Dutch Flanders became one great sea,
with the towns rising, as it were, on islands, in the
vast expanse of waters.   It was a desperate expedient:
the Dutchmen's own flocks and herds were drowned
before they could be got in; even for those that had
been got in there was not sufficient provender to last
long, and famine threatened the inhabitants.

The Prince of Orange was now elected Stadtholder
by the Provinces of Holland and West Friesland;

though not as yet by all the United Provinces. Nor were his supporters satisfied without wreaking their vengeance upon the leaders of the opposite faction. They cruelly tortured one of the De Witts in prison and they subsequently assassinated both him and his brother in a very barbarous manner. "The Prince of Orange, whose partisans had made him this horrible sacrifice," according to Ramsay, "seemed touched with the unfortunate end of the two illustrious brothers : he made the Pensioner's eulogium, though coldly enough, and he ordered the murderers to be prosecuted ; but the clemency he showed them gave cause to suspect that he had countenanced the murder. The real advantages he drew from it did not a little contribute to strengthen the suspicion. Scarce were the De Witts dead when the Magistrates of all the United Provinces declared the young Prince, as those of Holland and Friesland had declared him some days earlier, Governor, Admiral, and Captain-General : so that by this event he became master of all the deliberations of the States."

Now that the country was under water, it was impossible to take Amsterdam and thus finish the war. In this respect the campaign had been unsuccessful ; but, if the paradox be permissible, in another respect it had been too successful.

The Dutch sued for peace, and France proposed terms ; but they were too hard to be acceptable. Turenne had recommended more lenient conditions ; and, if his advice had been followed, the French frontier would have been advanced to the Rhine, and six years of war would have been saved; but Louis XIV. was overpersuaded by Louvois. When the negotiations for peace failed, the whole of Europe became alarmed at the conquests made by France and the ambitions of Louis XIV. The Emperor ordered all the members of the Empire to unite for the protection of the Germanic body; and even England began to waver. Louis XIV. returned to Paris, leaving Turenne in command of his army.

In August the Elector of Brandenburg advanced to the assistance of the Dutch with 25,000 men; and the Imperial army of 18,000 started for the same purpose, under Montecuculi and the Duke of Bournonville. They all marched towards the Rhine apparently with the object of crossing it and carrying on the war to the west of that river. Turenne, knowing that the support of those two allies of France, the Elector of Cologne and the Bishop of Münster, was essential to the honour of his King, and highly important to the protection of his country, left Holland to intercept the enemy and marched up the Rhine, until he reached its junction with the Lahn, after which he marched in an easterly direction towards the enemy. With some reinforcements which he received and the troops of Münster and Cologne, Turenne's forces were nearly equal to those about to confront him. Meanwhile Condé, who had now sufficiently recovered to take the field, was stationed in the South with 18,000 men, for the defence of Alsace.

The soldiers under Turenne, most of whom had been under arms since April and all through the long

campaign in Holland, showed great discontent at being
ordered to make long, tiring marches up the right bank
of the Rhine, in September, for what looked very
like being a winter campaign.   Napoleon says that
Turenne's march, "to support the King's allies was at
once politic and military: he was insensible to the
murmurers of his army.   The soldiers were reluctant
to commence a winter campaign in a distant country,
at a moment when they were anxiously expecting to
go into winter quarters.   His marches from the gates of
Amsterdam to those of Münster, Cologne and Trèves,
were rapid and worthy of remark."

In October began one of those series of marches
and counter-marches of which Turenne was so able a
master.   His success in them was chiefly owing to the
importance which he placed upon scouting, the large
use which he made of spies, and his encouragement of
deserters from the enemy.   "Spare neither promises,
pardon, nor recompense," he is reported to have said,
"to deserters, though accomplices in treason, if they
will discover it.   Never slight the intelligence given you.
Something may seem very improbable which nevertheless may happen.   Therefore you should watch the
event. . . .   Have in the enemy's camp some spies. . . .
You should have secret intelligence with some of the
inhabitants, officers or soldiers (of the enemy) gained
with money or fair promises, but you must take care
you are not deceived or drawn into some scrape, by
their seeming to accept your proposals; so you should
always have some hostage or security for his or their

fidelity. . . . Spies are attached to those who give them most, he who pays them ill is never served.   They should never be known to anybody; nor should they know one another.   When they propose anything very material, secure their persons, or have in your possession their wives and children as hostages for their fidelity. Never communicate anything to them, but what it is absolutely necessary that they should know."

The Elector of Brandenburg and the Imperialists were manœuvring to cross the Rhine and Turenne was endeavouring to prevent them from doing so. The enemy tried to give him the slip; but he had scouts in all directions.   He found it prudent to re-cross the Rhine to its west side, with the object of preventing the enemy from crossing its bridges, and when he entered the Electorate of Trèves, or Trier, the Elector made a great show of perfect neutrality. Turenne, however, having discovered that he had been intriguing with the Court at Vienna, felt no scruple in laying his country under contributions to provision the French army.

The Grand Elector of Brandenburg then retired to Coblentz, where he received an Imperial garrison; and shortly afterwards he was joined by the Imperial army.   The allies proposed to cross over the bridge at Coblentz; but, to their surprise, they found that Turenne was waiting in force, on the opposite side, to receive them.   They then marched fifty or sixty miles up the river on its east bank, hoping to cross it at Mayence. But here again they were foiled; not this time by

Turenne, but by the Elector of Mayence and the Elector of the Palatinate, who, intimidated by the news that Turenne would arrive in a day or two, feared the consequences of giving his enemies a passage; and, when the Imperialists showed signs of taking the law into their own hands and crossing the bridge at Mayence by force, the Elector broke it down.

The Imperialist armies then started on the long march of more than a hundred miles, in a southerly direction, up the Rhine, with the object of crossing the river by the bridge at Strasburg. Turenne, having discovered their intention, sent couriers to inform Condé, who, as has been observed, was stationed in Alsace. Thereon Condé sent messengers to the Governor of Breisach, with orders to send boats loaded with combustibles down the river to burn the bridge at Strasburg; and when the Imperial troops reached that city, they found the bridge destroyed.

The Imperialists then turned back again and made a hurried march all the way to Mayence, and, as there was no bridge unbroken there, they made one for themselves of boats. Just as they were going to cross the river, on the 30th of November, Turenne appeared on the opposite bank, "so that they were constrained to continue in a ravaged country, though very much wearied by sickness, want, and useless marches and counter-marches ".[1]   And now inhospitality was added to scarcity, for the Electors of Mayence, Trèves and the Palatinate complained to the Emperor that the Im-

[1] Ramsay.

perial troops were ruining their electorates by marching
backwards and forwards through them, and consuming
everything that was eatable; therefore, to prevent the
resentment of those three electors, the Imperial army
and its allies were ordered to make their winter quarters
in Westphalia and in the territories of the Elector of
Cologne and the Bishop of Münster.

It was now near Christmas and Louvois wrote to
Turenne telling him that the King "positively commanded him" to put his troops into winter quarters.
Turenne replied "that it would be prejudicial to the
King's service" to do so; and that, if the enemy were
not prevented from invading the territories of the
Bishop of Münster, that bishop would be certain to
ally himself to the Emperor. Then Turenne went
privately to see the Bishop of Münster, confirmed him
in his allegiance to the King of France, and assured him
of a guarantee against any pressure or raiding by the
troops of the enemy.

Up to the end of the year 1672, this long and
wearying campaign consisted, like several of Turenne's
other campaigns, in a series of marches and counter-
marches with very little fighting. It may indeed be
said to have been a campaign in two parts: the first
in Holland, and the second in Germany; the one
against the Dutch, the other against the allied armies
of the Emperor and the Duke of Brandenburg.
Ramsay says that great astonishment was expressed at
so great a general as Montecuculi never hazarding a
battle during the whole of this campaign. "Some pre-

tended [again] that Prince Lobcourtz, the Emperor's
Minister, had counterfeited the Imperial Seal, in order
to forbid Montecuculi to fight. The Minister was
afraid of engaging his master in a war, at a distance,
while the Ottoman Porte on the other hand, threatened
to invade the Hereditary dominions." And well he
might! For grave indeed would have been the position of a monarch who had "the most Christian King"
pommelling him in the face and "the Unspeakable
Turk" kicking him in the back.

CHAPTER XXIII.

POSSIBLY the frequent restraint alleged to have been put on the pugnacious instincts of Montecuculi by Prince Lobcourtz may have got upon his nerves; for he became ill in January, 1673, and had to relinquish his command. In his absence, the Elector of Brandenburg and the Dukes of Lorraine and Bournonville were in command. These generals had a suspicion that Turenne would join his troops to those of the Bishop of Münster, and they consulted together as to the best method of preventing such a juncture. Their army had been reduced from 40,000 to 20,000 by garrisons left in fortresses, losses in minor attacks, and sickness; but they advanced towards Soest, a curious old walled town, on the road between Hamm and Paderborn, hoping thereby to intervene between the army of Münster and that of Turenne, which they imagined to be upon the banks of the Rhine. Great was their surprise when they heard, on the 3rd of February, that Turenne had already effected his juncture with the army of the Bishop of Münster, and that he was besieging Unna, a town about twenty miles to the west of Soest.

Some of Turenne's battalions volunteered to take

Unna by storm, sword in hand, but he was anxious to save his men, so, refusing this gallant offer, he ordered the town to be bombarded by five mortars, while eight siege guns fired on the walls until a breach was made. When this had been done Unna surrendered. Turenne occupied Hamm and several other places, including Soest, the Imperial troops retreating before him, and then he resolved to pursue the enemy and to take possession of all the towns in Westphalia belonging to the elector.

That winter was very severe in the Westphalian Highlands. The country was mountainous with narrow valleys, and in most cases there were fortified passes in these valleys which had to be forced, an operation which Turenne always effected with success. When his army was passing slowly through one undefended pass, Turenne, exhausted by fatigue and anxiety, lay down to take a short sleep behind a bush, although snow was falling heavily. Some soldiers, seeing him lying exposed to the weather, cut down branches of trees, stuck the ends into the ground, and, laying their cloaks upon them, made a sort of hut to shelter him. Their well-meant exertions woke him up, and he asked them what they were doing. "We want to take care of our father," they replied, "for if we should lose him, who would lead us back again to our own country?"

Throughout this long march—for a very long march it proved to be, in a difficult country and in terrible weather—Turenne, as his historian tells us, "was

present everywhere, and supported his soldiers under
their fatigue by sharing it". He chased the Imperial
armies from post to post, and drove them out of Westphalia into the Bishopric of Hildesheim, which was a
little south of Hanover. The Imperialists then moved
still farther east; but were there opposed somewhat unexpectedly. The Dukes of Brunswick, Wolfenbüttel,
and Lunenburg-Zell did not fancy being involved in a
war in which they took no interest, or having hungry
troops overrunning their territories; so they blockaded
the valley which served as the main entrance to their
dukedoms with 12,000 men. This left the Imperialists
and their allies no alternative but to divide and retreat.
Towards the end of March the Grand Elector of
Brandenburg made off to Berlin, his capital, and the
Emperor's troops retired into Franconia, or what is
now the north-western part of Bavaria.

Napoleon gives unqualified praise to Turenne's
winter campaign in 1672-73. "The Marshal," he says,
"made longer marches in this campaign than in the
preceding one. During the winter of 1672-73, he
marched from the Lower Rhine to the Weser, braving
the frosts of the Northern regions. 1st. He saved
the Elector of Cologne and the Archbishop of Münster,
the King's allies. 2nd. He defeated the Prussian
army, and compelled the Grand Elector to detach
himself from the Emperor and to make his peace.
He therefore made good use of his time and turned
his forced marches and severe fatigues to good
account."

Having no longer any enemy to fight, Turenne returned to Soest, in the Duchy of Marck, and placed the Westphalian territories that belonged to the elector at the discretion of his troops, a discretion of which they availed themselves very freely. "They found there abundance of provisions, put all under contribution, and enriched themselves. The Viscount was the only man who did not make advantage of the spoils of the enemy, and evidenced throughout the whole of this famous expedition a disinterestedness as great as his valour."[1] A certain general suggested to Turenne a method by which he could obtain for himself 400,000 livres in fifteen days, without any possibility of discovery by his Government. " I am very much obliged to you," said Turenne, "but as I have often had opportunities of thè same nature without ever taking advantage of them, I think I ought not to change my line of conduct, at the age of sixty-two." Near the place where this occurred the inhabitants of a large city offered to give him 100,000 crowns if he would not march through it. "You need offer me no money," said Turenne, "for I do not intend to lead my army through your city."

In this campaign Turenne had a young Englishman of the age of twenty-three among his officers; namely that John Churchill who became one of the most famous of English generals and was created Duke of Marlborough. Turenne used to call him "the handsome Englishman". In the course of the

[1] Ramsay.

campaign a column of the enemy attacked and captured an outpost from which a French colonel retired without fighting. Turenne made a wager that "the handsome Englishman" would retake it with half the number of men that had been under the command of the French colonel, and he won his bet. In his *Life of Marlborough* Lord Wolseley calls Turenne Marlborough's "tutor in war" (vol. i., p. 146).

The Grand Elector of Brandenburg, alarmed at the successes of Turenne, and not considering himself safe even in Berlin, offered to make terms with France. After some negotiations a treaty was signed, on the 10th of April, by which the Grand Elector renounced his alliance with Holland and all the engagements into which he had entered against the interests of France, and promised to remain neutral for the future. The King of France, by the same treaty, agreed to restore to the elector Wesel and all the towns in Cleves, which had been retained for many years by the States-General, as well as all the fortresses belonging to the elector which Turenne had taken in Westphalia.

Leaving Westphalia, Turenne went south through the Duchy of Berg, and thence south-east through Hesse-Darmstadt, encamping in the beginning of June, 1673, at Wetzlar, near Frankfurt, so as to be in readiness to prevent the Emperor's troops from advancing to the Rhine, which he had reason to believe was their intention.

Meanwhile Louis XIV. entered Brabant with an army of 40,000 men, and, with 7,000 more, for which

he sent to Turenne, he invested Maestricht and took
it, on the 23rd of June, thirteen days after opening the
trenches.   It was in this siege, which was engineered
by Vauban, that parallels were used for the first time
in Europe, although they had already been employed
by Italian engineers, in the service of the Turks before
Candia.   Condé advanced against Utrecht, but his
operations were frustrated by a further flooding of the
country.   The King then left Condé with an army
of 20,000 men to keep watch on Flanders, and proceeded himself to the frontiers of the Empire.

The 7,000 men borrowed from Turenne returned
to him after the fall of Maestricht.   He remained at
Wetzlar till the 14th of August, and the surrounding
country inevitably suffered during its long occupation
by idle troops.   Cases of disorder committed by the
soldiers, in neutral territory, were complained of by
German princes in communications with the King of
France.   Louvois wrote sternly to Turenne, requiring
him to keep his men under stricter discipline.   Turenne
replied that the country was suffering as little as any
country could possibly suffer when occupied by a
strange army.   As a matter of fact, the valley of the
Main got off lightly in comparison with the district of
Trèves, which was occupied by the army of the King
himself, a district which suffered such ill-treatment that
its elector bitterly complained to the Diet of the miseries
endured by his country at the hands of the army of
Louis XIV.

On the 30th of August a fresh alliance was made,

at the Hague, between the United Provinces, the
Emperor, Spain and the Duke of Lorraine against
France. Certain conditions were made by Spain, but
they scarcely concern the history of Turenne. The
Emperor collected an army of 30,000 men in Bohemia,
and placed them under the command of Montecuculi,
who had now completely recovered his health. A little
later the armies of the Elector of Saxony and the Duke
of Lorraine joined him with 10,000 men, bringing up
the force to 40,000. To oppose this army, Turenne
had a force, including the troops of Münster and
Cologne, amounting to only 20,000, but he had hopes
of being joined by the troops of the Elector of Bavaria ;
hopes, however, which were destined to be grievously
disappointed.

The prospects of Louis XIV. were much clouded
by his having followed the advice of Louvois to garrison
the fortresses he had taken, thus seriously reducing his
armies in the field, instead of following the advice of
both Turenne and Condé to demolish all, but some half-
dozen, of the fortresses, and to keep his soldiers for
active use in his campaigns.

The Prince of Orange gained a success in Holland by retaking Naarden. Dupas, its governor, surrendered it sooner than the French military regulations
permitted, and the King ordered him to be sentenced
to death. On hearing of this Turenne, who knew
Dupas to be a brave man, interceded for him, and
obtained remission of the death sentence as well as
the King's consent that he should serve as a volun-

teer at Grave, where he died nobly, at the siege of that town.

Being anxious to drive Montecuculi from the country bordering on the Rhine, Turenne asked for reinforcements, but Louvois, in the name of the King, refused them. The friction between the Marshal and the Minister of War increased until it became a quarrel. Turenne represented that many of his men had deserted, that his English and Irish contingents were gradually disappearing, and that his soldiers were ill and dying from want of food. To these representations Louvois paid no attention, and Turenne was suffering more now from want of reinforcements than he had suffered from the same cause even in the days of Mazarin.

Montecuculi, with his allied armies of 40,000 men, advanced towards Nuremberg, from whence it was open to him either to march south-west to the Upper Rhine and invade Alsace, or to proceed north to the Lower Rhine and effect a junction with the Prince of Orange.

Although his enemy possessed double his own numbers, Turenne, who was now at Aschaffenberg, was in a good position to prevent Montecuculi from marching to the north, as he had fortified all the passes on the Main, and had obtained a promise of strict neutrality from the Bishop of Würzburg. Montecuculi remained inactive, and Turenne, after waiting some time, advanced to meet him. He passed the river Tauber, at Marienthal, a place with which we are already well acquainted, and he found the Imperial

army encamped near Rottenburg.   With forces of
only half the strength of those of Montecuculi, Turenne
had no desire for a pitched battle, for its own sake ;
but he was anxious to block the way to the Rhine, and
to block it in the place where it might be easiest for an
inferior force to make a successful stand against a
superior.

Montecuculi wished to avoid an action, to give
Turenne the slip, to hurry to the north-west and to
effect a junction with the Prince of Orange ; but, even
with his numerical superiority, he had no fancy for
fighting rearguard actions throughout a long march.
To conceal his intentions, he began to put his first line
in order of battle, as if preparing for a general action ;
and Turenne did the same.   Meanwhile Montecuculi
made his second line file off, with all its transports, to
the rear, under the concealment of a neighbouring
mountain.   Turenne had not long drawn up his army
in battle formation when, to his surprise, he saw his
opponent's army filing off.   He immediately pursued
it, attacked its rear, and captured some stores and
ammunition, yet without succeeding in bringing on a
general engagement.   His enemy having escaped him,
he encamped upon high ground, beside a Carthusian
monastery, while Montecuculi took up a position behind the morasses between Würzburg and Oschen-
furth.   The two armies remained near each other for
a fortnight, and then Montecuculi, who had privately
induced the Prince Bishop of Würzburg to break his
promise of neutrality to Turenne, quietly led his troops

away to Würzburg and marched them by its bridge over the river Main. The perfidy of the Prince Bishop thus enabled Montecuculi to make himself master of the right bank of the Main, from Würzburg to Wertheim, where he seized an immense quantity of provisions which had been collected there for the use of Turenne's army. This completely upset all Turenne's designs, and there was nothing left for him to do but to march down the left bank of the Main. While he was doing this, in October, he was slightly encouraged by receiving a reinforcement of 4,000 men.

The whole aspect of the war was now altered. The Prince of Orange, hoping to meet Montecuculi, marched with 25,000 men up the left bank of the Rhine and invested Bonn, while Montecuculi marched down the right bank of the Main as far as Mayence. The Dutch and the Imperial armies were now within eighty miles of each other. By crossing the bridge at Würzburg so unexpectedly, and before Turenne had been aware of it, Montecuculi had stolen such a march upon him that he had reached Mayence by the north bank of the Main when Turenne had only got as far as Miltemburg, a place by the river's bank and on the south of it, some sixty miles short of Mayence. By forced marches Montecuculi could probably have joined the Prince of Orange at Bonn before Turenne could have caught him up; but he was too wise a general to run unnecessary risks, and he determined to practise a further deception on Turenne before proceeding. He

therefore selected a place on the Rhine, where there
was an island, made a bridge to the island, and then a
flying bridge from the island to the opposite side.   As
soon as it would bear horses to pass in single file, he
began to send his cavalry across it to the west bank,
as if he intended to march into Alsace.

News of this was at once conveyed to Turenne, as
Montecuculi wished that it should be.   Turenne had,
from the first, expected Montecuculi to attack Alsace
and Lorraine, which were almost undefended, unless
indeed Condé had already returned from Holland to
Alsace, which seemed doubtful.   Accordingly, so soon
as he heard that Montecuculi was crossing the Rhine
and pointing for Lorraine, Turenne left the river Main
and hurried in a south-westerly direction, with the
object of crossing the Rhine at Philippsburg, and intercepting Montecuculi in the north of Alsace and
Lorraine.

As soon as Montecuculi had sent enough cavalry
across his temporary bridge over the Rhine in a
southerly direction to make Turenne's spies gallop off
to inform Turenne that Montecuculi was marching
towards Alsace and Lorraine, he shipped his infantry
on boats, at Mayence, sent them down the Rhine in a
northerly direction towards the Prince of Orange at
Bonn, and sent orders to the cavalry, which had
crossed over the bridge, to recross it and follow them.
The Prince of Orange, having heard of the advance
of Montecuculi, went up the Rhine to the south, and
effected a junction of the Dutch and Imperialist armies,

near Coblentz. Then they all went to Bonn,[1] which fell in a few days. The French troops were now obliged to retreat from Holland, which then closed its sluices and gradually emerged from the waters.

Turenne put his army into winter quarters in Alsace, Lorraine and Hainaut; then, with "an air of thoughtfulness and melancholy," he went to the Court of France. The King received him with great esteem and affection, and deplored the bad advice which he had received from Louvois and had, unfortunately, followed. This gave Turenne a splendid opportunity of avenging himself upon his enemy; but all he said was: "The Marquis of Louvois is capable of doing your Majesty admirable service, in the Cabinet; but he has not yet had sufficient experience in war to take upon himself the direction of campaigns".

The King told Turenne that he would never again employ the Marquis d'Abre, because he had written to Louvois severely blaming the strategy of Turenne and saying that, if he had been consulted, he could have saved Bonn without endangering Alsace. "Why did he not tell me how he could do so?" said Turenne. "I should have listened to him with pleasure and perhaps I might have profited by his advice." Then he made excuses for D'Abre, praised him, mentioned good services which he had rendered, and persuaded the

---

[1] Bonn had undergone a severe siege in 1584 by Archbishop Ernest of Bavaria, who had been deposed from his see for heresy; and it was subsequently besieged and taken by Marlborough in 1703. Its celebrated university was not established until 1818.

King to give him a gratuity and not to deprive himself
of the services of so able a lieutenant-general. We
shall hear of him again.

Napoleon severely blames Turenne's conduct of the
summer and autumn campaign of 1673 : " Montecuculi
completely deceived and imposed upon Turenne. He
got rid of him and sent him marching into Alsace,
whilst he proceeded to Cologne, and joined the Prince
of Orange, who was besieging and taking Bonn.
Turenne's conduct on this occasion has been censured :
1st He manœuvred at too great a distance from his
enemy: 2ndly He did not act according to Montecuculi's movements, but ascribed to him an intention
of entering France, without any foundation whatever.
Yet Holland was the centre of the military operations.
No one knew better than Turenne that war is a con-
jectural art : he ought to have regulated his movements
by those of his adversary, and not by his own ideas:
3rdly Montecuculi would have been insulated in Alsace
and would have had to engage the united armies of
Condé and Turenne, whilst under the walls of Bonn
he found himself on the grand rendezvous, where the
momentous question was to be decided, far from Condé's
army, and covering Holland and Belgium. This march
established the reputation of Montecuculi. The error
committed by Turenne on this occasion was a blemish
to his glory ; it was the greatest fault of which this distinguished Commander ever was guilty."

Once more, and for the last time, we have had to
consider, in the latter part of this chapter, a campaign

in which Turenne had no fighting beyond skirmishing; but a campaign wherein, for the first time, instead of outmanœuvring his enemy, he was outmanœuvred himself. Yet in Montecuculi Turenne met a foe worthy of his steel. He was three years older than Turenne and had displayed great military genius under his uncle during the Thirty Years' War. He had distinguished himself in campaigns against the Swedes in Silesia; he had commanded a successful expedition against Prince Rakoczy in 1654; he had assisted Denmark against Sweden with such effect as to obtain the peace of Oliva in 1660; and, in 1664, he had defeated the Turks so decisively that they concluded an armistice for twenty years. In his leisure time, he had written several military works of considerable importance, and he was an ardent lover of science. A few years later than the date with which we are dealing, he was made a Prince of the Empire by the Emperor Leopold, and Duke of Melfi by the King of Naples.

CHAPTER XXIV.

Louis XIV. has been aptly entitled *Le Grand Monarque*, but at the time which we are at present considering he had managed to make his country intensely unpopular throughout the greater part of Europe, and nearly every European King and Prince his enemy.

The ill-fortune of Turenne in his last campaign had shaken the adherence of those fair-weather friends, the Archbishop of Cologne, the Bishop of Münster, and Charles II. In the spring of 1674 all the German Princes, with the exception of the Electors of Hanover and Bavaria, allied themselves with the Emperor against France. The Elector of Cologne, the Bishop of Münster, and, later, the Elector of Brandenburg, broke their treaties with France and turned against her. Charles II. of England was bullied by his Parliament and his Ministers into withdrawing from his alliance with France and recalling the English regiments which had been fighting under her banner; but those regiments were devoted to Turenne and refused to leave him.

Louis felt obliged to evacuate all the places he had taken on the Rhine and the Meuse in the two previous campaigns, except Maestricht and Grave. He then resolved to recompense himself for the loss of the United Provinces, by acquiring Franche-Comté, the large province lying to the south of Lorraine, which was then Spanish. Having taken a large army thither in April, he eventually conquered it, and made it a part of France, which it has ever since remained. About the same time he sent another army, under Schomberg, to the frontiers of Spain, and he gave Condé 40,000 men wherewith to advance against the Prince of Orange. To Turenne was consigned the guardianship of the Rhine, with a very much smaller army than that of Condé. Turenne's being entrusted with so heavy a task with so inadequate a force was the work of his bitter enemy, Louvois.

It is not impossible, even if it be improbable, that there may have been some collusion between Louvois and Condé. In his *Siècle de Louis XIV.* (vol. i., p. 133) Voltaire declares Condé to have been jealous of Turenne, and he describes a certain scheme which Condé once confided to Louvois, which was to be to the advantage of Condé and to the disadvantage of Turenne, adding that, on hearing of it, Louvois eagerly embraced Condé. Undoubtedly Turenne and Condé admired each other as generals; and in a certain sense they were friends, even great friends; but there are several sorts of friendships, and it may be that the particular variety of friendship which Condé felt for Turenne did not altogether exclude sentiments of jealousy. He loved Turenne, he loved him much; but he loved himself and his own interests still better.

Turenne encamped near Saverne, or Zabern, a
town about twenty-two miles to the north-west of Strasburg; and he had to consider the very serious question
of how he was to guard the Rhine from Coblentz to
Basle, a frontier of some two hundred miles. Early
in June he learned that two armies were on the march
to effect a junction with the object of crossing the
Rhine, one a force of about 9,000 men, under Count
Caprara and the other of about the same numbers,
under the Duke of Bournonville.

Turenne was anxious to defeat one of these armies
before it could be joined by the other. To this end
he started on the 12th of June, made forced marches
with little or no transport, crossed the Rhine by the
bridge at Philippsburg on the 14th, and thence hurried
forward with 9,000 men, six guns and three days'
provisions to Hockenheim, where he encamped. On
the way his men came in for some very sharp skirmishing. One night, fearing a surprise, he went out
in the dark to see for himself that all the men were
at their posts, and, in passing a tent, he heard some
young soldiers complaining at his having made them
take such a long and useless march. Then he heard
an old soldier, who had been wounded in one of these
skirmishes, say: "You do not know our father: he would
not have exposed us to so much fatigue, if he had not
some great thing in view, of which we as yet know
nothing".

The next day Turenne proceeded to Wiesloch,
having marched nearly ninety miles in four days. This

was a tiring march; but he started again between three and four o'clock the next morning. After marching for nearly five hours, he discovered the enemy on a hill, on the farther side of a small town of the Palatinate, called Sintzheim, about half-way between Philippsburg on the Rhine and Heilbronn on the Neckar, and situated itself on the river Eltzbach. The rival armies were pretty equal in point of number, as Turenne had only 9,000 men with him, having left strong garrisons to occupy Hagenau and Saverne in order to protect the north of Alsace, and having sent a strong detachment to Belfort. While Caprara had far more cavalry than infantry and no artillery, Turenne had six guns and almost as much infantry as cavalry, a great advantage in the kind of country where the battle was to take place. Caprara, on the other hand, had two advantages over Turenne: his position on a hill with steep sides was excellent, and his men were fresh, whereas Turenne's had just completed a march of about 100 miles in four days and as many hours.

The enemy sent one detachment into the town and another into an old abbey, fortified like a castle, which lay between the town and the hill. On the hill the army was drawn up in two lines, the first commanded by the Duke of Lorraine,[1] and the second by Count Caprara. Behind them was a large wood.

The position of Turenne was hazardous, for, in

[1] Lorraine's army, which used to be 10,000, was now only 2,000.

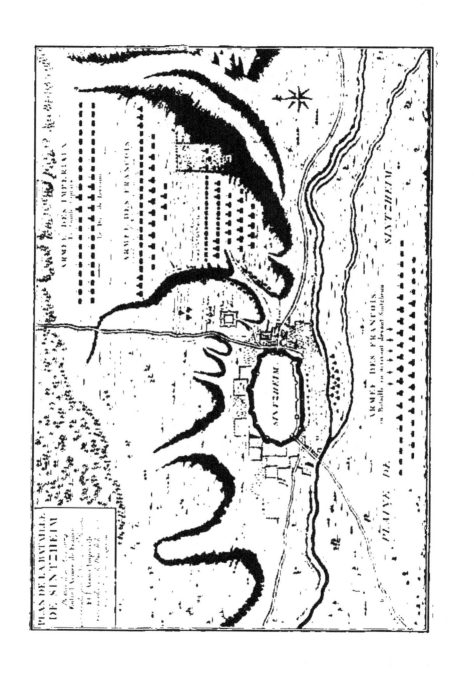

PLAN DE LA BATAILLE
DE SINTZHEIM

ARMÉE DES IMPÉRIAUX

ARMÉE DES FRANÇOIS

SINTZHEIM

ARMÉE DES FRANÇOIS
en Bataille, en arrivant devant Sintzheim

PLAINE DE

case of defeat, the retreat would have been very difficult in an enemy's country deeply wooded; but it
would have been still more hazardous to allow Caprara
and Bournonville to join their forces.

Two branches of the river Eltzbach had to be
crossed, and Turenne effected this crossing under
cover of the fire of his artillery.   Then followed fierce
fighting, first in the suburbs, and next in the little town
itself and at the abbey beyond it; but after an hour
and a half the French troops had driven the enemy
both out of the town and out of the abbey.   After that
there was some stubborn fighting in the suburbs, the
vineyards and the hedgerows.   The troops of Caprara,
which had been defending the town, then retreated
from it to the east, and ascended to the plateau upon
which his main body was drawn up.

From the town there was a narrow defile, which
led up the hill on Turenne's left.   Here his great preponderance of infantry proved invaluable; for his musketeers scrambled up the ascent, and, lining the defile on
both its sides, protected his troops, while they passed
through it up to the sloping plateau above.   He also
succeeded in getting three battalions into a vineyard on
this plateau by a passage up a steep bank on his extreme
right.   Even allowing for Caprara's weakness in infantry, it is difficult to understand why he could not
prevent troops from ascending a hill of which he held
the command with an equal number of men, especially
as the ascent had to be made by a narrow defile on
the one side, and by a steep climb on the other; and

Caprara's men were fresh while Turenne's were wearied by forced marches.

Once on the hill, Turenne drew up his cavalry in lines and placed platoons of infantry between them. He had a vineyard on his right and a hedge with a steep declivity on his left. General d'Abre, of whom we lately heard, commanded the right wing of the first line, and he imprudently advanced beyond the line of cavalry on his left and the farther end of the vineyard on his right, thus exposing both his flanks. Taking advantage of this imprudence, the enemy immediately attacked his front and each of his flanks, thereby throwing his ranks into confusion. D'Abre himself was mortally wounded. Seeing what had happened, Turenne galloped up and just saved the situation. The ground being very dry, the charges of cavalry raised clouds of dust, and, under their cover, he took the opportunity of extending his front until he had eighteen squadrons in his first line, with three battalions of infantry on either wing. The enemy was in a reversed position, having four battalions of infantry in his centre, with eight squadrons of cavalry on either side.

Very sharp fighting followed. Every squadron of cavalry charged several times, and every charge raised more dust, until it was difficult to distinguish friend from foe. Turenne, who kept in the forefront of the battle, encouraging his men by voice, gesture and example, suddenly found himself in the midst of the Emperor's cuirassiers, and some time passed before he was able to get clear of them and return to his own

men. Although now sixty-three, he showed magnificent
personal courage in this action. Well might Napoleon
say of him: "Turenne is the greatest of the French
Generals: he is the only one who became bolder with
age".

It was long doubtful, amidst the thick clouds of dust
and smoke, which side was getting the best of the
battle; standards and colours were taken and retaken
on either side, and great was the slaughter; but gradually the Imperial troops wavered, fell back, broke up,
and retired. The wood at their back now came into
view, through the dusty air, and they retreated into
it, after making a weak defence on its outskirts. Then
the German soldiers disappeared among the trees. To
pursue them through an unknown forest was impracti-
cable, and the Marquis of Renty, who was sent with
400 men to attempt it, failed to effect his purpose.

The battle, from the first crossing of the river by
Turenne to the flight of the enemy into the wood,
lasted four hours. During that time, the French lost
nearly 200 officers and 1,100 men, and the Imperialists
lost nearly 2,000 in killed, besides large numbers of
wounded, 500 or 600 prisoners, and forty waggons.
When Turenne's principal officers congratulated him
and admired his personal courage in the battle, he
replied: "With such splendid soldiers, a general need
never hesitate to attack; for he is certain of victory!"

Of these operations Napoleon says: "In this campaign, contrary to his usual custom, Turenne engaged
in several actions and fought one great battle. His

march against Caprara, when he passed the Rhine at
Philippsburg, to surprise him previously to his junction
with the Duke of Bournonville, was admirable. Caprara
thought him forty leagues off, when he discovered him
with his army formed in line, opposite his camp. The
numerical superiority of the infantry secured him the
taking of Sintzheim and the passage of the defile.
Caprara committed an error in accepting battle : he
ought to have repassed the Neckar and marched to
meet and join the Duke of Bournonville."

A few days after his victory at Sintzheim, Turenne
returned to Philippsburg, recrossed the Rhine and encamped in a very rich plain near Neustadt, a town about
eighteen miles to the north-west of Philippsburg—it
may be well to have mentioned its whereabouts as there
are thirty places bearing that name.   Here he received
considerable reinforcements.   Meanwhile he sent detachments to gain information about the enemy, to discover passes through the mountains and to spread
various false reports as to his own intended movements.
After making a false march to the west, in the direction
of Kaiserslautern, to deceive the enemy, he turned back,
marched south-east to Philippsburg on the 3rd of July,
again crossed the Rhine and then marched nearly due
north to Weiblingen, a village on the Neckar between
Mannheim and Heidelberg.   He was now accompanied
by an army of 18,000 men.

By this time Caprara, with the remains of his army,
had joined Bournonville, and their united armies
numbered about 15,000.   They were some miles north

of the Neckar and were marching on Mannheim, when
they discovered the army of Turenne a few miles off,
and, not desiring a battle just then, they retired towards
Frankfurt, two hours before Turenne had learned that
they were within reach of him.   He sent cavalry in
pursuit ; but it was too late.

Being unopposed on the north of the river Neckar,
Turenne was master of the Palatinate.   And now we
come to an incident in his career for which he has been
severely criticised.   He allowed his troops to live at
their discretion, which they used so freely that in a
month they had consumed all the food and forage in
the country.   Most of the peasants abandoned their
houses and went elsewhere in search of provisions;
before doing so, large bodies of them revenged themselves upon the soldiers by surprising them whenever
they could find them single, or even in twos and threes,
murdering them and torturing them with abominable
cruelty.   They burned them to death over slow fires,
or left them to die hanging by their feet from trees with
their heads downwards, or tore out their hearts and
entrails, or maimed them in various ways and left them
exposed alive on the high-roads : in some rare instances they contented themselves with putting out
their eyes.

It was but natural that the soldiers should retaliate
upon the peasants for the terrible cruelties which had
thus been perpetrated upon their comrades.   This re-
taliation is said to have been begun by the English
soldiers serving under Turenne, and Ramsay says that,

22

when they saw what horrors had been committed upon some of their comrades, they became like madmen, and taking torches in their hands set fire to villages and even to some small towns before their officers could restrain them. "Had not the threats and orders of Turenne put a stop to their fury, they would have laid waste the whole country. He exemplarily punished those who began the burning, though they were the bravest soldiers of his army. He could not condemn them to death without doing great violence to himself: but, as the maintaining of discipline was concerned, he made clemency give way to severity."

Napoleon, on the contrary, says that Turenne "set fire to two towns and twenty-five villages, by order of Louis XIV." Most historians have attributed this incendiarism to Turenne's own initiative and have considered it a stain on his memory. But, even if it had been by his orders, which cannot be definitely proved, it must be allowed that his provocation at the hideous cruelties practised upon his soldiers was immense ; and in addition to this, it should be remembered that, if he had not laid the country waste, the enemy might have foraged in it, on his way to attack Philippsburg, Hagenau, Saverne, or other French positions of importance near or on the river Rhine. Captain Hozier says that "an English army, in order to compel Massena to fall back from Lisbon, wasted a friendly country and thus turned the tide of the Peninsular war ".[1]

---

[1] *Turenne*, p. 187.

And, even in our great Boer War, farms were burned, crops were destroyed, and districts were cleared of provisions.

Louis, the Elector Palatine, who watched the conflagrations from the tower of his castle at Mannheim, was exceedingly enraged at the devastation of his territories, more especially because Turenne was a relation of his own and had hitherto been on friendly terms with him. He wrote to Turenne saying that he understood the burning of the towns and villages to have been by his orders. " I am at a loss to find out a reason for it. . . . I cannot help being surprised at a procedure so little conformable to the laws of wars amongst Christians and to the assurances you have so often given me of your friendship." Then he said that he did not believe the alleged atrocities to have been committed by his peasants, and he continued : " But granting that it had been my subjects, I cannot see how the inhumanity of some private men, whom I would have severely punished had I known the authors of it, could have obliged you to ruin so many innocent families, and consume even the very churches of your own religion. Actions so contrary to the improvement you pretend to have made in the practice of Christianity by your conversion "—this was evidently intended to be a particularly nasty slap—" make me believe that they proceed from some prejudice or spite you have conceived against me ; but it would have been easy for you to have taken satisfaction from me by ways more usual among men of honour." And he ended his letter by requesting

Turenne to send by the bearer a letter naming a time and a place for a duel.

Turenne immediately wrote in reply: " I have received the letter your Electoral Highness did me the honour to write to me; I can assure you that the burning of some of your villages was without my order, and that the soldiers who found their comrades killed after a very strange manner, did it at hours when they could not be hindered. When your Electoral Highness shall be sufficiently informed of the fact, I doubt not but you will continue to honour me with a share of your favour, since I have done nothing that can be a reason for depriving me of it." He altogether ignored the challenge to a duel.

Ramsay states that when the elector inquired further into the matter, he "found it such as the Viscount had represented and was ashamed of having been so much transported with passion ".[1]

When his army had consumed everything that was eatable in the Palatinate, north of the Neckar, Turenne again crossed the Rhine and encamped south-west of Philippsburg. Sickness having broken out among his men, he spent much time in going among them, doing

[1] When Napoleon was about fourteen he was conversing with a lady about Marshal Turenne and extolling him to the skies. " Yes, my friend," she answered, " he was a great man, but I should like him better if he had not burnt the Palatinate." " What does that matter," Napoleon replied briskly, "if burning was necessary to the success of his plans ? " (*Table Talk of Napoleon Buonaparte.* Sampson Low & Son, 1868).

all in his power to comfort them and provide for their wants. Occasionally, when he had spent for this purpose what money he happened to have in his pockets, he borrowed some from his officers and told them to ask his steward for repayment. The steward sometimes suspected that they demanded larger sums than they had lent, and, hinting at this to Turenne, he suggested that when he borrowed money from his officers he should give them written orders for the exact amount. "No," replied Turenne, "give all they ask for. It is impossible that an officer should demand a sum which he has not lent—unless he be in great want, and in that case it is but just to assist him."

While Turenne was for the moment at a standstill, Condé fought one of his greatest battles, the battle of Seneff, in which with 45,000 men he encountered the Dutch and Spaniards who had nearly 60,000, under the command of the Prince of Orange. Both sides claimed the victory and chanted *Te Deum* in their cathedrals. On both sides, again, the slaughter had been enormous; it was said that the battle-field was strewn with 27,000 corpses; and in such personal danger had been both commanders-in-chief that Condé and the Prince of Orange had each more than one horse killed under him. Condé's energy in this great battle was the more meritorious on account of his ill-health. For some years he had been obliged to live chiefly on milk.[1] After the battle of Seneff, at which he spent seventeen

---

[1] Desormeaux, vol. iv., p. 208.   Mahon's *Life of Condé*, p. 266.

hours in the saddle, he had such a severe attack of gout
that, when he went to present himself to the King, he
could scarcely crawl up the great staircase at Versailles.
But we must return to Turenne, who also was to fight
a great battle in a few weeks.

The Imperial army, which had meanwhile been encamped between Mayence and Frankfurt, was largely
reinforced by German levies, until the Duke of
Bournonville had 35,000 men and thirty guns under
him by the end of August. With this large army he
forced the bridge at Mayence and crossed to the west
of the Rhine.

Both Louis XIV. and Louvois were much alarmed
at hearing of this advance of the Imperial army, and
Louvois laid all the blame of it on Turenne. He
urged the King to withdraw his troops, to abandon
Alsace, and to fall back into Lorraine. Louis XIV.
consented and sent pressing orders to this effect to
Turenne ; upon which Turenne sent back a respectful
remonstrance. "The enemy," he wrote, "how numerous soever their troops be, cannot think of any other
enterprise this season but that of making me leave the
Province I am in : they have neither provisions, nor
the means of passing into Lorraine, till I be driven out
of Alsace. If I go away of my own accord, as your
Majesty orders me, I shall do for them what they would
find it difficult to make me do. When a General has a
reasonable number of troops, he need never quit a
country ; though the enemy may have a great many
more. I am persuaded that, of the two, it would be

less prejudicial to your Majesty's interest that I lost a battle, than that, abandoning Alsace, I should repass the mountains into Lorraine: for, if I were to do so, Philippsburg and Breisach would soon be obliged to surrender. The Imperialists would take possession of the whole country from Mayence to Basle, and very possibly they might invade Franche-Comté, Lorraine and Champagne. I know the strength of the Imperial army, the Generals who command it, and the country in which I now am. I am prepared to take the whole responsibility and I will answer for the event."

The King so thoroughly trusted Turenne that he told him to do as he pleased, reinforced him with eight battalions and ordered Louvois to submit.

Bournonville now marched south and made a bridge of boats six miles from Philippsburg. Turenne was uncertain whether Bournonville intended to besiege Philippsburg, or to recross and march up the Rhine, or merely to make a feint of crossing the Rhine and then turn back to the west. In this uncertainty, Turenne made elaborate arrangements for watching his movements. Four guns were to be fired as a signal if he did one thing, and six guns if he did something else. A detachment of 500 infantry, specially told off to observe his proceedings, was under the command of "the handsome Englishman".

In spite of all the precautions of Turenne, Bournonville managed to give him the slip. He recrossed the Rhine on the 20th of September and hurried up the river, by its right or eastern bank, to Strasburg.

Turenne followed him on the left bank, being anxious to reach Strasburg before his enemy, in order to confirm its magistrates in their neutrality; not that he had much anxiety on that point, as they had refused the Imperialists a passage over its bridge a few months earlier, and they were not likely to run any danger of incurring the wrath of Louis XIV. or of having their city made the centre of a great war. And Turenne was very nearly right, so far as the magistrates of Strasburg were concerned; for they refused point-blank to permit Bournonville to cross over their bridge; but Count Hohenlohe, who had undertaken the negotiation, on failing with the magistrates, had tried his luck with the people, and with such effect that they rose against the magistrates, took possession of the bridge, and gave the Imperialists a free passage over it. The army of the Empire then crossed the river on the 26th of September, Turenne arriving only six hours too late to stop them.[1] After crossing the river, the Imperial army turned to the south, up the Ill, a river which flows into the Rhine below Strasburg, and encamped between that city and Gravenstadt, a small town about three miles to the south, on the Ill.

"By this disposition," Ramsay tells us, "the Imperialists became masters of the country, from the Rhine to the mountains of Saverne, and by consequence of all Upper Alsace, where they found provisions in abundance to support a very powerful army, a long time,

---

[1] So at least says Napoleon.

and from whence they might easily make an irruption into France."

Of these operations Napoleon has this to say: "The Duke of Bournonville surprised Turenne, by gaining several marches upon him and taking possession of Strasburg. The French ministry had been remiss in not ordering the occupation of Strasburg. What had they to hesitate about? Nearly the whole Empire was at war, and the hostile disposition of the citizens of Strasburg was known: the possession of the place was indispensable to the security of the frontier. But Turenne ought to have watched this important point. He was on the left bank of the Rhine, and the enemy on the right: he ought to have kept a division near Strasburg so as to have been able to anticipate the enemy, particularly as there was no other point on this whole frontier calculated to excite his solicitude in a similar degree."

The position now was exceedingly critical. The army of the Empire already greatly outnumbered that of Turenne, and the Elector of Brandenburg was expected in a fortnight with a reinforcement of 20,000 men. Turenne had only 22,000 men, and with little more than half the numbers of the enemy he had to cover Saverne and Hagenau, places as important as they were weak. A retreat would have been dangerous and its consequences fatal, including the loss of Breisach, Philippsburg, Alsace and possibly also Franche-Comté and Lorraine. Likely enough, again, it might have been followed by the pillaging of Champagne. If Brandenburg joined the Imperial army, Turenne's force would meet with almost certain destruction from one nearly three times its number.   Turenne's only chance of success, and that a poor one, seemed to be to attack the enemy at once, before Brandenburg could join him.

CHAPTER XXV.

IT must have put a severe strain upon the spirits of
even so brave a soldier, and a man of such an equable
temperament, as Turenne, to prepare for attacking, with
a comparatively small army, a large and splendid army,
which was soon to be very considerably reinforced.
But one of Turenne's maxims was to "appear more
gay than ordinary in the time of the most imminent
danger". St. Evremond wrote of him, while he was
still living : " He is never elevated in good, never cast
down in bad fortune".

While the enemy was encamped three miles to the
south-west of Strasburg, Turenne encamped about as
far from it on the north-east, at Wanzenau, on the
Ill, a little above where that river flows into the
Rhine. Although he could calculate on only fourteen
days before the arrival of 20,000 fresh enemies to join
the forces greatly outnumbering his own, already
present, he wisely gave his own men a three days' rest
before beginning his operations.

Early in the night of the 2nd of October he sent
off three regiments of dragoons, at midnight he decamped himself, but the main body of his army does

denburg joined the Imperial army, Turenne's force would meet with almost certain destruction from one nearly three times its number.   Turenne's only chance of success, and that a poor one, seemed to be to attack the enemy at once, before Brandenburg could join him.

CHAPTER

Iᴛ must have put a severe strain upon the spirits of even so brave a soldier, and a man of so imperturbable temperament, as Turenne, to prepare for attacking, with a comparatively small army, a large and splendid army, which was soon to be very considerably reinforced. But one of Turenne's traits was to "appear more gay than ordinary in the time of the most imminent danger". St. Evremond wrote of him, while he was still living: "He is never drunk in good, never cast down in bad fortune".

While the enemy was encamped three miles to the south-west of Strasburg, Turenne encamped about as far from it on the north-east, at Wantzenau, on the Ill, a little above where the river flowed into the Rhine. Although he could calculate on only four or five days before the arrival of more fresh enemies, to join the forces greatly outnumbering his own, already present, he wisely gave his own men a three days' rest before beginning his operation.

Early in the night of the 1st of October, he sent off three regiments of dragoons, at midnight he was encamped himself, but the main body of his army de...

not seem to have started till the next morning. It
marched first due west and then to the south-west of
Strasburg, his cavalry keeping next to that city, his
infantry in the centre and his transports on the farther
side. Torrents of rain fell during the night, and, as a
good deal of ploughed land had to be traversed, the
marching was very heavy. At four o'clock, in the
afternoon of the 3rd, Turenne encamped on high
ground above Achenheim, a village near the river
Breusch, over which he was fortunate enough to find
a bridge unbroken at Holtzheim. He at once crossed
the river with some cavalry, and used the rest of the
daylight for reconnoitring. He discovered the camp
of the enemy, about three miles due south of his own,
on the opposite side of Ensheim, a village some half-
dozen miles to the south-west of Strasburg. On the
Strasburg side, that is to say at the enemy's right
flank, was a very large wood ; and, in front of his
right wing, separated by a wide passage from this
wood, was a vineyard. In front of his left wing was
a small wood which seemed to Turenne, and, as it afterwards turned out, to Bournonville also, the most important point in the coming battle. In front of the Imperial
centre was the village of Ensheim, with two open
spaces of from half a mile to three-quarters of a mile
each, one between the village and the vineyard on the
right, and the other between the village and the small
wood on the left.

Knowing that he had not a moment to lose,
Turenne made his army begin to file over the small

bridge at Achenheim as soon as possible that evening,
and to continue this movement throughout the night.
As quickly as his troops passed over the river Breusch,
he drew them up in order of battle, on the farther side of
the village of Holtzheim, which stood upon the south
side of the river. Thus occupied, he spent the whole
night in the saddle.

Soon after six o'clock, on the morning of the 4th BATTLE OF
of October, both the French and the German armies 4th October,
were in order of battle. It was a gloomy morning, 1674.
and a fog, with which the day began, soon developed,
first into a drizzle, and presently into a steady downpour
of rain which lasted till the evening. Lord Wolseley
says (*Life of Marlborough*, vol. i., p. 140) that Turenne,
theoretically, with an army little more than half the
size of that of his enemy and with a river which could
only be recrossed by one bridge behind him, ought not
to have attacked at all ; but, he adds, Turenne knew
that he could depend upon a want of agreement between "the many serene Highnesses in the Imperial
army," which was made up of contingents from many electorates and provinces commanded by their own princes.
"None but a master in the practice of war," says he,
"knows when to discard theory ; the instinct which
prompts him to do so at the right moment is the hall-
mark of real military genius." Making all allowances,
however, Lord Wolseley is of opinion that Turenne
was scarcely "justified in the attack upon which he
now resolved".

Both armies had infantry in their centres and

cavalry on their wings; but with this important difference, that the Imperialists placed the whole of their
infantry in their centre, while Turenne placed a few
battalions in his centre and divided the rest into platoons,
which he placed between the squadrons of cavalry.
Napoleon would probably have been the first to
acknowledge that musketry was, at that time, in a very
experimental and transitional stage, and that little
blame could be laid upon Turenne for making a mistake
in its use; but he says: "The plan of mingling platoons
of infantry with cavalry is bad and produces nothing
but disadvantages: the cavalry loses its activity and is
obstructed in all its movements; it loses its power; the
infantry is endangered and, on the first movement of
the cavalry, remains without support".

Turenne[1] "posted himself in no particular place,
intending to go wherever his presence should be
necessary";[2] but Bournonville, who was commander-
in-chief of the Imperial army, "placed himself at the
head of the main body". Before the action opened,
Bournonville sent troops with guns to occupy the small
wood which stood before his left wing and ordered the
position to be entrenched. He also had the village entrenched and armed by artillery. In the open spaces,
on the right and left of the village, he placed infantry
concealed by lying in hollows and behind banks. Then
he quietly awaited the French attack. The first line

[1] Ramsay.
[2] Turenne, nevertheless, is reported to have once said: "A
general who ' is everywhere ' is nowhere ".

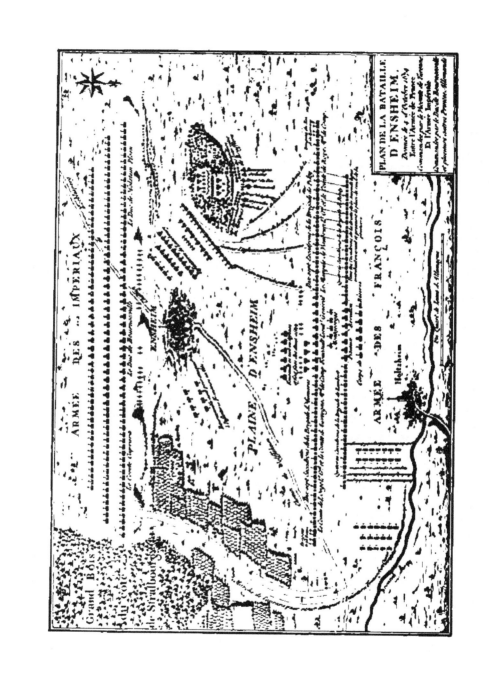

PLAN DE LA BATAILLE
D'ENSHEIM.

of the French was as long as that of the Imperialists; the second was shorter than theirs; but the French reserve was only about a fifth of that of the enemy, which, in his case, was to all intents and purposes a third line of battle. The two armies were drawn up about a mile from each other.

It seemed to Turenne that the first thing to be done was to take, if possible, the small wood on his own right and on the Imperialist left; and he began the action by sending the Marquis Boufflers, with eight squadrons of dismounted dragoons, to attack it. The artillery on either side cannonaded each other for some time, the Imperialists using "cartridge shot". Under Boufflers, and with Monmouth's force, fought the future Duke of Marlborough, who was commanding a regiment, the nucleus of which, says Lord Wolseley (*Life of Marlborough*, vol. i., p. 135), were drafts of fifty men from each of the three regiments of English Foot Guards. Sir F. Hamilton, in his *History of the Grenadier Guards* (vol. i., p. 194), says: "The men of the three companies of the King's [Grenadier] and Coldstream Guards, forming part of Monmouth's original Royal English Regiment, had . . . been drafted into the other companies of that corps still remaining in the French King's service, and . . . more than half of each of the Guard's companies of Skelton's battalion were similarly drafted into Churchill's corps". An Englishman, in writing about Turenne, may be excused for dwelling upon these details and for feeling proud that some of the hardest fighting, in one of the

hardest-fought battles of Turenne, was the work, and
the successful work, of his fellow-countrymen.

Both Bournonville and Turenne constantly sent
reinforcements to this important position.   At last
Boufflers, sword in hand, marched up to the entrenchments, stormed them, drove the enemy out of them,
and took two guns; but, on advancing through the
wood, he was surprised and staggered at being confronted by a second entrenchment, a little distance
behind the first, from which no less than six guns
opened fire.   For three hours the French struggled
against this fire, without being able to make any way.
Turenne then sent further reinforcements; but a blind-
ing storm of rain for some time interfered with the
attack.   Then the French made a most vigorous onslaught.   The bloodshed was terrible on both sides.
As they fought, many of the living were standing upon
the bodies of the dead; but the French persevered
until they carried the second entrenchments, captured
the six guns, and drove the enemy out of the wood.

Bournonville, as will presently be seen, did not
concentrate his attention too exclusively upon the small
wood where there was such terrific fighting; but he
still considered it of the utmost importance, and he sent
a strong force and six guns in hope of recovering it.
Turenne sent about an equal number of men to repel
them, but, at first, no artillery.   These rival reinforcements came into contact between the wood and the
village of Ensheim, but the Imperialists had strong
support, being close to their own lines, whereas the

French troops were quite unsupported and suffered great losses from the Imperial artillery. As Napoleon describes it, "the carnage soon became dreadful". Turenne himself led this attack, one horse was shot under him, and several of his staff were killed at his side. The personal courage which he exhibited did much to animate his troops, and they fought with extraordinary valour. When the guns which had been captured by the French in the wood had been brought up and reversed against the Imperial forces, they did much to turn the tide of the battle, and the Imperial troops were gradually driven back, until they sought shelter behind the entrenchments which had been made at the village of Ensheim.

When the battle had been at its hottest, Bournonville had observed reinforcement after reinforcement leaving the French centre and even the French left to support the attack between the small wood and the village, until the French left became considerably weakened. He then conceived what Napoleon calls an "able manœuvre". Advancing himself, at the head of several carefully chosen squadrons, he led them between the village of Ensheim and the vineyard on his right to make a demonstration of charging the French centre. Before starting he had sent Caprara, with a much stronger body of cavalry, by a way invisible to the French, between the vineyard on his right and the large wood, to make a sudden attack on the French left flank.

When General Foucault, the oldest of the French

23

lieutenant-generals, saw the Imperial cavalry advancing across the plain, he immediately suspected Bournonville's design, and prepared for an attack upon his flank or rear. Perceiving that Foucault had made a formation accordingly, Bournonville, thinking that his plot had been discovered, instead of charging, retired; the brave Caprara, however, faithfully carried out the orders that he had received, and emerging from between the cover of the vineyard and the large wood, he charged the flank of the second line of the French cavalry almost before his approach had been noticed, broke up several squadrons of Turenne's cavalry and attacked the rear of the French infantry. If Bournonville had executed his share of the manœuvre, the left wing of the French army would have been in a most perilous condition; but, failing that charge, the French left and centre, although weakened by withdrawals for the great battle that was going on between the small wood and the village of Ensheim, and no longer supported by any right wing, was just sufficiently strong to withstand the attack of Caprara's cavalry, which had at last to retire.

Cavalry and infantry, on both sides, had now had about as much fighting as they could well endure. The remainder of the daylight was used for cannonading; and it soon became too dark for further action on this cloudy, dreary day, during which the rain had hardly ever ceased. The Imperialists then withdrew to their camp, close at hand, where they had provisions awaiting them; while Turenne, who had no food for his men, led the main body of them back, past Holtzheim, and across the river to his camp at Achenheim.

Both armies ended this severe day's fighting by retaining their positions; Turenne left twelve squadrons of horse and four of dragoons to hold the battlefield before retreating to Achenheim; but the Imperialists decamped during the night, leaving behind them a number of wounded, a considerable quantity of provisions, with two guns, and retired to Strasburg. Their loss in the battle had been 3,000 killed on the spot, besides many who died on the day after the action, in addition to other wounded. The French loss was 2,000, including many officers; but they captured eight guns, several standards and colours, and many prisoners.

In the opinion of Napoleon, if Turenne "had joined to his extreme left, all the infantry which he injudiciously dispersed amongst his squadrons: had he placed them in the wood with some cannon, covering them with entrenchments and trees cut down, the left of his cavalry would have had an *appui;* this would have compensated for his inferiority in cavalry. The best way of protecting cavalry is to support its flanks. . . . If, after the taking of the little wood, which the enemy had defended with all his means, Turenne had pushed his advantage, the battle would have been decisive. He might, at all events, have lain on the field of battle, but he fell back a league and a half, the same day. On this occasion, he carried his circumspection so far that it amounted to timidity."

It was little that Turenne gained by the battle.

23 *

Indeed it was almost waste of energy, if his own maxim be correct, that "actions ought not to be valued on their own account, but only for their consequences". True, the enemy had withdrawn to Strasburg; but what of that? The Germans, again, had lost more in numbers than the French, but their original numbers having been much greater, their proportionate preponderance over the French had been little, if at all, reduced by their losses in the battle. And in a few days the Grand Elector of Brandenburg arrived at Strasburg and reinforced the Imperial army with 20,000 men, bringing up its numbers to between 50,000 and 60,000, while Turenne had now scarcely 20,000. So confident then were the German allies of victory, that they brought with them the Electress of Brandenburg and several other princesses, who declared that they were going with the Imperial army to Paris to make the acquaintance of the French ladies, and learn manners from the politest of nations. The German generals, also, fully looked forward to advancing through France and capturing its capital.

As one more example of the courtesies of warfare at that period, it may be observed that, during this campaign, Turenne sent his nephew, a lad of fourteen, to convey his compliments to the Duke of Lorraine, who was fighting against him. "My young Cousin," said Lorraine, "you are too happy in seeing and hearing M. de Turenne every day. Kiss the ground whereon he treads. Be killed at his feet."

Turenne now fell back upon his fortress of

Hagenau, about seventeen miles north of Strasburg,
and that of Saverne, some twenty miles to the north-
west of the same city, the distance of twenty miles
between Hagenau[1] and Saverne being of great importance because it covered the principal entrance to
Lorraine and Northern France. He broke the bridges
which lay between the two fortresses, spoiled the fords
and placed scouts to watch the narrow valleys by
which the few roads led towards Lorraine. On his
own retreat towards Saverne, or rather towards Dett-
weiler, which lies a few miles to the east of it, he was
attacked by the enemy, which dogged his footsteps;
but 6,000 horse of the French Reserve, supported by
a number of French Dragoons who dismounted and
fired on the Imperialists from the cover of hedges,
held a narrow defile until the main body of Turenne's
army reached a camp on a very strong position, after a
most creditable retreat in the presence of a hostile force
nearly three times its size. At several points during
this retreat the Germans had opportunities of either
coming up with the French army, or of placing themselves between the French and either Saverne or
Hagenau; and it is doubtful whether their failure to
take advantage of those opportunities was owing to
ignorance of the country, bad generalship, or want of
resolution. As to generalship, indeed, they had now
too much of it; for they had so many generals that
there is likely to have been a bewildering diversity of

[1] Hagenau is about eight miles from Wörth, the scene of the
great battle between the Prussians and French on 6th August, 1870.

counsel. On the other hand, Turenne was a general
who was a past-master of the very difficult art of
making a retreat.

Great was the alarm in Paris when the position of
Turenne was realised. The King insisted upon
strenuous levies ; and, by degrees, Turenne was largely
reinforced. The report of these reinforcements, raw
levies as they were, had the effect of making the Imperialists more cautious. In connection with these
levies a story is told which shows something of the
character of Turenne. Noticing an officer in one of
them exhibiting great military zeal, a zeal very far from
being shared by his weary, woebegone steed, Turenne
insisted upon changing horses with him, pretending
that the officer's screw, being quieter than his own
spirited and valuable charger, would suit a man of his
age much better.

At the end of November the Imperialists, observing Turenne's inaction, thought that he had abandoned
Alsace, that the campaign was over, and that there was
nothing left for them to do but to divide their forces
into detachments, and select winter quarters in the
most fertile districts of Alsace.

Louvois complained bitterly to the King of the
conduct of Turenne. Reinforcements, said he—large
and repeated reinforcements—had been sent to him,
his army was now a formidable one, yet he was doing
nothing. Admitting that the army of the Empire exceeded Turenne's in numbers, Louvois reminded the
King that Turenne had undertaken the entire re-

sponsibility of keeping the Imperialists out of Lorraine and Franche-Comté; yet now he had allowed them to overrun the whole of Alsace, and they were waiting at the very gates of Franche-Comté and Lorraine to enter those districts and ravage them, if not to take possession of them, as soon as the coming spring might permit.

At this time Turenne was the subject of much abuse among the military critics of Paris. But he had a champion in St. Evremond, who wrote of him: "Nature has bestowed on him as much sense, capacity, and merit, as on any man living, but has denied him that fire of genius, that openness and freedom of mind, which makes it appear bright and agreeable. He must be destroyed before we can know his value; and it will be at the loss of his life that he will obtain full justice to his reputation."

The Imperialists scattered themselves over different parts of Alsace, so as to give plenty of room for foraging to each detachment of their large army. They all felt safe from any danger of attack, but those who felt most secure of all were they who were in the extreme south of Alsace. They knew that Turenne was in the north of Lorraine, fifty or sixty miles off. The great chain of the Vosges Mountains, many of them from 3,000 to 4,000 feet in height, protected the whole of the western side of Alsace, and, between the south and the north of Alsace, detachments of the Imperial army were quartered in all directions. The Grand Elector of Brandenburg had sent for his wife to spend the winter quietly with him at Colmar, a town half-way between Strasburg and Basle, with the mountains of the Black Forest and the Vosges ranges about ten miles off on either side.

Some of the Imperial troops were in the extreme south-west, close to the frontier, where the army of the Empire was intended to pass between the Jura and the Vosges ranges, through Southern Lorraine, to invade Franche-Comté, in the early summer; but now there was snow down to the very foot of the hills, and all warfare was in abeyance. Christmas came, and the Prussian and Austrian soldiers joined with the Alsatian villagers in the customs and festivities of that season so dear to Germans. All was now "Peace on earth, and good-will towards men!" Many messages came in for the officers on the south-west frontier, most of them being good wishes of the season; but this monotony was suddenly and violently varied by a despatch to the effect that Turenne was only eight miles off, at Belfort,[1] with a very large army, and that, if they wished to escape capture with their detachments, they had not a moment to lose. Belfort is the gateway from mid-eastern France into Germany and Switzerland, being situated in the gap between the Vosges and the Jura ranges known as the "Trouée de Belfort". Well might the astonished Imperial officers ask how the —— Turenne could possibly have got there!

Early in the last Boer War, when the Boers were

---

[1] It was at Belfort, in 1871, that Bourbaki, with 100,000 men and 240 guns, made a desperate attempt to relieve the garrison which was besieged by Werder and Manteuffel. After his failure to do so Bourbaki tried to commit suicide.

holding Magersfontein and the English army was making no apparent progress towards taking it, an American, who was discussing the position with an English friend in London, said: "Is there no way round?" That was exactly the question which Turenne had asked himself in Northern Lorraine at the end of October, 1674, and he had answered it in the affirmative.

He conceived the idea of marching to the west of the Vosges Mountains through what are now the French departments of Meurthe-et-Moselle and Vosges, but what was then Southern Lorraine, and entering Alsace in the south-west. Early in December, leaving sufficient troops to garrison Saverne and Hagenau, he divided his army into detachments, and ordered them to march by different routes, which he carefully specified, and finally to concentrate at Belfort. They all met there, at about the time intended, after three weeks of marching, sometimes over mountains covered with snow, sometimes through valleys flooded by overflowing rivers, sometimes by roads almost impassable with mud. This long march was unknown to the enemy until it had been accomplished.

On the appearance of the French army, the Imperial troops in the extreme south retreated ; some of them were driven across the Rhine, at Basle, and 5,000 or 6,000 Imperial cavalry were attacked by Turenne, who put them to flight, after a sharp engagement, capturing twenty officers, 300 prisoners and eighteen standards.

Several days were passed by Turenne, either in dispersing the German troops in the south of Alsace, or

in giving his men a rest before advancing north against
the enemy.   In the meantime the Imperial generals
had received intelligence of his appearance.   There-
upon the Duke of Bournonville joined the Grand
Elector of Brandenburg, near Colmar, and together
they drew up their troops between that town and
Turckheim, another four miles to the west of it.
They had a splendid position.   On their left they had
the rivers Lauch, Thur, and Ill; on their right they
had the river Fech and a branch of that river ran
across their entire front.   On their own side of this
branch of the river, in their front, they made parapets
and erected batteries of artillery.   They also placed
some guns on their left, just north of Colmar.

BATTLE OF
TURCK-
HEIM, 5th
January,
1675.   On the morning of the 5th of January Turenne
advanced — Napoleon says with 40,000 men, but
Ramsay says with only 30,000—against, according
to Napoleon, 50,000 of the enemy, drawn up on the
very strong position just described.   The battle began
at eleven o'clock.   Turenne put his right wing under
his relative, Comte de Lorges, with orders to extend
it along the entire front of the enemy, as if intending
to attack Colmar.   This had the effect of making the
Imperialists neglect Turckheim and turn all their attention to concentrating their forces to their left, to
oppose any attempt by the French right upon Colmar.
Meanwhile Turenne, with his left, lay concealed behind
a hill, in a gorge, which led between two spurs of the
Vosges Mountains, in the direction of Turckheim and
the Imperial right.   As soon as the enemy was seen to

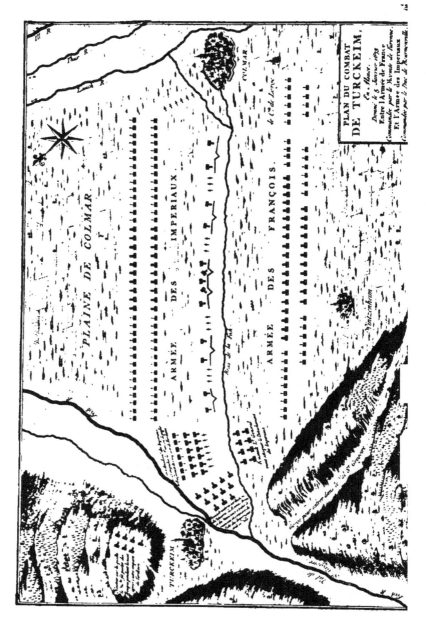

PLAN DU COMBAT
DE TURCKEIM,
En Alsace.
Donné le 5 Janvier 1675.
Entre l'Armée de France
Commandée par le Mte de Turenne.
Et l'Armée des Imperiaux
Commandée par le Duc de Bournonville.

be moving his troops towards Colmar, Turenne led his men through the gorge to his left, in the opposite direction to Colmar and towards Turckheim. The Imperialists had expected the battle to be the battle of Colmar, and it was exactly because Turenne saw that they expected it to be the battle of Colmar, and had made all their preparations for a battle of Colmar, that he determined to make it the battle of Turckheim.

As soon as the Imperial generals perceived Turenne's tactics, they despatched six guns, twelve battalions and several squadrons of cavalry to their extreme right to prevent Turenne from crossing the Fech and occupying Turckheim. Against this force, Turenne sent Foucault with eight battalions, and soon afterwards reinforced him with four others ; but, instead of taking advantage of having arrived before the enemy's reinforcements, he ordered Foucault not to begin the attack till an hour before sunset, as he hoped that the Imperialists might retire without fighting. Accordingly, after enduring the artillery fire patiently for some time, at three o'clock Foucault crossed the arm of the Fech, and, after a very brilliant attack, in which he was killed, his troops drove their opponents towards the Imperialist centre. The delay, ordered by Turenne, in the delivery of this attack, is rather difficult to understand.[1] As the sun set at four o'clock

[1] The following is Ramsay's account of this incident : " The Viscount made Lieutenant-General Foucault advance with eight battalions and attack the post which the enemy had seized along the brook, ordering him, in case he should drive them from thence,

darkness soon came on and the battle ended; but the French army had gained a position on the Imperial flank, behind its entrenchments.

Turckheim was now completely undefended, and Turenne sent seven battalions to occupy a hill beyond the town, immediately above the Fech and commanding the entire right flank of the enemy. But when the sun rose the next morning, the Imperialist army had disappeared. Turenne then occupied Colmar, where he found 3,000 wounded, sick and stragglers.

The most remarkable features of the battle of Turckheim were that, although what fighting there was was fierce, only a comparatively small number of the troops upon the battlefield fought at all; that the fighting was only in one place; and that the space upon which the action occurred was a very small portion of a very large field of battle. Neither side appears to have desired a general engagement.

The Imperial army continued to retreat, and Turenne followed it till it came to Strasburg, where it crossed the Rhine and retired into Germany. Turenne had thus driven the enemy entirely out of Alsace and also out of Strasburg, to whose inhabitants he gave a promise to forgive and forget all that was past. .

not to follow them nor take their cannon, in order to avoid a general battle; he likewise forbad him to begin the attack till an hour before sunset, that the enemy might take counsel in the night and retire by favour of it to prevent being attacked next day in front and flank ".

The whole of Europe was astounded at Turenne's success, and greater still was the astonishment when it became known that he had foretold it two months earlier. The King read before his whole Court a letter which Turenne had written so early as the 30th of October to Le Tellier, the Chancellor and Secretary of State, in which he had said: "Pretending not to be able to resist the enemy after his junction with the Elector of Brandenburg, I will still retire before them, to give them the greater confidence. I will retreat into Lorraine, after which they will not fail to extend themselves all over Alsace, then I will fall upon their quarters, by a way by which they will never expect my approach to surprise them: and I may perhaps oblige them to repass the Rhine and take up their winter quarter in their own country."

In fact Turenne was acting upon what is reputed to have been one of his own maxims: "Seem sometimes to show fear, to give a greater confidence to the enemy in their own strength, and to make them more negligent and less distrustful of you".

It might be supposed that Napoleon would have nothing but the highest praise to offer to the memory of Turenne in relation to this splendid strategy. Yet he found a good deal to criticise, and very interesting are his criticisms. He says: "It was on the 27th of December, that Turenne reached Belfort, and it was on the 5th of January that he fought the battle of Turckheim, being nine days after his arrival, and six days too late. . . . The cantonments being once mustered at Belfort, the manœuvre was unmasked, there was not an hour to lose. Had Turenne marched with more rapidity, he would have obtained important successes; but the enemy's troops had time to rally from all their quarters, so that he found all their army united on the field of Colmar. He ought to have prevented this junction. The whole spirit of this operation consisted in reaching the bridge of Strasburg before the army had rallied. Turenne failed in this; such a manœuvre would have been fruitful in grand results, and certain of success, if, instead of debouching by Belfort, that is to say by the extremity of the Vosges, Turenne had debouched by the middle of the Vosges, direct on Colmar[1] and Strasburg, he would have arrived before the cantonments could have rallied. On this occasion, he evinced more talent in the conception than in the execution of this fine plan." And he hints that Turenne might have been defeated at Turckheim, if the Grand Elector of Brandenburg had thought the risks of a great battle worth running for the sake of retaining Alsace, a place 250 miles from his own dominions, from which it was separated by a number of small states.

The Grand Elector, Napoleon declares, "ought to have given battle at Colmar. He was in an excellent position, his whole army had rallied, and his retreat on Strasburg was secure. The possession of Alsace was

[1] There is a pass, rather less than half-way between Strasburg and Belfort, through the Vosges Mountains to Colmar, by St. Marie-aux-Mines. Its height is 2,625 feet.

undoubtedly worth a battle, but not to him or to the princes of the North of Germany. There was nothing to compensate them for the risks they would have run and the losses they would have suffered in accepting battle."

This question whether the Imperial army voluntarily retreated, owing to differences of intention in the allies composing it, or fled through defeat, is an interesting one. The people of Brandenburg, or Prussians, were the chief of the German Protestants; and although in some sense allied to the Empire, they were, at heart, rather the enemies than the friends of the Austrians. They had been glad enough to make common cause with them in curbing the ambitions of Louis XIV. and they were ready to help them in driving the French out of Alsace, so long as the united armies were in something like the proportions of three to one to the French army. But it was quite a different thing to run the risks of a great battle solely for Austria's advantage, when the proportions were reduced to five to four.

For the opposite supposition—that the Germans, at any rate after the battle of Turckheim, retreated from necessity and not from choice—it may be argued that the French, by establishing themselves inside the right flank of the Imperial army, and thus getting partially behind their entrenchments, had rendered a large portion of those entrenchments useless, and that a simultaneous attack upon the Imperial right front and its weak and unprotected right flank, on the following morning, would have exposed its army to very serious risks.   Moreover, now that the French troops had advanced some distance on the high ground north of Turckheim, it was possible that they might have harrassed the retreat of the German army towards Strasburg, although, as Napoleon says, they might not have been able to cut it off.

CHAPTER XXVI.

ON his return to Paris, and more or less in every town through which he passed on his way thither, Turenne was received in triumph. Whenever he appeared in public he was surrounded by a crowd who cheered with joy. Louis XIV. could not show him enough favour or affection, and he obliged Louvois to make him an apology for all the trouble he had given to him.

Far from being proud of all the honour that was paid to him, or from enjoying the public proofs of his popularity, his one desire was to escape from them. Indeed he intended to retire altogether from military and public life, and to make a prolonged visit to the House of the Fathers of the Oratory at Paris. He said that having spent nearly all his life in heresy he was anxious to devote one or two years exclusively to the study and practice of the Catholic religion. Two priests of the Oratory, Père du Castel and Père St. Denis, had accompanied him as chaplains in the campaigns which followed his reception into the Catholic Church. The Parisian Oratory was founded in 1611 by Cardinal Bérulle, who also founded fifty colleges, seminaries and houses of retreat in connection with it; but the French

CPSIA information can be obtained
at www.ICGtesting.com
Printed in the USA
BVOW06*0538200317
478896BV00010B/81/P